# The Rebel Tours

# The Rebel Tours

## Cricket's Crisis of Conscience

Peter May

Published in Great Britain by
SportsBooks Limited
PO Box 422
Cheltenham
GL50 2YN
United Kingdom

Tel: 01242 256755
Fax: 0560 3108126
email: info@sportsbooks.ltd.uk
www.sportsbooks.ltd.uk

First published October 2009



Cover design by Alan Hunns.

Cover photograph of Mike Gatting, David Graveney and John Emburey from PAPhotos.
Insert of South African protester from Getty Images.

A catalogue record for this book is available from the British Library.

ISBN 978 1899807 80 2

Printed and bound in England by
Cromwell Press Group.

# Acknowledgements

This is not a topic that people are desperate to talk about so special thanks are due to all who agreed to be interviewed: Dennis Amiss, Norman Arendse, Jimmy Cook, Michael Holding, Geoff Humpage, David Kenvyn, Peter Kirsten, Adrian Kuiper, Garth Le Roux, Mike Procter, Barry Richards, Greg Shipperd, Mike Terry, Vince van der Bijl, Bob Willis and Sir Nicholas Winterton. Numerous players across all tours were invited to contribute but ignored or declined my enquiries; only one offered the unimprovable, irony-free response, 'What's in it for me?'

I am grateful to Randall Northam and SportsBooks for both the opportunity and support. My colleague Tristan Holme was less a research assistant than a sorcerer, conjuring up outstanding material time and again. Lerato Malekutu at Cricket South Africa was a great help in the southern hemisphere. Interviews with Sky Sports commentators Michael Holding and Bob Willis were courtesy of James Motley and Sky. Richard Burgess kindly dug out and dispatched a copy of his BBC radio documentary.

In addition I have been fortunate to rely on a support team so numerous they put the modern England set-up to shame. Lynda Thompson helped me get started.

Tom Ezard, Stephen May, Dave Roche and Pete Webber provided insightful commentary from the early drafts; Carl Cullinane, Guy Fletcher, John McGee and Ben Parsons joined the fray later with valuable new perspective. Lucy Jefferson was an indispensable friend, flat-mate and purveyor of terrible 1980s cop films. Kevie and Dave Gordon graciously offered bed, breakfast and Baltimore on countless occasions. Pete Manson has the finest air mattress in London and don't let anyone tell you otherwise. Their time and generosity, and the backing of many other friends and family members, are hugely appreciated.

Endless gratitude is due to Nóra Bairéad, the one person without whom this would never have been completed. She is my favourite for her patience, belief, encouragement and humour. Finally I thank my parents for their constant interest and support.

All errors and omissions are, of course, solely my responsibility.

Peter May
May 2009

# Contents

# Introduction

The rebel cricket tours to apartheid South Africa rank among the most extraordinary sporting ventures. Between 1982 and 1990 seven teams defied international boycott action to visit the republic, prompting anger and condemnation throughout the world game and far beyond. The tours threatened the future of international cricket and brought those who took part public opprobrium and in some cases personal and professional ruin. Despite the intense controversy, the rebel tours have received little retrospective examination. This is the story of one of the greatest cricket crises.

The genesis of the tours was the D'Oliveira affair, which in 1968 brought apartheid to the attention of many people for the first time. South Africa was excluded from international competition until it dismantled racism in cricket; the game was then appropriated as a tool to exert pressure on the South African government in other ways. International condemnation of apartheid was all but universal, but there was intense disagreement on the commitment to and effectiveness of competing efforts to bring about its demise. Accusations of hypocrisy, racism and appeasement were rife. Once placed on the front line in the battle against apartheid, cricket remained there until the fall of the regime more than two decades later.

The rebel tours were South Africa's answer to isolation. Administrators secretly agreed huge salaries with unofficial international teams to play acclaimed 'Tests' and 'one-day internationals' against officially recognised Springbok XIs. When the first rebel tour, by an English squad, revealed their plans by arriving in Johannesburg in February 1982, the reaction was sensational. Few sporting ventures have generated such extensive front-page coverage while the fury in India, Pakistan and the West Indies threatened a 'black–white' split in international cricket. In subsequent seasons the South African authorities continued to provoke international anger with unofficial tours from Sri Lanka, the West Indies and Australia. Each visit boasted its own characteristics and costs, but all renewed cricket's instability while feeding a wider atmosphere of antagonism.

Behind the international outrage and domestic hype, the matches represent an anomaly in the game's history. They provided a platform for great figures such as Graeme Pollock, Barry Richards and Mike Procter, and a new challenge for a forgotten generation of outstanding players led by Clive Rice, Peter Kirsten and Vince van der Bijl. While the least among the tourists are understandably forgotten by cricket history, some illustrious names visited the republic: Graham Gooch and Geoffrey Boycott; Lawrence Rowe and Colin Croft; Kim Hughes and Terry Alderman. There were some dramatic contests and outstanding individual contributions but the matches were repeatedly undermined by other influences. Player strikes, poor umpiring and schedules driven by commercial rather than common sense all conspired. World-weary cricket followers might think these make the tours all too ordinary but the shadow of the South African government never fully receded.

Apartheid remained entwined with international cricket to the very end when a final rebel party, led by Mike Gatting, was tempted to the republic in 1989–90. Cricket and politics collided with formidable force once again. As FW De Klerk prepared to release Nelson Mandela from his cell on Robben Island, non-white South Africa began to vent decades of frustration and fury with English cricketers the focal point.

This book traces the full history of these remarkable tours, beginning with the sporting boycott (Chapter 1) and tumultuous 1970s (Chapter 2) before detailing the on- and off-field story of the tours themselves (Chapters 3 to 9) to provide a comprehensive account of their organisation, conduct and fall-out.

## Chapter 1

# The Sport that Rocked the World

*'When one side in a cricket match insists on the right to select both sides, then reality has degenerated into Mad Hatterism.' – Benny Green*

Nineteen sixty-eight was 'the year that rocked the world'. Momentous events proliferated: the end of the US civil rights movement, the beginning of the end of the Vietnam war, the assassinations of Martin Luther King and Robert Kennedy, and the first manned Apollo missions, Apollo 7 and Apollo 8; Swaziland, Mauritius and Equatorial Guinea attained independence as European colonial influence continued to disintegrate across Africa and Asia; in Paris *mai '68* brought the country to the brink of revolution and ultimately proved a watershed for French society; demonstrators the other side of the Iron Curtain were not so fortunate in defeat as the Soviet Union met attempted reforms in Prague with brutal military force and Polish political unrest was repressed through anti-Semitic purges.

Against this backdrop a cancelled cricket tour might have been a frivolous diversion but instead boasted profound consequences, a remarkable tale born of endeavour and resilience that changed not only cricket but the world far beyond. Among the most celebrated episodes in sporting history, it is now known simply as the D'Oliveira affair.

Immediately after scoring a feted 158 against Australia at The Oval in August 1968 Basil D'Oliveira was omitted from the MCC's England squad to tour South Africa the following winter, a decision roundly denounced as a political betrayal. The ruling National Party government in South Africa had since 1948 legislated the policies of apartheid – literally 'separateness' in Afrikaans; this amounted to institutional segregation of the population by spurious racial groupings, with the ruling white minority afforded economic, political and social supremacy over the other race classifications, 'blacks', 'Indians' and 'coloureds'. Cape Town-born all-rounder D'Oliveira was a brilliant right-handed batsman who had been classified as coloured and thus excluded from first-class cricket despite spectacular success in the non-white leagues. He had emigrated in 1960 to fulfil his ambition to become a professional cricketer, gaining British citizenship during a rapid rise from the Lancashire League to county side Worcestershire and then the England Test team. The prospect of his appearance for the MCC in the republic – and particularly that of a 'Cape coloured' hitting the white Springboks to the four corners of Newlands, where D'Oliveira's peers were segregated in an area known as The Cage and allowed onto the field only to tend the grass – tormented the South African government.

Much later it became public that the omission was indeed politically influenced, with the South African Prime Minister BJ Vorster himself actively lobbying the MCC committee throughout 1968.[1] But the public controversy in England was too great for Lord's to resist and, following Warwickshire all-rounder Tom Cartwright's timely withdrawal through injury, D'Oliveira was called up as his replacement.

This belated about-face provoked ire among the South African establishment, who, though unsuccessful in separate, secret one-to-one attempts to bribe D'Oliveira to stay away, thought they had done enough backroom manoeuvring with the MCC to ensure his exclusion. On the day that D'Oliveira's selection was announced, Vorster was speaking at the National Party Conference in Orange Free State. In a speech since immortalised in an oft-repeated television clip, the visibly affronted Prime Minister launched into a furious rebuke of the decision and those who had demanded it:

> *'The MCC team as constituted now is not the team of the MCC but the team of the Anti-Apartheid Movement [...] We left the MCC to make their choice. We did not want to play selection committee for them. The ultimate decision was theirs and theirs only, and they made their choice on merit. There was an immediate outcry because a certain gentleman of colour was omitted on merit, as they themselves said. From then on D'Oliveira was no longer a sportsman but a political cricket ball. From then on it was political bodyline bowling all the way. From then on the matter passed from the realm of sport to the realm of politics.'*[2]

The National Party congregation was predictably delighted by this denunciation of their enemies, rising to a fevered standing ovation, but the implications of its wider reception had not been understood by Vorster or his party. While there was no question that their position would be emphatically undermined by D'Oliveira's presence on the same field as the white home XI, any rejection required deft diplomatic treatment rather than a bold challenge to apartheid's enemies.

Even before the D'Oliveira affair these had been growing in number. The Anti-Apartheid Movement, the British-based pressure group leading international opposition to the South African regime, had enjoyed qualified success while always striving for greater public awareness.[3] The tour cancellation provided that, raising the profile of the Vorster Government's position and paranoia and making it easier for the AAM and its associates to rally their cause. The reality of apartheid policies were increasingly subjected to the light of public scrutiny: separate schools, hospitals, beaches and buses; prohibition of mixed-race marriages; restrictions on the movement and employment of non-whites; and disenfranchisement of non-white voters. Although no specific laws were created with regard to mixed-race sport, the Group Areas Act (1950) assigning different residential, social and commercial sections to different racial groups achieved this de facto. Racial integration was a vexed social issue in many western nations – not least the UK, where Enoch Powell had delivered his infamous 'Rivers of Blood' speech just five months earlier – but since World War II segregationism had all but perished as a viable political platform in national European elections, where there was no shortage of racial tension yet widespread contempt for apartheid policies. That contempt only grew the greater exposure these received.

In adopting this bellicose stance South Africa had misjudged how far their allies might indulge 'tradition'. The republic's history of racial oppression stretched back centuries, conventions merely formalised by apartheid from 1948 onwards, and that had been reflected in a dishonourable sporting canon. In 1894 the coloured fast bowler Krom Hendricks was left out of the first-ever South Africa tour to England on political orders and two years later Charles Llewellyn, born of a black mother and white father, played Test cricket for the Springboks only because he was light-skinned enough to pass as white. In addition to whites-only national teams, segregation was practiced at every level, effectively excluding non-whites from the facilities, coaching, competition and recognition deserved by the highest levels of sporting achievement. The insanity of such organisation was vividly illustrated in the case of Papwa Sewgolum, a self-taught golfer classified as Indian who had preceded D'Oliveira in answering apartheid exclusion with success abroad. As a two-time Dutch Open champion, Sewgolum got special dispensation to play in the 1963 Natal Open and promptly won the tournament. The Group Areas Act forbade his entering the clubhouse except as a servant and so while his fellow Natal Indians served drinks at the presentation ceremony he stood outside in the rain, receiving his trophy through an open window.[4]

A catalogue of such injustices across social and political life had long established 'the South African question' of whether relations with the republic ought to be maintained, a problem many simply ignored. The MCC, co-founders of the International Cricket Conference with Australia and the whites-only South African Cricket Association in 1909[5], had long-standing friendships with their southern hemisphere counterparts and had never opposed the Springboks' selection policy. Indeed since 1961 South Africa had not even been an official international team. The republic's withdrawal from the Commonwealth had invalidated its ICC membership and India, Pakistan and the West Indies had vetoed a constitutional change to allow their re-entry. England and Australia turned the practised blind eye, simply awarding caps and classifying matches with South Africa as official Tests in any case.[6]

Such attitudes were by no means unique to cricket.

Answers to the South African question were divided throughout the sporting and political world. Just six months before the D'Oliveira affair South Africa had been excluded from the 1968 Olympics in Mexico after 50 nations had threatened to withdraw despite Vorster's concession that a mixed-race committee would choose a mixed-race team. This had been enough to mollify the 'white' Western nations, who like the MCC were open to accommodating South Africa where possible, but not the 'black' and communist states who overcame an International Olympic Committee voting system weighted towards the West to demand an exclusion. Congolese representative Jean-Claude Ganga told the IOC, 'We do not wish that the blacks of Africa appear like costumed apes presented at a fair and then, when the fair is over, sent back to their cages.'[7]

South Africa had met the IOC rejection with complacent expectation that their return would prove a formality. Now it was not their enemies taking issue, but a long-standing ally. In 1929 the MCC had excluded Anglo-Indian KS Duleepsinhji during a tour of the republic at their hosts' request, but in a more enlightened and professional era SACA and the MCC had no choice but to call off the tour. The established pattern of official collaboration, which had acknowledged injustice neither on nor off the field, had been pushed to breaking point, as the writer Benny Green reflected: 'Although the D'Oliveira affair embodied a vital issue of political morality, it remained perfectly possible to reach conclusions about the crisis within a frame of reference which excluded politics altogether. When one side in a cricket match insists on the right to select both sides, then reality has degenerated into Mad Hatterism.'[8]

The D'Oliveira affair galvanised the anti-apartheid movement, establishing sport as the most visible means of registering protest. When the MCC in early 1969 announced their intention to proceed with South Africa's scheduled tour of England in June–August 1970, anti-apartheid campaigners immediately resolved to build on the success and exposure granted by D'Oliveira, planning opposition and honing their tactics at smaller-scale events. Four young Liberals led by Peter Hain interrupted the July 1969 Davis Cup tie between Great Britain and South Africa with a sit-in that ended swiftly in their arrests. And a strong, all-white cricket tour party funded by Johannesburg businessman Wilf Isaacs was the subject of numerous small-scale interruptions and demonstrations through pitch invasions and sit-ins.

In white South Africa the interlopers were dismissed as a minority collection of nutcases, drug-takers and paid agitators, but the on-ground reality was of a growing number of protestors coalescing and organising themselves under the banner 'Stop the Seventy Tour'. The STST committee announced its formation a year on from Vorster's furious conference speech, with Hain, the presumptive chairman, outlining their intentions to 'mount a sustained campaign against apartheid in sport [...] working for the cancellation of the 1970 tour to Britain by a white South African cricket team':

> *'We will be organising mass demonstrations and disruptions throughout the tour ... next summer's cricket season could collapse into chaos should the tour take place. We are fighting British collaboration with racialism in sport. And this is a fight we are confident of winning. We are today issuing a clear warning to British sports authorities: that their complicity in apartheid sport will no longer be tolerated – all future tours, including the rugby tour starting in November, will be severely disrupted.'*[9]

The rarefied cricket world suddenly found itself on the front line against apartheid, identified as a battleground that suited the AAM's strengths and agenda. The campaign would undoubtedly gain some publicity in the UK and more importantly contribute to the isolation of the apartheid government in South Africa. In the first instance it was hoped that this pressure would end apartheid in sport, leading to the selection of mixed-race South African teams, but underlying this stated ambition was a fundamental belief: that sport could not be separated from society, and white South Africa's acceptance of non-racial sport would lead inexorably to integration in other spheres.

Unexpectedly an earlier opportunity to apply pressure had already presented itself: the impending UK and Ireland tour by white South Africa's favourite sporting sons, the rugby union Springboks. Such had been the power of the D'Oliveira affair in focusing apartheid opposition on the next summer's cricket, protestors had given little thought to the rugby tour due to start within seven weeks. Initially intended as a 'trial run' for the cricketers the following summer, the momentum for rugby tour protests grew startlingly quickly on their own initiative. STST had envisaged focusing efforts on a one-off demonstration ahead of a Twickenham Test on 20th December, but it quickly became clear that each of the 25 scheduled matches would be the subject of some protest action. The opening tour game at Oxford University was scheduled for 5th November yet cancelled on 23rd October, a week before the Springboks had even landed in the UK, after weedkiller was sprayed on the Iffley Road pitch spelling out 'Oxford Rejects Apartheid' in five-foot letters.

The tourists were met with derision on arrival at London airport and that seldom relented until their departure on 2nd February 1970, 95 days later. With

Oxford no longer suitable, the opening fixture was moved to Twickenham itself on 5th November but attempts to keep the new location secret failed and there was a mass demonstration. Although the match itself went ahead with minimal delay, it did so in farcical circumstances with an almost empty stadium witnessing the clearly unnerved visitors defeated by moderate opposition. The national press, for the most part initially ambivalent to the STST, began to carry the story on their front pages as a matter of course and spontaneous growth of protest bodies spread across the UK and Ireland.

Throughout the next three months the STST hounded the Springboks from Aberdeen to Exeter and across the Irish Sea. Hundreds and thousands of demonstrators appeared at each match, and though only one, in Northern Ireland, was cancelled and another two relocated, the opposition was uncompromising. The South Africa team coach was blockaded in some places, pelted with eggs and stones in others; players' hotel room doors were gummed shut. In some cases match-day protests were limited to marches outside the stadium and attempted pitch invasions; in others dye, smoke bombs and tacks were thrown onto the field.

Guerrilla tactics and containment measures evolved rapidly as the tour progressed. Two colleagues of Hain, Mike Findley and Peter Twyman, erected a pole in a back garden to practise shinning up goalposts and handcuffing themselves to the crossbar in the build-up to the Twickenham Test, while police began to perform match-day duties in football boots to aid their pursuit of pitch invaders. Another Young Liberal, Michael Deeney, hijacked the Springbok coach at their Park Lane Hotel on the morning of the England Test and, having handcuffed himself to the steering wheel, promptly crashed it into a Post Office van, earning a broken jaw from one of his passengers for his trouble. Upon their belated arrival at

Twickenham South Africa were beaten 11-8 following multiple interruptions; among them, Findley succeeding in chaining himself to one set of posts while the slower-footed Twyman was felled by a boisterous constable on the five-yard line.[10]

The wisdom of some of these measures remains open to debate, but their effectiveness does not. Their every move subject to outside interference, South Africa were plainly distracted on the field and would not win any of their four Test matches, losing 6-3 at Murrayfield and recording only draws in Cardiff and Dublin, 6-6 and 8-8 respectively. The latter two matches, towards the end of the tour in January, would not even have taken place had the Springboks had their way. After the Twickenham Test the players voted to return home but their call went unheeded by the management, whose decision was doubtless backed by the government back in the republic. South African Rugby Board President Danie Craven told the press the following day that the tour would continue 'for the sake of next year's cricket tour', indicating that the South African establishment too was steeled for a long fight. Off the field the campaign gained media coverage on a scale unimaginable three months previously, ensured that the tour was a colossal financial failure and, perhaps most importantly in the minds of the STST committee, had proved an educational trial run for their true target: South Africa's cricketers later that year.

The value of sport as a platform for protests was now inescapable. The STST trial run had been successful in raising the profile and quality of debate on apartheid as well as inflicting discomfort and cost on the white South African XV and their hosts. Yet despite the unprecedented size of the rugby campaign – Hain estimated 50,000 demonstrators in total – public opinion in the United Kingdom still showed trenchant views on both sides. At a time when political rebellion was purportedly in the air around the world, the UK had show itself characteristically uninterested in revolution. Anti-war protest groups galvanised by Vietnam were both powerful and active in comparison to most other nations, and the Anti-Apartheid Movement would prove perhaps the most successful protest group anywhere in the world since the Second World War. But the aggregated view of the whole population would be more accurately reflected in the June 1970 general election, which voted in a Conservative government led by Edward Heath. Despite some success for the AAM and their economic boycott, the UK remained a key trading partner for South Africa. De Beers diamonds filled jewellers' windows, market stalls groaned under the weight of Cape fruits and thousands of Britons holidayed in the republic each year. In addition two-thirds of foreign investment in the republic – amounting to £1.5billion – came from UK companies, and if public condemnation of apartheid as neither moral nor practicable was routine then this did not always affect individual choices.[11]

Nor was there a shortage of support at Westminster and Lord's for continued alliance with South Africa. Sir Nicholas Winterton MP, a vocal supporter of South African links throughout this period, explains his reasons for favouring engagement over isolation: 'I am quite prepared to accept that conservative elements controlled South African sport for too long and they made a grave error with Basil D'Oliveira. They could not tell us who to select for England. However, to my mind Peter Hain's approach was very negative. I was strongly of the view that establishing boycotts was wrong. I much prefer to bring about change by education and example. Exposure to countries where integration had occurred, as with D'Oliveira, was very valuable. I always believed that the Springboks overseas would see people with a different colour of skin treated as equals quite normally, quite naturally, and would think, "Oh, they're not devils after all" and that this would get back to South Africa. I also supported trade, for example in financial services, precious metals and minerals. It is a hugely prosperous country with the potential to improve the way of life for people of all backgrounds. We were not showing support for the National Party government in Pretoria.' This commercial co-operation extended to the military sphere: the closure of the Suez Canal and growing naval power of the Soviet bloc had made the Cape route valuable and South Africa an expedient ally for the West.

From the AAM perspective, engagement equated to collusion. When the rugby and cricket Springboks came on tours they were treated as honoured guests and their hosts did not raise political issues. As in the economic or political spheres, in the view of isolationists sporting co-operation was a comfort rather than a challenge to apartheid. Indeed, it was felt that a pro-engagement stance often indicated implicit support for the status quo. Certainly many considered that a preference at Lord's for continued engagement, embodied by the former Prime Minister and MCC President Alec Douglas-Home, was born from appeasement and apathy as much as any belief in the value of 'bridge-building'. The Conservative opposition did little to reverse this perception in campaigning to end a government embargo on selling arms to South Africa, or its influential Monday Club retaining close links with National Party leaders.

Home Secretary James Callaghan called it simply, 'one of the few issues of recent times where public opinion has been divided right down the middle', exercising as it did politics and sport in an unprecedented fashion. If the Soviet Union regime was scarcely more palatable than the South African, why did the STST not feel moved to throw broken glass onto the stage of the touring Russian ballet? Were those who advocated links with BJ Vorster, who had been imprisoned during World War II for supporting Nazi Germany, any wiser than Neville Chamberlain? The debate filtered down and played out on countless parochial levels; the Bishops of Stepney and Peterborough argued publicly on whether it would be more 'unchristian' to accept the tourists and thus apartheid, or to reject them and thus prove unwelcoming hosts to one's fellow man.

There were many who expressed their abhorrence of apartheid but could not support the illegal tactics of trespass, damage and menacing behaviour; on the opposing side was an audible conservative disdain for 'post-hippy' protestors and a desire to sustain the cordial Test history between England and South Africa, which had previously been uninterrupted despite racialism in the republic. While the STST were trying to force public enquiries and lodge official complaints on police brutality and civil liberties breaches, there were plenty who thought robust measures justified:

> *Sir,*
> *In your third leader today you suggest that the South African cricket tour may be cancelled. If it is, should we not clear our minds of cant and realize true reason?*
> *It will not be because the British public wants to sever sporting connections with South Africa – there's no evidence that they do. It will not be because a minority of conscientious folk feel strongly enough about apartheid to gather in peaceful demonstrations. No: it will be, overwhelmingly, because we cannot control thugs and hooligans who attach themselves to any cause which gives them an excuse for vandalism. It will be because public and police together cannot*

> *protect such national institutions as Lord's and Old Trafford against young louts who don't shrink from scattering broken glass on Rugby grounds or digging up cricket pitches.*
> *Unfortunately the vandals have been encouraged during the Springboks tour, by the patronage of muddle-headed clerics and MPs who seem to have accepted two principles usually associated with Hitler and Stalin: (i) if you oppose a political system, persecute and insult any individuals in any way connected with it, even if they are quite unrepresentative, even if they may be its critics; (ii) use any means, whatever, towards an end which you imagine to be good.*
> *So if the cricket tour is cancelled we shall have signalled to the world that Britain cannot keep order at home and cannot prevent hundreds of thousands of her citizens from being deprived of an innocent summer pursuit by a small minority of barbarians. Such an admission would be a natural sequel to our recent failure to protect our Springbok guests from repeated insult and persecution by the uncivilised: but surely it is an admission we should do our utmost to avoid?*
> *(Letter to The Times, 5th February 1970)*

At the same time, in the manner beloved of the English chattering classes, there followed endless speculative laments at the cost to the taxpayer. Typically these revolved around the considerable expense of heightened police presence while more imaginative fiscal hawks wondered how many of the STST agitators were funded by student grants.

If views on the STST were mixed in the UK then they were naturally more robust in white South Africa, where the hysterical complaints of the Isaacs tour were magnified many times by this affront to the iconic Boks.

The pro-government *Die Beeld* published this editorial following the opening tour match between Oxford University and South Africa at Twickenham:

> *'We have become accustomed to Britain becoming a haven for all sorts of undesirables from other countries. Nevertheless, it is degrading to see how a nation can allow itself to be dictated to by this bunch of left-wing, workshy, refugee long-hairs who in a society of any other country would be rejects.'*[12]

And just as the South African establishment sought to dismiss the protestors, they were also at pains to establish their own sense of right. Upon their return Danie Craven insisted, 'We despise the conduct of the demonstrators, the way in which rugby matches were turned into chaos, the childishness and banalities of the demonstrators. We would like to put it clearly and openly that if these people think they can influence us or that we shall change our way of life because of demonstrations, they are making a grave error.'

But, as the South African historian Albert Grundlingh later noted, 'Craven was wrong.'[13]

Despite the extraordinary events surrounding the rugby tour, South Africa's cricketers were by March 1970 still largely unaware of the welcome being prepared in England. Life in the white South African bubble raised men with a sense of entitlement and most saw little wrong with apartheid. Barry Richards and Mike Procter have both written candidly of how international travel unseated their complacency and revealed the barbarity of their own government.[14] Not only did the bubble desensitise whites to the inhumanity of apartheid, it conditioned them to believe that the system was intractable. After BJ Vorster's D'Oliveira speech the anti-apartheid activist Donald

Woods, a rare white South African who rejected the status quo, asked the veteran Springbok all-rounder Trevor Goddard to denounce the government. But Goddard refused: 'I agree with a lot that you said, but we cannot speak out. We are in a very difficult position.' Woods replied, 'No, you are not in a difficult position. You are in a very safe position. You are national heroes and you won't be thrown into jail if you speak up.'[15]

It is not always reasonable to expect sportsmen to moonlight as political revolutionaries. One of the essential aspects of the D'Oliveira affair was its chief protagonist's motivation. He did not leave South Africa with the intention of becoming a cause célèbre to a liberal elite or an iconoclast to apartheid; he went as a cricketer to maximise his extraordinary potential wherever that was possible. If fulfilled, his desire to return to South Africa as an England player would have placed him in collaboration with the all-white Springbok team. As such Hain considered D'Oliveira to have come out of the 1968 imbroglio 'very badly'[16], which indicates the standards by which single-minded activists will judge others. Nevertheless the South African cricketers of the era might have done far more to voice dissent. Unlike other leading sportsmen, including the rugby union captain Dawie de Villiers[17] and the golf star Gary Player[18], they were not publicly supporting apartheid. But nor were they providing meaningful opposition. The captain Ali Bacher has since conceded that despite his disagreements with the government, and even the occasional public pronouncement, he was 'simply making the "right noises."'[19] And batting maestro Richards says, 'In those days it was a Nationalist government and it was almost a frightening experience to go against them so you just tended to keep your head down and your arse up rather than ask any questions. You tended to just say "Right, I'll just play my cricket and get on with it."'

The attraction of focusing on cricket was understandable, since it was something they did with formidable style. Bacher's side had grown impressive reputations throughout the 1960s, losing only one of their latter seven series in the decade. But it was in early 1970, around the time that their rugby counterparts were being hounded out of Ireland, that they had grasped the mantle of the world's best team by beginning a comprehensive 4-0 Test series defeat of Australia. The claim that they were truly the best, the 'undisputed champions of the world', is debatable. Certainly most observers inside the republic and around the world shared this view but there were others, notably the West Indies batsman Clive Lloyd, who were vocal in their disagreement. It is an insoluble point. The inaugural World Cup was five years away and since 1888 South Africa had played Tests only against the 'white' nations, England, Australia and New Zealand. At the political level, the idea of contests between a white-only South African XI and India, Pakistan or the West Indies was equally unpalatable to all sides.

What is beyond question is that Bacher's team contained some of the finest players in the game's history. Most prominent among these was Graeme Pollock. A tall middle-order batsman, Pollock was endowed with a rare combination of power and grace. He used his natural size and strength to get onto the front foot at every opportunity and was a forceful striker of the ball, particularly through the off side. At the same time he retained the elegance of a 'classical' left-hander, a combination that had led Donald Bradman to describe Pollock as the greatest 'southpaw' he had ever seen. That approval is apposite as in 1970, and for over three decades thereafter, Pollock had only the great Australian to look up to in the Test averages. He was the head of an exclusive club of those to average over 60 in pursuit of The Don, with fellow members limited to the West

Indian George Headley and England's Herbert Sutcliffe, both contemporaries of Bradman. Upon the 4-0 humbling of Australia, Pollock was, at the age of 26, quite simply the world's leading batsman.

The closest challenger to that title was another left-hander, Garry Sobers, but the West Indian was eight years older than Pollock and past the peak of his immense powers. The most likely heir to Pollock's world batting crown had only just emerged on the international stage: his fellow South African, Barry Richards. Richards' first – and, as it would prove, last – series had only just come against Australia but after four Tests many already considered the 24-year-old to be touched by greatness. A right-handed opener of flawless eye and technique, he and Pollock had written themselves into South African cricket history with a devastating partnership in the second Test at Kingsmead, Richards making 140 off 164 balls before watching his partner reach 274 in an emphatic innings victory. In the countless 'what if?' conversations among cricket fans during South Africa's subsequent international exile, no-one would be the subject of so much debate as Richards, who repeatedly earned inclusion in 'dream teams' of all-time South African and World XIs, including that of Bradman himself. When in 2002 the distinguished cricket journalist Christopher Martin-Jenkins was asked by *The Times* to choose an England XI and a Rest of the World XI from his 50 years watching the game, four-cap Richards was selected to open with India's Sunil Gavaskar ahead of the great West Indian Gordon Greenidge, who had played 108 Tests: 'seeing the ball early and playing with the full blade of a straight bat, he found batting easy and made it look ridiculously so.'[20]

Procter was also established as a key member of Bacher's side. Though not quite in the exalted class of Pollock and Richards, he was a formidably talented all-rounder whose seven-Test career had better showcased his right-arm fast bowling than his muscular batting.[21] His action was unorthodox, seemingly delivering the ball off the wrong foot[22], but a treacherous proposition for batsmen. Procter had formed an opening partnership with Peter Pollock, Graeme's elder brother, to which Australia had no answer in 1970. The pair of relentless fast bowlers had taken 41 wickets in the whitewash. Perhaps their only cricketing weakness was that eternal South African failing, lack of a top-class spinner. But with these four spaced evenly throughout the team, as well as three all-rounders of the calibre of Goddard, Eddie Barlow and wicketkeeper batsman Denis Lindsay, they felt well equipped to secure success on English soil under Bacher, an astute leader adept at both maximising his own strengths and exploiting opponents' weaknesses.

This was a more than fair assumption – England were inconsistent throughout the late 1960s, and had not held the Ashes for 14 years – but never put to the test, as the STST campaign gathered irresistible momentum. While the public focus had been drawn to events surrounding the rugby tour in autumn 1969, the STST campaign had not lost sight of its established main objective. Letters of protest had begun to arrive at Lord's as the rugby Springboks arrived and the Test and County Cricket Board, recently established to administer the professional game in England under the auspices of the MCC, met in December to establish the wisdom of proceeding with South Africa's visit. But as then secretary Jack Bailey later wrote of the prevailing MCC view, 'The argument for retaining contact through the game, linked with an old-fashioned notion of not letting down those in South Africa who had contributed so much to the game internationally, were principles to which the majority adhered.'[23] Clasping their 'old-fashioned notion', they resolved to proceed.

Given the growing reach and boldness of the STST campaign, this made a pitched battle that summer inevitable and both sides began mobilising forces. The very next week SACA attempted to placate opposition with the promise that a non-racial touring side would be selected on merit, in reality a fatuous promise readily dismissed by campaigners in the UK and South Africa. It was almost impossible for a non-white player to reach the required standard for international cricket with non-existent facilities and coaching, and as Basil D'Oliveira had shown, when a hero emerged from the shadows he was not afforded any respect. SACA would never identify a non-white player for inclusion on the imminent tour.

By early 1970, as the relieved rugby players set off home, those seeking to persevere with the tour were facing setbacks on all fronts. The Commonwealth Games, due to be hosted in Edinburgh in July, were placed under ever-growing international pressure as African and Asian nations expressed their opposition to South African ties. An MCC tour to East Africa was cancelled by the host nations Kenya, Uganda and Zambia in protest at the TCCB acceptance of South Africa. Within the UK, there were echoes of those October protests at Oxford in a co-ordinated trespass at 14 of the 17 county cricket clubs nationwide; messages were writ large in paint and weedkiller. And, just as it did with Vorster's outburst amidst the D'Oliveira affair, the South African government's folly made them their own worst enemy.

On 28th January Arthur Ashe, a black American tennis player and the first ever US Open champion two years previously, was refused entry to compete in the South African Open. As he was a prominent civil rights advocate and anti-apartheid campaigner, it could be argued that excluding Ashe was a necessary measure for Pretoria. But since the decision was made public less than 48 hours after he had won the Australian Open, one of tennis's four Grand Slam events, it was the kind of hapless posturing at which the National Party was uniquely adept.

These events were all fuel on the STST fire and within a fortnight their pressure was brought to bear. A meeting of the Cricket Council on 12th February decided to curb the tour schedule from 28 matches to 12, reducing the number of venues from 22 to eight. The thinking behind this was at least in part to reduce the area which the authorities were required to control. Cricket pitches lend themselves more readily to interruption than rugby, with greater circumference and piecemeal stadium structures, and just weeks after the Springboks' departure they were aware that keeping the tour going would prove a formidable task. In hindsight, however, as the anti-apartheid campaigner and *Guardian* cricket correspondent John Arlott had argued, they were probably wrong to consider that they still exerted control over the situation at all. He wrote, 'They are arranging a tour that can give neither pleasure nor profit to anyone … it is clear that the future offers even greater and more dismal threats. No-one has won.'[24]

Public momentum for the protest campaign had begun to snowball and on 22nd February the Prime Minster Harold Wilson, who along with Home Secretary James Callaghan had declined to take a position on the rugby protests, spoke out against the tour taking place at all. He would later use a television interview to support peaceful demonstration. Sympathetic public support was provided by players past and present: the Bishop of Woolwich, David Sheppard, an England captain himself in 1954 whose brief tenure had been ended by a refusal to lead a touring party to South Africa, and Michael Brearley, then an uncapped Middlesex batsman who would later rank among the most celebrated England captains, each collaborated with the STST despite a shared opposition to their direct action policy. Coverage of the matches would also be a problem as the Association of Cinematograph, Television and Allied Technicians announced their opposition, the National Union of Journalists considered a media blackout and John Arlott indicated he would not cover the matches for the *Guardian* or BBC radio. The international sporting community continued to exert pressure too as on 20th May Kenya and Zambia withdrew from the Commonwealth Games, bringing the total of absentee countries to 18.

The Pakistan Cricket Board first instructed its county-employed professionals not to participate in tour matches against South Africa and would later call off an under-25s tour of its own to England scheduled for later in the summer. In early May the International Olympic Committee would vote to expel South Africa at their meeting in Amsterdam; they were the first nation ever to suffer the fate and, having already missed Tokyo '64 and Mexico '68, would not compete again until the 1992 games in Barcelona.

The 1970 county cricket season therefore got under way as the unlikely eye of a global political storm. Matches were played out on pitches surrounded by barbed wire, and the STST, though still half expecting the belated cancellation of the tour, continued to prepare themselves. The unprecedented nature of the opposition would be vividly evidenced by the personal protest of David Wilton-Godberford, a biology student happy to ally his learning to reading matter of an older vintage where the occasion called for it. *The Times* cricket correspondent John Woodcock reported:

## PLAN TO DISRUPT CRICKET TOUR WITH LOCUSTS

*A London University student said yesterday that a plan had been devised to wreck the South African cricket tour with an army of locusts. By the time the tourists arrived 500,000 would be ready for release on cricket pitches so that they would eat the grass, he said.*
*Mr David Wilton-Godberford, a biology student aged 20, already has 50,000 of the insects at his home at Colwyn Bay. He said that friends were also breeding them in secret in other parts of North Wales.*
*The breeds he intends to use are the desert locust and African migratory locust. They will be up to 1½in. long, harmless to human beings, and unable to fly.*
*In a brick building behind his home rows of small glass-fronted cases contain thousands of locusts, kept warm by the heat from electric bulbs. There are also scores of bottles containing eggs.*
*Mr Wilton-Godberford, who said he was against violence, explained: "I abhor apartheid and this is to be my personal protest. Anything up to 100,000 locusts will be let loose at any particular ground and I think the plan is foolproof. They will ravage every blade of grass and green foliage. The greatest care will be taken to ensure that they are in the correct physiological stage. So that their insatiable appetites will not be impaired they will not be fed for 24 hours before the moment of truth.*
*"It takes 70,000 hoppers 12 minutes to consume one cwt. of grass. The crack of a solid army of locusts feeding on the grass will sound like flames. The South Africans are going to dread this trip; they will see more locusts than they have ever done back home."*
*He said the insects would probably die within a month because of the climate and certainly before their wings developed.*[25]

Wilton-Godberford embodied the remarkable development of the STST: he was young, committed, and enterprising. More circumspect observers of the movement would comment that he was also typical of the self-regard among their number.

Wilton-Godberford was in any case not required to make good on his threat as the tour was cancelled, though not without the obligatory moral and organisational confusion from Lord's. Home Secretary Callaghan had made it clear that the MCC need not delegate responsibility for calling off the tour: 'It is not unfair to the Cricket Council to throw responsibility upon them. They invited the South Africans and they can uninvite them if they choose to do so.' The Cricket Council would not oblige, however, and continued to insist that the tour would go ahead, while each of their pronouncements left the door ajar for government intervention.

On 19th May the Cricket Council met for the last time before South Africa's anticipated arrival at the end of the month and delivered one final obfuscation. In a nonsensical compromise that suited absolutely no-one, it announced that all future tours by South Africa would be cancelled until teams were selected on a multi-racial basis – but that the 1970 team should proceed as planned. Ignoring events of the D'Oliveira affair and the rugby union tour, the Council effectively professed to exist in a political vacuum, strictly limiting its responsibilities to within cricketing parameters.

This insistence on keeping cricket and politics notionally separate was by now demonstrable nonsense: barbed wire surrounded the outfield at Lord's and the AAM's 'small minority of barbarians' were at the Grace gates. Once it was clear that administrators would not intervene, Callaghan stepped in. Following a meeting with the MCC and Cricket Council, he announced on 21st May that the government demanded withdrawal of SACA's invitation.

A second successive series between England and South Africa had been cancelled.

The expected £200,000 revenue was no longer slated for the MCC coffers and cricket fans who had not supported the STST movement despaired at being deprived of their summer fix. In a quick turn of foot not typically associated with the TCCB, an innovative and attractive solution was quickly put together. As had been mooted throughout the spring, a Rest of the World XI would play England in a five-match series instead. The RoW side was a formidable one, not least thanks to the inclusion of five South Africans who had been scheduled to visit the UK: Barry Richards, Graeme and Peter Pollock, Mike Procter and Eddie Barlow. Alongside these were four West Indian legends-in-the-making – the all-rounder Garry Sobers, batsmen Rohan Kanhai and Clive Lloyd, and spin bowler Lance Gibbs – as well as the glamorous Indian wicketkeeper-batsman Farokh Engineer, Pakistan's intelligent leg spinner Intikhab Alam and Australian fast bowler Garth McKenzie.

Under the captaincy of the great Sobers the RoW XI recorded a 4-1 series victory, a highly competitive contest after an innings victory for the visitors at Lord's. England levelled the series in Nottingham and played their part in three keenly contested matches at Edgbaston, Headingley and The Oval. D'Oliveira and Tony Greig, the colourful Eastern Cape-born all-rounder who had emigrated to the UK in the mid-1960s and qualified to play for England through his Scottish mother, each made major contributions that offered further indications of cricket's strength in the land of their birth. South Africa's additional potency with these two and any number of disenfranchised non-whites would have brought an abrupt conclusion to any debate over South African claims to be the world's best side. Richards and Procter played their part, and Graeme Pollock made a century in the final Test, but South Africa supplied a star attraction in Barlow. The boisterous, bustling all-rounder was alone in considering himself the equal of the most talented players on either side but scored centuries in the opening two matches and claimed 12 wickets at Leeds.

The series was loved by many, earning fulsome praise from EW Swanton: 'The Tests were contested with the utmost rigour, and produced some of the best Test cricket seen in England. I suppose that the 1948 Australians might be thought to match this side [...] nine men who might make a hundred, every type of bowling represented and the height of virtuosity in the field.'[26] And Procter recalls, 'It was very, very special indeed. I must say it's one of the greatest sides I've ever played for but, to me, what was so great about that side was that we all got on so well – it was the best spirit of almost any side I've played in. We had a lot of fun and played some fantastic cricket together, having Garry Sobers as captain was tremendous and it was just a wonderful experience.'

There had been no little entertainment and an obvious statement in the Pollocks, Barlow, Richards and Procter thriving alongside West Indians, Pakistanis and an Indian. It is doubtful that Vorster cheered his compatriots on the BBC World Service or enjoyed the picture of Sobers and Graeme Pollock sharing a 165-run partnership at The Oval. At the same time the matches were awkward to classify as an identical substitute for Test cricket and though they were initially afforded official Test status this was later withdrawn. Most of all the South African players yearned for restoration to the Springbok green and gold, and upon leaving England at the end of the 1970 summer they fully expected a rapid return to national colours.

This expectation was quickly and emphatically dashed. The D'Oliveira affair and subsequent STST success would prove a watershed in anti-apartheid protest with sport a low-risk, low-cost, richly symbolic means of arranging opposition. Football, tennis, athletics, boxing, netball and basketball by now had all suspended international relations with the republic along with a host of minority sports including judo, wrestling, weightlifting, fencing and cycling. South Africa's cricketers had begun 1970 by establishing themselves as the world's leading Test team, apparently heralding a new era of dominance; they ended it as pariahs, not only deposed as kings of the cricket world but exiled altogether.

Their next date was a 1971–72 tour of Australia but trenchant international opposition made preparations for the trip wildly optimistic. In a dramatic if tokenistic gesture SACA invited their non-white counterparts to nominate 'two players on merit' for the tour, but the government ruled out the possibility. SACA pressed on with a trial match to select a touring party and, anxious to distance themselves from Pretoria, the leading players planned a protest of their own. The first ball of the match was bowled to Richards by Procter, pushed for a single, and then batsmen and fielders walked from the field, leaving the umpires in the middle. A subsequent statement, backed by almost all players present, including the RoW quintet, read: 'We cricketers feel that the time has come for an expression of our views. We fully support the South African Cricket Association's application to include non-whites on the tour to Australia if good enough and, furthermore, subscribe to merit being the only criterion on the cricket field.'

Their gesture infuriated the National Party establishment and provoked a brief public furore inside South Africa, but critics of players' political apathy saw their condemnation confirmed: it was too little, too late. Natal bowler Vince van der Bijl, who took part in the walk-off and was selected for the Australia tour, recalls, 'Contextually we thought we were being quite brave but we weren't really. We never said, "We will not play cricket unless there is multi-racial sport." And if I look back on it I regret we didn't have the insight, as opposed to the courage, to do something like that. But at the time it was a stand that flabbergasted many people including the administrators. They were appalled and the Minister of Sport, would you believe, cancelled a *braaivleis*[27] and refused to give us our medals – really pathetic, reflecting their stupidity and arrogance.'

A chaotic Springbok rugby tour to Australia soon afterwards hammered the final nail into the coffin. Protestors built on the tactics and success of STST to envelop the visitors in chaos, adding their own twists such as the provocative dressing of Aboriginal protestors in Springbok green and gold. Although the three-Test series went ahead, and the visitors competed with greater composure in securing a 3-0 win, the off-field maelstrom was spectacular with the third match moved from Melbourne due to mass protests and Queensland declaring a state of emergency. Security and policing costs, coupled with the knowledge that cricket matches are far harder to police and protect, prompted Australian Cricket Board chairman Donald Bradman to withdraw the invitation in early September.

The reality had penetrated even the bubble, as the *Rand Daily Mail* lamented 'The first big achievement of Mr Vorster's sports policy. South African cricket, at the height of its brilliance, has been destroyed.'[28] It would be another 12 years before the Springbok emblem was worn on the cricket field – and only then in sparking a new and vociferous controversy that rocked cricket and the world far beyond. Cricket's age of revolution had only just begun.

1 Oborne (2004).
2 Front, *The Times*, 18 September 1968.
3 The AAM protested through consumer boycott, economic sanctions, arms embargo, cultural boycott, academic boycott and sports boycott. All of these were under way by 1968 and had enjoyed significant but mixed fortunes, eternally battling not only apartheid but entrenched political and business recalcitrance in the UK, and limited by the size and structure of the AAM. (pp 67–127, Fieldhouse 2004)
4 pp 38–9, Hain (1971).
5 In 1909 this was founded as the Imperial Cricket Conference; it had been renamed the International Cricket Conference in 1965 and would become the International Cricket Council in 1989.
6 pp 123–4, Oborne (2004). When the ICC became the International Cricket Conference in 1965 it began accepting 'associate members', who would play international cricket without Test status. The first were the United States and Fiji (1965), and Denmark and the Netherlands (1966). South Africa was not considered as they would not be permitted to play international matches at any level. (p 218, McGlew and Chesterfield (1995).
7 p 97, Booth (1998). The South African Non-Racial Olympic Committee (SANROC), run by Sam Ramsamy from a small office in north London, was integral to the Olympic exclusion and would also play an important role in co-ordinating rebel tour opposition.
8 p xiii, Green, ed. (1983).
9 p 122, Hain (1971).
10 pp 142–3, Hain (1971).
11 p 87, Fieldhouse (2004). 'This financial investment,' adds Fieldhouse, 'was as much a form of support for the apartheid regime as trade or military collaboration.' After South Africa's 1961 withdrawal from the Commonwealth, successive UK Governments fought to protect its preferential trade tariffs. In March 1968, shortly before the D'Oliveira Affair, the House of Commons Board of Trade outlined plans to expand trade with South Africa on account of its 'economic potential and likely political stability'. The UK was South Africa's biggest export market and South Africa in turn the UK's second biggest international customer. Relations covered minerals, finance, communications, manufacturing, food, tobacco and tourism. The only omission of note was arms following a 1963 United Nations embargo – but this measure itself was not watertight

and military trade to South Africa continued. Meanwhile the Conservative Party, Confederation of British Industry and other groups continued to campaign for relaxation or abolition of all restrictions with mixed success.

12 *Die Beeld*, 9 November 1969, replicated p 132, Hain (1971).
13 pp 98–9, Booth (1998).
14 p 11, Procter (1981); p 80, Richards (1978).
15 pp 80–1, Bose (1994).
16 pp 83, Hain (1971).
17 De Villiers was a member of the highly secretive Afrikaaner Broederbond, which exerted great influence on the National Party, and was later appointed ambassador to Britain. In that role in 1980 he explained all-white Springbok teams thus: 'Blacks have really only known Western sports for the past ten years.' (p 137, Booth 1998)
18 Although he later recanted Player was a repeated apologist for the apartheid system that had so benefited him. For example: 'I am of the South Africa of Verwoerd and apartheid.' (p 59, Booth 1998)
19 p 126, Hartman (2004).
20 Christopher Martin-Jenkins, *The Times*, 13–27 July 2002.
21 In seven Tests Procter made 226 runs at 25.11 without a half-century and took 41 wickets at an exceptional 15.01.
22 p 100, *Wisden*, 1982.
23 p 56, Bailey (1989).
24 p 21, *Guardian*, 13 February 1970.
25 p 2, *The Times*, 11 May 1970.
26 p 369, Swanton (1983).
27 Southern African social custom most easily translated as 'barbecue'.
28 p 10, *Rand Daily Mail*, 9 September 1971.

## Chapter 2

# Making the Unthinkable Thinkable

*'We're really on our own.' – Ali Bacher*

South Africa's international sporting exclusion intensified the post-D'Oliveira pressure on the National Party government. It was a high-profile overseas embarrassment, an external mark of their internal reality. And white South Africa, a society that placed particular cultural and historical significance on sporting achievement, rounded on Prime Minister Vorster for inviting their exclusion.

As early as 1971 the boycott's impact was illustrated in two polls: 'in the first, 925 prominent South Africans were interviewed and a full 79% favoured sports integration; in the second 276 out of 292 top white cricketers said they were prepared to play with or against blacks at league level.'[1] Prior to 1970 only a handful of prominent whites inside or outside sport had publicly espoused integration.

Exclusion also hurt the 'white South African in the street', communicating the disapproval of the outside world, even if many remained convinced that they were the 'victim of a vendetta', most likely a communist conspiracy.[2] The National Party needed a policy that was compatible with their own extreme ideology while encouraging the international readmission that so many of its voters craved.

For cricket, the ICC stipulated two conditions for readmittance: teams selected on a multi-racial basis and investment in under-privileged areas. By South African standards these represented a revolution and the earliest attempts to meet them were perverse. Vorster, apparently blind to the irony in demanding politics be kept out of sport during the D'Oliveira affair, had already responded to the Mexico '68 exclusion by hosting two tournaments under the Olympic symbol: a white South African games at Bloemfontein in 1969 and a black games in Soweto the following year.[3] These had been followed by South Africa's expulsion from the IOC but with impeccable consistency he sought to better establish the policy of 'multi-nationalism'.

Vorster's principle was that the South African population would be divided into 'nations' rather than racial groups. South Africans could compete against each other in multi-racial 'open international events', representing their respective 'nation', but not as members of an integrated South African team. Thus, in the International Datsun Double Wicket competition in September 1973 Edmund Ntikinca and Edward Habane represented 'South African Africans' (i.e. black South Africa) against 'South Africa' (i.e. white South Africa) and international pairings.[4] At the 1973 South African Games overseas athletes competed against four South African teams representing the different racial classifications.[5] And in the 1975 Durban to Pietermaritzburg marathon the six non-white South Africans in a 1500-man field were obliged to wear Nazi Germany-echoing tribal arm-bands.[6]

It was also permissible for foreign teams to field multi-racial sides in the republic – against separate white and black South African teams at segregated stadia. Among the first to take advantage of these changes was

Derrick Robins, a flamboyant businessman and briefly a Warwickshire batsman who organised private tours to the republic. The first of these in early 1973 featured five England internationals, including the young fast bowler Bob Willis, and attracted big crowds: 6,500 saw Barry Richards hit a century against the Robins XI at Johannesburg.[7] But it was the second tour, in 1973–74, that was most notable as government inivtations were extended to Younis Ahmed of Pakistan and the West Indian John Shepherd, two Test players and the first non-whites to play in South Africa in a SACA-sponsored side. In line with 'multi-nationalism' the schedule featured the South African African Cricket Board XI, the first time black South Africans had faced a team containing white foreigners since 1892. The home team, including Ntikinca, Habane and the 20-year-old all-rounder Khaya Majola, were outclassed in a 220-run defeat as experienced Test batsmen John Edrich and Graham Roope scored centuries, and Australia spinner John Gleeson claimed 7-33.[8]

In addition, the 'international' theme was embraced with three 'mini-Tests' against a South African Invitation XI. Captained by Eddie Barlow following Ali Bacher's retirement, this was effectively a full-strength white South African XI that included Mike Procter, Barry Richards, Graeme Pollock, Vintcent van der Bijl and Hylton Ackerman. Despite a general sense among South African cricket that they had not shown their full strength, they prevailed 1-0 in the 'mini-Test' series. Third and fourth tours went ahead in successive years, and with distinctive popularity among cricketers, for whom South Africa was always a popular touring destination. Australian internationals including Trevor Chappell and Bruce Francis, GB Troup of New Zealand, and current and future England caps including Tony Greig, Derek Randall and Mike Hendrick all helped to maintain a high standard.

In 1976 an International Wanderers XI managed by Richie Benaud toured the republic and the willingness of leading cricketers to maintain relations was clear. The hugely respected Benaud led a party including not only West Indian international Shepherd but also Australians Dennis Lillee, Alan Hurst, Gary Gilmour, and Ian and Greg Chappell; current England players Mike Denness, Phil Edmonds, Bob Taylor and Derek Underwood; and New Zealander Glenn Turner. The Wanderers XI produced the best standard of cricket played in the republic in the 1970s, as Vince van der Bijl recalls: 'That was a really strong team. We knew it wasn't Test cricket because they were invitational, but the experience was fantastic.

'I remember Dennis Lillee bowling to me. I go out to bat and we're in deep shit at 99-7, and I join 'Tich' Smith[9] and as I walk to the wicket Dennis looks at me and says, "Hiya, Vince. I'll give you one to get off the mark." And I said, "Thanks Dennis." And then as I get down – no helmet, nothing – I suddenly realise he means a bouncer and start to think, "This guy could kill you." So as he starts to deliver, I duck and thank God this blur goes past me. Smith strolls down the wicket and says to me, "Lucky he bowled you a slower one!" But we put on about 60[10] and had the privilege of playing against the best in the world.'

Off the field SACA and their government proclaimed great progress through the tours. The South African press hailed the SAACB XI v Robins XI match as historic, garnering column inches alongside the Yom Kippur War and Watergate scandal, while Bruce Francis believed that attitudes to non-whites were civilised by the trip, recalling two white South Africans' glowing review: 'We had dinner with John Shepherd and Younis Ahmed and they are far classier people than we are.'[11]

Certainly they provided welcome stimulation to

isolated white cricket. Richards described them as the most enjoyable matches of the season[12] and the historian Ray Knowles wrote, 'Although not to be compared with official tours, Derrick Robins provided the South African public with cricket at a time when it was much needed. In a return to the origins of such touring, entrepreneurs saw possibilities in South Africa's isolation.'[13]

The picture beyond white cricket, as ever, was rather different. The 'multi-national' policy was a matter of semantics, a 'new name for an old game', in the words of leading activist Dennis Brutus. For all the Vorster government contortions to appease international opposition, 'multi-nationalism' perpetuated categorisation by race. And the Robins tours softened the boycott's impact on the 'white man in the street' since international cricketers were apparently still happy to visit the republic and play matches against an all-white South Africa XI. While *Wisden* reported that Shepherd and Ahmed were 'accepted and acclaimed wherever they went'[14], non-white political campaigners were dismayed by their presence. David Curry, coloured Labour Party deputy leader, rebuked the pair: 'We do not view your visit with gratefulness. We will not be used as the white man's tool for crawling back into world sport – and if he wants to crawl back into world sport let him crawl on his underbelly, not on the backs of blacks.'[15]

Majola, the iconic black South African cricketer of the 1970s, would later regret his involvement in the SAACB XI, citing youthful naivety. The following year he refused to partner Habane in the Datsun Double Wicket in a high-profile line-up including Barlow and Richards, Ian and Greg Chappell, and Greig and Keith Fletcher. He instead joined those battling for non-racial sport from the outside: '[The SAACB XI] was clearly a show for the government and the white cricket board.'[16] That viewpoint was strengthened in 1975 when a South

African Africans XI was invited to enter the Gillette Cup, the premier domestic one-day competition. Examination of the small print revealed that they would be pre-drawn against the Currie Cup champions Natal and in the unlikely event of victory forbidden from playing in the next round.[17]

Unity in South African cricket remained out of reach. Following the ICC's decree, SACA had sought in 1972 to unify the three 'national' bodies under an umbrella organisation, the Cricket Council of South Africa. The black SAACB had accepted the alliance, albeit reluctantly, to ensure access to the best facilities and equipment for their members. But the Asian and coloured South African Cricket Board of Control (SACBOC), led by the charismatic Hassan Howa, declined to join as long as membership remained 'multi-national' instead of unified.[18]

'Multi-nationalism' had done nothing to mollify isolationists inside or outside South Africa and the enduring pressure was brought to bear on the Vorster Government. In 1974 it was announced that multi-racial sport would be allowed in domestic as well as international events – in those sports where South Africa was forbidden from international competition. It was an emphatic victory for the boycott, which had achieved its original aim startlingly quickly. In five years there had been a paradigm shift in the legality and public perception of multi-racial sport in South Africa, and in January 1976 cricket became the first major sport to embrace this new 'normality'. The SAACB, SACBOC and SACA all accepted the proposal of 'participation of and competition between all cricketers regardless of race, creed or colour in cricket at club level under one provincial governing body', the South African Cricket Union (SACU).

'The "normal cricket" agreement created great excitement,' wrote the historian Andre Odendaal. 'However, [it] was destined to end in failure. During the off-season, on 16 June, the Soweto uprisings began, fundamentally changing the course of South African history. As the country went up in flames, the concession of black and white being able to play cricket together on weekends while apartheid continued unabated in other areas of life seemed a triviality.'[19]

The limitations of the ICC's instruction to make cricket in South Africa multi-racial were now laid bare. While reversal of the sports boycott was listed third in a poll of desired change among white South Africans, it is doubtful if the same would have registered in the top 100 items for blacks, for whom maltreatment in sport was one part of a wider political and social denigration.[20] Non-white cricketers merely became 'white for the weekend', freed of tyranny temporarily, while at lower levels – for example in schools cricket – segregation remained necessarily dominant. Integration was also practised only in those sports where a boycott was in place. International rugby union – the game of the Afrikaaners who provided the foundation stone of National Party support – had continued to recognise an all-white Springbok XV. In 1970 New Zealand's All Blacks had been allowed to include Maori players as 'honorary whites' in their touring party for the first time on the 'informal understanding that they won't send us any very dark ones just now.'[21] The following year a visiting France team echoed the D'Oliveira affair in omitting the black wing Roger Bougarel from a South Africa touring squad then reinstating him; but there the similarities ended as the tour went ahead. But when outstanding South African rugby players the Watson brothers left their white board to play in integrated competition they were arrested by the authorities and became a target for violent reprisals. Government commitment to integration, and the singular impact of the boycott, were clear.

The stated aims of sporting isolationists now changed: removing apartheid from sport was not enough; only the abolition of apartheid itself would validate multi-racial sport. Despite the unprecedented sporting opportunities that 'normal' cricket now offered non-white cricketers in South Africa, the overwhelming majority remained loyal to the wider struggle. For Hassan Howa there could be 'no normal sport in an abnormal society' when there were 'still 387 racial laws in South Africa where a black person's skin was equated with a statutory crime.'[22] The official black and Asian boards joined the whites in the newly-formed, non-racial South African Cricket Union, but a majority of their members instead signed up with Howa in the South African Cricket Board. Where 'normal cricket' was tried, provincial boards offered hugely variable commitment to the scheme – Edward Habane was refused permission to play for a white club by Transvaal Cricket Union – and SACB dismissed SACU non-whites as traitors conspiring with the white plutocracy. With two rival boards largely defined by the racial make-up of their members, any notion of normality was strictly relative.

Overseas isolationist efforts were now bolstered by the leadership of national governments. Jamaican Prime Minister Michael Manley, whose 'love of cricket was rivalled only by his commitment to political decolonization'[23], ensured reluctant Caribbean states such as thebmore conservative Barbados joined his and Guyana's hard-line stance against South African engagement. Manley then led the negotiations among Commonwealth governments at Gleneagles in 1977, brokering a deal in which leaders 'accepted it as the urgent duty of each of the Governments vigorously to combat the evil of apartheid by withholding any form of support for it, and by taking every practical step to discourage contact or competition by their nationals with sporting organisations, teams or sportsmen from South Africa.'

The Gleneagles Agreement was not legally binding but it changed an issue of sports administration to one of national and international government. In doing so it completed a drastic shift from the origins of the sports boycott seven years earlier. Sporting links with South Africa were no longer equated with appeasing racism in sport; they would instead be viewed as direct support for the apartheid regime itself.

For white South Africans who just wanted to play cricket, the greatest frustration was obvious. The Springboks' status as the world's best team was hardly challenged. Bill Lawry was sacked as Australia captain after losing the Ashes in 1970–71 and though Ian Chappell inspired a resurgence as the decade gathered momentum he failed to regain the urn 18 months later despite the emergence of Dennis Lillee. England were beaten at home by the West Indies, who in turn had lost to Australia and India. Bishen Bedi's side perhaps made the most compelling case for a brief time in the early 1970s after back-to-back series successes in the Caribbean and England, but those victories were bookended by defeats against the same opposition as well as a heavy home loss to Australia.

This tit-for-tat atmosphere at the top of the world game only strengthened South African conviction that they were the default world champions, a belief evidenced further as their cricketers made formidable contributions in the first-class game. Mike Procter continued his relationship with Gloucestershire throughout the decade, forging an association so close that fans knew the county as Proctershire. He was the sort of player that demands iconic status: a ferociously fast bowler whose run-up seemed to start in the Bristol suburbs, headband straining to contain a mane of light brown hair; a fine slip fielder and a powerful batsman whose quick scoring belied a correct technique. Though it is impossible to bracket any player with Garry Sobers, few have come closer than Procter in terms of all-round talent. With Gloucestershire he became the first man to take a hat-trick and score a century in the same match twice; in Currie Cup cricket he was no less destructive, moving between Natal, Western Province and Rhodesia, and in 1970–71 equalling the record for six consecutive first-class centuries held by Donald Bradman and CB Fry. When his pace bowling yielded only a single wicket for Rhodesia against Transvaal in October 1972, he switched to off-spin and won the match with a career-best 9-71.[24]

Procter was one of a handful of South African cricket professionals who sought career satisfaction overseas, mostly in the English county championship. By the late 1970s other notables included Clive Rice, the fiery Nottinghamshire all-rounder; Ken McEwan, a prolific right-handed batsman with Essex; and Peter Kirsten, a commanding number three and outstanding cover fieldsman with Derbyshire. The majority, however, continued to play as amateurs and were largely unrecognised outside the republic. Among these the figurehead was Graeme Pollock. Scarcely a year older than Procter, his earlier start in Test cricket, announced with a century against Australia aged 19, had afforded him 23 caps and the opportunity to prove himself on the biggest stage. Like most Currie Cup players he played first-class cricket around a full-time job and he remained prolific in the South African domestic game, becoming a figurehead to a generation raised on 1960s Test cricket but destined never to enjoy exalted Springbok status. These were lamented in the South African press as 'God's forgotten cricketers': Arthur Short and Gary

'Chaka' Watson, who were the first to miss out after being selected to visit England in 1970; and players of the 1970s including Vince van der Bijl, Dassie Biggs, Peter de Vaal and Hylton Ackerman.[25]

And then there was Barry Richards, the professional who would find isolation the most difficult of all. As a near-contemporary of Pollock he had missed earlier chances to play for South Africa – notably in 1967, after an altercation with a doorman during an official reception for the touring Australians. A displaced flower pot cost Richards three rand to repair but three years of Test cricket as the Springbok administration took a dim view and neglected to pick an identified troublemaker. Five times in the 1970s he scored more than 1,000 runs in a South African season and he became the first South African to score more than 1,000 Currie Cup runs twice. In 1970–71 he played a season in Australia's Sheffield Shield and made the most notoriously competitive of domestic competitions look like a Sunday knockabout, setting a South Australia record of 1,538 runs in the season. For Hampshire, he partnered Gordon Greenidge in one of the county game's greatest ever pairings, winning the championship in 1973. Proclaiming that top cricketers ought to earn the same as golfers and tennis players, he toured the world relentlessly, playing all year round, but an unabashed willingness to accept the right cheque also brought derision, notably when he left Natal for grade cricket in Australia and later played in a privately financed deal in the Netherlands. In 1977 he went so far as to make a public plea for the scrapping of the Currie Cup B-section so that the money could be spent in wages and bonuses for top players.[26]

This attitude brought criticism from the South African public, who felt that Richards did not always give his all in domestic cricket. Certainly it was true that he did not hide his struggles for motivation and in an 18-year career he played only 79 Currie Cup matches. But in averaging 60.40, he scored 36 centuries, a feat put into context by Graeme Pollock's 35 centuries in 157 Currie Cup matches. Moreover, Richards was not motivated solely by money. He embodied the brilliance and frustration of white South African cricket, and by the mid-1970s he endured growing disillusionment at life without the personal and professional fulfilment of international recognition. Particularly after his 30th birthday, which followed quickly the 1975 World Cup, he experienced a deepening futility: 'In 1967 no young man could have loved cricket more than BA Richards; ten years later there could be no more disenchanted player in the first-class game ... *Wisden*, my childhood bible, seems as interesting as reading the dictionary ... by 1977 I had become so disenchanted that even a hundred before lunch left me with no sense of elation.'[27] For a man who had found batting so easy against even the very best, there were no more worlds to conquer.

That first World Cup was another defining moment for South African cricket. Within the republic it was not afforded great interest, as if a shallow diversion, but the world game embraced a successful, if disconcertingly commercial, innovation: two weeks of highly competitive, often spectacular cricket, and won on the very final ball by the West Indies, who would soon replace the 1970 Springboks as the decade's outstanding team. Two years later at the Centenary Test in Melbourne, South Africa was on the outside again. At a showpiece match between Australia and England to mark their first ever meeting at the MCG in 1877, self-congratulation was everywhere but one of the ICC's three founder members went unacknowledged. The game itself was bizarre with both sides making less than 150 in the first innings then more than 400 in the second as Australia won by 46 runs. Former England captain Colin Cowdrey wrote fondly in *The Times*, 'It will be much the same 100 years from now.'[28]

Others at the Test had different ideas.

Within two months of the Centenary Test, cricket as Colin Cowdrey and the rest of the world had known it was finished. The Australian media tycoon Kerry Packer had been frustrated in attempts to buy television rights to international cricket as the Australian Cricket Board, in keeping with the cricket authority tendency towards cosiness over strategy, extended their long-standing relationship with the Australian Broadcasting Corporation. And so Packer did the unprecedented: he secretly signed 35 elite players – among them Greg Chappell, Tony Greig and Clive Lloyd, the respective captains of Australia, England and West Indies – for a new, unauthorised competition, World Series Cricket.

This was the greatest of all cricket crises, denounced at the time by writers, administrators and fans alike. England sacked Greig as captain and the ICC placed a ban on all participants returning to first-class and international cricket. But the ban was unsustainable. WSC would prove an archetype of creative destruction, the breakdown of monopoly power among honorary authorities opening new earning opportunities and ways of organising professional cricket. Coloured clothing, floodlights and helmets were all used seriously for the first time; on-field microphones and multiple camera angles were among the notable experiments in pioneering television coverage.

Cricket had edged towards full-time professionalism throughout the 1970s, tentatively embracing new sponsorship and one-day formats. But progress had been slow and even the England captain Greig was said to earn less than £10,000 per year. West Indian players were poorer paid still, unable to make a living out of the game without a county contract or regular international appearance fees. The previous year Pakistan's squad had threatened to strike before a tour of Australia, securing better pay for their efforts. The enduring administrative complacency had been epitomised gloriously in 1972 by Alan Barnes, ACB secretary, who had said of a potential strike by the national team: 'These are not professionals … they were all invited to play and if they don't like the conditions there are 500,000 other cricketers in Australia who would love to take their places.'[29]

That complacency was exploded in May 1977, and the gulf between professionals and administrators laid bare in the dramatic breakaway. Chris Harte wrote in *A History of Australian Cricket*, 'The fact that not one player, nor any state official who was in the know, passed on any hint or information showed the disdain in which cricketers held the board.'[30] In total 28 Australians, 18 West Indians and 22 others signed up as Packer ransacked international set-ups by offering three-year contracts worth AUS$60,000–90,000, supplemented by sponsorship deals. But it was also noteworthy that the powerful mogul treated his new employees with a respect and sympathy seldom associated with national boards. As each season lasted only around 12 weeks, albeit characterised by an unprecedented intensity, the rewards had been unimaginable within the game at large. The Series proceeded with three teams – Australian, West Indies and Rest of the World XIs under the respective captaincies of Ian Chappell, Lloyd and Greig – playing 'Supertests' and one-day matches for five-figure prize money.

After an unsettled first season the second campaign was a notable success for those taking part while wreaking havoc on the game outside. The Chappells' Australians included ten of their Centenary Test XI and Alan Barnes' threat was laid bare by two miserable years for the establishment loyalists under Kim Hughes and Graham Yallop, culminating in a thumping 1978–79 Ashes defeat to an England side themselves deprived of Greig, Derek Underwood, Alan Knott, Dennis Amiss, John Snow and Bob Woolmer. The 1977 Australians became known as 'the team Packer poisoned', and even if their problems extended beyond WSC, the impact was still enormous.

The West Indies by contrast were singular beneficiaries. With the inspirational World Cup-winner Lloyd staunchly in the Packer camp, and quick to recruit his team-mates to the cause, the West Indies XI extended the development they had undergone throughout the 1970s. Michael Holding says, 'We became a lot more professional because Packer demanded it. We were given a dedicated fitness trainer for the first time and we became a lot fitter, more focused and more professional. And it served its purpose. We went back to playing for the West Indies and we dominated the world. It was not the first time the West Indies had produced talented cricketers but it was the first time we had dominated the world.' Of the West Indies team that retained the World Cup against England at Lord's in 1979, only Alvin Kallicharran had not played WSC and that was not for want of trying; he had helped broker deals for team-mates and hoped to sign up himself before eventually honouring a deal with Queensland radio station 4IP.

No other national team was quite so affected by loss of personnel but WSC caused a fundamental restructuring of the world game. The TCCB and ICC had tried to bar Packer players from all first-class and international cricket, and were challenged in the High Court. After a 31-day hearing, in which Greig and Mike Procter defended the players' freedom to trade and Geoffrey Boycott was among those supporting the establishment, the High Court in London found in the rebels' favour.

The judgement that no-one had a monopoly on the world game was an unwelcome and costly shock to the national boards, who paid in wounded pride and £200,000 legal fees. Unrest about the wisdom of the venture, and the clandestine manner in which it had been conducted, would ensure rippling consequences but the matter, officially at least, was closed.

Throughout, South Africa stood apart. Packer's chief lieutenant Greig had made use of his South African connections to sign eight players in total: in the first raft of signings in April 1977 established stars Procter, Barry Richards, Graeme Pollock and Eddie Barlow were joined by Western Province leg spinner Denys Hobson; aggressive all-rounder Clive Rice was signed for the second season along with two outstanding young players to emerge since isolation, teenage opening batsman Kepler Wessels and fast bowler Garth Le Roux.

And while WSC was able to circumvent the international cricket establishment, it too required an answer to the South African question. Jamaican Prime Minister Michael Manley was in the process of brokering the Gleneagles Agreement and was determined to meet his own obligations in the discouragement of South African links. Michael Holding says, 'When I signed it was with the stipulation that I would not have to play with South Africans who had not played outside South Africa. I told them then and there that I could not be involved with those South Africans as my Prime Minister Michael Manley would not allow me to play.'

Pollock and Hobson were therefore persona non grata. Despite Packer's personal intervention, and Pollock's participation in Rest of the World Test series with England and Australia, Manley remained consistent to political principle. For Pollock the financial aspect was secondary to a surely final chance, at the age of 33, to play international cricket, but he returned to South Africa with good grace citing 'scheduling problems'. Hobson withdrew on the public grounds of a 'shoulder injury' but evidently found the Cape recuperative. He strengthened his reputation as the country's best slow bowler during isolation with a fruitful Currie Cup campaign including a career-best 9-64 against Eastern Province.[31]

For those who did play, and in particular Richards and Procter, the WSC proved an exhilarating release. Seven and a half years after last pulling on the Springbok colours they were afforded the opportunity to play with and against the world's leading players at an intensity approaching international standard. These two were lynchpins in Greig's Rest of the World XI, a hybrid of English, South African and Pakistani players that also included the rising star Imran Khan and Procter's Gloucestershire colleagues Zaheer Abbas and Sadiq Mohammad. At certain stages they joined forces with the West Indians to form a collective opposition, while New Zealand star Richard Hadlee later appeared in something approaching a truly representative RoW XI against the Australians.[32]

Both Richards and Procter took the opportunity to demonstrate their excellence. Even at 32 and with contact lenses to correct myopia in his left eye, Richards finished behind only his namesake Viv in the Supertest averages – and managed to eclipse the West Indian tyro with a masterful 207 when the two batted together in the fifth match at Perth in January 1978.

The WSC also offered the opportunity for personal appearances and sponsorship, but it was the professional fulfilment that mattered most. He says, 'World Series Cricket was an opportunity for the South Africans to test themselves against the best. For us at the end of our careers, or certainly for me at the end of my career, it was an opportunity to prove myself. And for guys like Garth Le Roux who was a generation apart, it was an opportunity to show that South Africa still had some of the best cricketers in the world.'

The strength of South African cricket's elite was still evident. Barlow, 37 before a ball had been bowled in the WSC, enjoyed a last hurrah, Le Roux emerged as the great unknown fast bowler of the world, and Rice and Wessels also confirmed their status as players of international class, the latter doing so for Australia after impressing in grade cricket. Australia's uniform did not immunise the teenager from political interference, however: when WSC Australians and West Indies made a difficult visit to the Caribbean at the end of the 1978–79 campaign he was forbidden as a South African from entering the islands.

For all the unique travails endured by the South African players during WSC, the conclusion of the tournament truly spelled out their singular status. Having signed for three-year contracts in 1977 they anticipated at least one more season of international cricket by another name. Procter had even shaken hands on a new three-year deal with Packer's right-hand man Lynton Taylor and left his kit in Australia. But for the rest of the world it was time to move on. Although it had come to embrace and admire the style and spectacle of WSC, the Australian cricket public desired a healing process to unify their team and in particular restore the traditional dominance of the Ashes. Packer had initiated the series as a business strategy first and foremost, and the ACB were now willing seriously to consider his broadcasting services for the first time.

For the players, too, it was time to restore the status quo; WSC had served its purpose. Test fees had risen markedly – England players went from £250 to £1,000 per match in the summer of 1977 as WSC recruitment kicked in – and there was a growing desire to return to national colours. Imran Khan wrote: 'For all the excitement of World Series Cricket, I had really missed the tension and commitment of proper Test cricket. Had WSC gone on for another season, as originally planned, I think a number of players – including me – would have dropped out.'[33] And Joel Garner echoed those sentiments: 'We remained at heart West Indies players. I felt this meant we should be playing West Indies Test cricket.'[34]

For Richards, Procter and co there was no such alternative. The three-year contracts were honoured in full for all Packer players but this was scant consolation to those for whom WSC represented the pinnacle of their post-1970 careers. Procter was 'dumbfounded… very upset' while the curtailment was perhaps hardest of all on Rice. The all-rounder, famed for his competitive on-field attitude, had been selected for the Springboks' abandoned 1971–72 Australia tour aged 22. Upon hearing the news the most bellicose of cricketers 'wept into his wife's arms.'[35]

While South Africa's leading players reeled at this classic one-two from hope and despair, their administrators had food for thought. As the cricket historian Gideon Haigh wrote in his definitive *The Cricket War*, Packer had 'made the unthinkable thinkable: that men would play for money rather than merely for national pride.'[36]

South Africa's cricket authorities now felt the impetus to act. The domestic game had entered a serious decline for the first time since isolation. Deprived of key players by WSC and denied the competitive and commercial engine of international cricket, standards and spectator numbers were falling. Ken McEwan, whose 74 first-class centuries is the second highest among those never to play Test cricket, joined Western Australia rather than rejoin Eastern Province in 1979. And Brian Davison, who played for Rhodesia and captained Leicestershire, moved to Tasmania the same season. While English and Australian cricket were professionalised and Packer-ised, it was not uncommon for key players to miss Currie Cup duty due to work commitments.

It had been a decade of frustration. Their greatest ever team had been thwarted by the boycott and, realising that for this they had only themselves to blame, the South African Cricket Union had dismantled racial barriers. This not only placed South African cricket in a more justifiable position than the 1960s, when a whites-only team had been acceptable to the ICC. It also put them far in advance of a contemporary South African society prescribed by apartheid policy.

Nevertheless it was clear that the Springboks would never be readmitted until apartheid had been dismantled in its entirety. The Gleneagles Agreement had established sporting links as an international political issue. Then in 1979 ICC representatives toured the republic and concluded that cricket had become completely integrated. It recommended 'that a strong team representative of as many countries as possible from the ICC be sent to South Africa to play a series of matches at the highest representative level during the 1979–80 season, and that any profits be used to further the cause of normal or non-racial cricket in South Africa.'[37]

This report went unpublished at the behest of India, Pakistan and the West Indies, whose boards matched their governments' South Africa position, and illustrated the entrenched views on both sides of the debate, much of which had not changed since Stop the Seventy Tour. For those who believed in bridge-building it was unanswerable evidence for abandoning the boycott. This had now achieved its goal and engagement would break down more barriers than isolation. A popular refrain became: 'Whose cause would be advanced by cricketers not touring?'

But to the boycott movement the mainly white ICC delegation had seen what their hosts had wanted them to see. As far as critics of engagement were concerned, multi-racial cricket was little more than propaganda. Moreover the debate certainly had changed since 1970: contrary to bridge-builders' expectations the boycott had exerted a measurable effect on the South African government. The boycott movement, and their supporters within the ICC, believed it might continue to do so. As TCCB chairman Doug Insole told SACU representative Ali Bacher, 'Until apartheid goes, you can forget about getting back into world cricket. England cannot support you. If we did, it would be the end of English cricket. The black nations would not play against us.'[38]

As professional administrators SACU did not recognise the non-cricket issues propagated by the boycott movement. Transvaal board member Mark Henning later said, 'We could hear Hassan Howa but we couldn't understand. He and his colleagues were part of a bigger power struggle, we were simply running cricket.'[39] Bacher, who did not believe apartheid would end in his lifetime, returned from his meeting at Lord's and told his colleagues, 'We can forget about getting back into world cricket through the front door. We're really on our own.'[40]

The back-door solution was fraught with difficulty. In bringing leading international cricketers to the republic SACU would have to ape Packer not only in trumping national pride with money, but in maintaining total secrecy. Rumours abounded throughout the late 1970s of attempts to approach Test players for trips to South Africa, though the waters were always muddy. The West Indies, as the world's best and most entertaining team, were the prime targets but their front-line players were always out of reach. Michael Holding had already taken a hard-line stance on South African engagement during World Series Cricket and his captain Clive Lloyd was a vocal critic of apartheid links.

Lloyd inspired great loyalty, and his judgement and intellect were hugely respected among his peers. But unlike WSC recruitment, when the team had followed Lloyd's lead, his guidance was less influential when it came to a South African tour. Most team-mates held strong personal views when it came to apartheid and leading players, notably Holding, Viv Richards and Joel Garner, repeatedly publicised their hostility to any tour.

'We were always being offered money to go to South Africa,' Lloyd said later. 'I mean huge amounts, massive amounts, hundreds of thousands of dollars. The sort of money that would have made me comfortable for the rest of my life. But money is not all.'[41] Though no intellectual, Richards had a keen interest in identity politics and was staunchly opposed to playing in the republic: 'Our people have been bought and sold throughout history. I don't care whatever anyone else does – I will never play cricket in South Africa. That kind of money goes to show you that things are not really right.'[42]

These clandestine approaches came from middlemen and so it was never clear how feasible the offers were and to what extent they had SACU's support. One such entrepreneur, Lancashire-born record producer Peter Cooke, would cross the threshold. A friend and business associate of Geoffrey Boycott, he had sounded out the Yorkshireman before England's tour of the West Indies in 1980–81 and was duly invited out to the team hotel on Trinidad during the first Test at Port of Spain. The Johannesburg resident arrived unnoticed on a British passport and after a promoter's pitch to the team found himself pushing against an open door.

Where Lloyd and Richards were vehement on the South African question, none of the English players had such reservations. Cricket remained a high-profile vehicle for anti-apartheid sentiment, driven by the Caribbean and Asian countries, but the commitment of its professionals to the boycott was always open to question. The assumption that South African business would sponsor any tour was neither substantiated nor challenged, with the English players accepting the idea readily: any trip would be about sport and commerce, but not politics.

On Trinidad Hilton notepaper Boycott, Graham Gooch, David Gower, Ian Botham, Graham Dilley and John Emburey provided written confirmation of their interest in a 'quiet, private' tour but expected little to come of a meeting that remained a closely guarded secret. Boycott had in mind nothing more than a high-class version of the Derrick Robins XI: 'The tour would involve as many current England players as possible and would be so arranged as not to clash with the county championship. It was never intended to be an alternative to established cricket and we genuinely believed that we could fit in a South African tour without breaking our county contracts and without disrupting the international Test schedule.'[43]

This belief was challenged within days of leaving the Trinidad Hilton when the second Test on Guyana was cancelled for an unrelated South Africa furore. Bob Willis, who would certainly have been invited to join the six signatories in Trinidad, had instead returned to England with an injury and was replaced by Robin Jackman, who had wintered in South Africa for 11 consecutive years.

During this time he had played for Rhodesia and Western Province in the Currie Cup, coached at various clubs and married a South African woman. His name was on a United Nations blacklist for sportsmen with close links to the republic. The UK government was adamant that, having played in South Africa as an individual rather than as part of a tour party, Jackman was not in breach of the Gleneagles Agreement and the British High Commissioner issued a forceful rebuttal: 'The whole thing is idiotic. The fact that Robin Jackman is here as part of a multi-racial England team to play in multi-racial Guyana against a multi-racial West Indies team is hardly a demonstration of apartheid.'[44] But the Guyanese government quickly revoked his visa and demanded he leave the country.

Evoking memories of the D'Oliveira affair – 'when one team in a cricket match insists on choosing both teams, reality has degenerated into Mad Hatterism' – England were adamant that they would not play the Test. The Guyanese had taken an extreme position, almost certainly otherwise motivated,[45] but an international diplomatic furore over an uncapped 35-year-old swing bowler reiterated cricket's position in the midst of the heated and emotive apartheid debate. Once Guyana's natural ally in these matters, Jamaica, confirmed that the Gleneagles Agreement did not apply, normal service was resumed. The West Indies eased to a 2-0 victory over four completed matches. For those who had just signed their interest in a secret tour of South Africa, it might still have served as a cautionary tale.

The hope that an unofficial South Africa tour might now be arranged without serious political disruption would have been charitably considered naive, more accurately obtuse. When a corruption scandal ended BJ Vorster's 12-year reign in 1978 he was replaced by PW Botha, but savage government and ruthless subjugation of dissent continued – and continued to be reported in the UK. Moreover English cricket had been returned to the forefront of the apartheid debate in the Jackman affair. Cricket had never instigated measures against South Africa; it had been repeatedly appropriated by those outside the game as a high-profile means of communicating international opposition to the apartheid regime. Any weakening of this opposition could expect a similarly high profile, particularly so when the AAM designated 1982 the International Year of Mobilisation for Sanctions against South Africa.[46]

Yet Peter Cooke's signatories remained extraordinarily detached. English cricketers going to South Africa to earn their living had been part of the professional game for decades and any offer from Cooke looked likely to increase the usual coaching salary by a multiple of 50 – with luxury travel and accommodation, and the use of tax-avoidance specialists among the added perks. The prospect of such returns only increased hostility to those pushing the political aspects. Geoffrey Boycott considered his recruitment offers 'a business proposition of the type that might be considered in any walk of life'[47] and the Essex and England seamer John Lever had previously summed up the 'cricketer's position' in writing: 'I just want to go out and play cricket and make a living and I can't stand those people who sit in dingy government offices telling me where I can and can't play the game and earn some money.'[48]

In addition to the prevailing apolitical atmosphere, there were further encouragements for would-be South Africa tourists. Commercial trade with the republic remained commonplace and lucrative, and Western nations played sport with regimes from the Soviet Union to Uganda. These inconsistencies appealed greatly and most thought that if travelling en masse to South Africa they would enjoy safety in numbers and escape serious sanctions. Few appreciated that as public figures they could expect an altogether different reaction.

For the moment this was a minor concern as Peter Cooke's signatories had returned home expecting nothing to come of the proposal. The stakes were raised again in the summer of 1981 when the Ashes series captured the public imagination. Leading 1-0 into the third Test at Headingley, Australia posted 401-9 declared in their first innings, bowled the hosts out for 174 and then reduced them to 135-7 following on. An England win was 500-1 with the bookmakers and Michael Brearley's side had booked out of their hotel a day early in anticipation of a premature conclusion to the match. But Ian Botham, with the unlikely help of tail-ender Graham Dilley, turned the game on its head with an unbeaten 149 as Australia were set 130 to win. The veteran pace bowler Bob Willis's 8-43 on the final day secured an 18-run victory and a defining place in Ashes history.[49] Only the second team to win a Test match following on, England were revitalised and would retain the urn 3-1 with their all-rounder's talismanic performances establishing the series sobriquet 'Botham's Ashes'. He was already a national celebrity, a familiar sight playing in the Bob Hope Classic with Sean Connery as well as in his whites, but this was an era-defining moment. England's cricketers, and Botham in particular, suddenly enjoyed iconic status in the national consciousness.

Despite Cooke's apparent inactivity, the shadow of apartheid was ever present and English cricket's commitment to the sporting boycott always in doubt. At the end of the 1981 season the TCCB discovered that John Edrich, an England selector, had been recruiting players for a 'Counties XI' tour of the republic. This was rapidly stamped out with an edict to county players that they would be 'placing their careers in jeopardy' by embarking on a private tour, an instruction that did not impress professionals who were contracted only from April to September each year. Beyond the few players fortunate enough to earn international recognition or coaching jobs during the winter months, most were grateful for any work they could get. Many had to satisfy themselves on the dole.

Then in September, Cooke's team re-entered the picture. The Holiday Inns company had offered a confirmed £500,000 budget to fund a short tour of

South Africa, money that lifted the eyebrows of even England's leading players.

The party swelled to nine as Mike Gatting, Alan Knott and Willis each confirmed an interest but plans to squeeze the trip into October were shelved while another South African debate raged. England's imminent tour of India hung in the balance over the fact that opening batsmen Boycott and Geoff Cook had both spent considerable time in the republic, in Cook's case coaching while Boycott had established Johannesburg as his favourite destination for a warming winter break.

Needless to say, if a strong English party had toured South Africa in the build-up this would have not only ended the tour but provoked a diplomatic catastrophe. Even given Cook and Boycott's minor involvement in South African cricket, the India tour went ahead only after considerable negotiation, with both men agreeing to denounce apartheid in public but refusing to rule out the possibility of future visits to South Africa. With a typically idiosyncratic flourish, on his arrival in Delhi, Boycott presented the Prime Minister Indira Ghandi with a signed copy of his recent book, which included a denunciation of apartheid.[50]

The India tour would prove less memorable for cricket than for chess. Sunil Gavaskar's side won the series in practised fashion, claiming the first of six Tests and then playing out five draws during which a positive match result was rarely if ever on the table. Bob Willis recalls, 'Gavaskar was bowling nine or ten overs an hour with his spinners. It was the most mind-numbingly tedious cricket you could imagine.' The tourists were also upset by the level of umpiring, and Gooch would later write that visiting India had bored and disillusioned him off the field as well as on.[51]

Those interested in a South Africa tour were using

a chess code to arrange their clandestine get-togethers: 'knights and castles meet in the bishop's room at nine', 'the chess tournament will now include this many matches', and so on. Quite improbably, the attendant press remained oblivious to these manoeuvres, which would prove a subject of some embarrassment later on.

The media instead were preoccupied with a favoured target in Boycott, a uniquely divisive figure after a decade and a half as an international batsman. It was said that for both Yorkshire and England he had made fewer friends than centuries, and he had never before travelled to the Asian subcontinent due to a distaste for the food and concern for his health. There had been little danger of him voluntarily missing out on the 1981–82 tour. He arrived in India just 230 runs behind Garry Sobers' all-time Test record of 8,032, passing it in the third Test in Delhi. He started the first day 81 runs shy of the milestone and reached it just before the close with a clipped single from Dilip Dohsi.

In the words of his biographer Leo McKinistry the tour 'could be described as a microcosm of Boycott's entire Test career: glorious achievement marred by crass and self-indulgent actions.'[52] After getting out late on the third day of the fourth Test in Calcutta, Boycott withdrew himself ill but spent the next day's play on the golf course rather than watching his team-mates bat. Even for a player who had long divided dressing rooms, fans and committee men alike it was an incredible action. Gooch later recalled that he could not remember such wholesale condemnation of a team-mate and after a fierce row with captain Keith Fletcher and the tour committee Boycott resigned his position in the party. The Yorkshireman flew home before the completion of the series, a more divisive figure than ever. Back in Headingley he would find matters no calmer as factions within the membership sought to have their greatest batsman sacked.

For Cooke and his business partner Martin Locke, Boycott's departure during the Holiday Inns negotiations was just the latest setback. Gatting had pulled out after the first Test but agreed to keep the plans secret. And then, during the second Test in Bangalore, a hammer blow: Botham withdrew too. The all-rounder had previously signalled an interest but when Cooke invited his advisers Reg Hayter and Alan Herd to India to complete the deal, they instead counselled their client against signing. Following 'Botham's Ashes' he was among the most sought-after sporting figureheads, earning lucrative deals with Shredded Wheat and Volvo. It quite simply did not make financial sense to pursue the South African option, which would have placed his international career and endorsements in serious jeopardy. Suddenly three of the biggest names in English cricket were out of the picture and when David Gower then decided shortly after Christmas that the tour did not make financial sense for him either, Holiday Inns withdrew their interest. Those who remained keen to tour were also increasingly vulnerable, as the 'safety in numbers' proviso no longer applied.

Cooke and Locke were undeterred, promising rebels continued interest from SACU president Joe Pamensky. As England embarked on a new tour in February 1982 – to Sri Lanka, for that nation's inaugural Test – Gooch was now perhaps the biggest attraction on the books and as such he and John Emburey began to play a bigger role in co-ordinating negotiations. The Essex right-hander had been a Test batsman for seven years without ever fully convincing the selectors, and perhaps himself, of his true credentials. After a torrid start against Australia in the 1975 Ashes he had shown a significant improvement and then a serious statement of intent in the West Indies in 1980–81: two centuries in eight innings against Clive Lloyd's pace attack, including a masterful 153 at Kingston.

But he had lost form again thereafter and was dropped during the 1981 Ashes before earning a winter recall through weight of county runs. His dislike of India as a touring destination, compounded by the dire on-field spectacle, had bred disenchantment and, along with close friend Emburey, another apparently preoccupied with self-doubt and security, he had convinced himself of the wisdom of touring.

The organisers then arranged a new sponsor, South African Breweries. Cooke, with only four confirmed players, began frantically calling cricketers around England and Sri Lanka to squeeze in the tour in March before the South African summer ended and the county season began. All the while the plotters kept their plans secret from captain Fletcher and recruited further members to the cause. Lever and Derek Underwood were also in Sri Lanka and, nearing the end of their careers, agreed to go; from outside the squad Cooke was also able to recruit four more men with Test caps: batsman Wayne Larkins, all-rounder Peter Willey, and bowlers Mike Hendrick and Chris Old. The veteran batsman Dennis Amiss, who had been a leading England player until joining WSC five years earlier, and the uncapped Leicestershire seamer Les Taylor swelled the numbers to twelve. Amiss says, 'I just loved playing cricket in South Africa, I had done it many times over the years with all the different coaching positions. I was particularly fond of South Africa and made a lot of friends there over the years. It's only a short career and this was another golden opportunity. We had to go for it.'

Upon the England squad's return from Sri Lanka on 24 February the story, improbably, remained a total secret from the press. Underwood's insistence to reporters that he needed a break from cricket was taken at face value. Instead he would be flying out first-class to Johannesburg four days later. In a whirl of last-minute activity, Willis withdrew. He says, 'It was an enormous amount of money. The telling fact, as with Packer, was that I wouldn't be able to play for England and that's all I was interested in. I went to Warwickshire and said, "Is there anything you can do to help me secure my future?" They changed my contract so I would be paid when I was injured. And I was able to carry on playing for England, which was what I wanted to do.' The TCCB had caught wind of the expedition ahead of the media and made contact with a number of players, apparently also persuading Geoff Cook not to sign up to protect his England career. At the same time, Cooke was able to convince the record-breaking Boycott, besieged and on the brink of being sacked by Yorkshire, to add his substantial name to the party.

The 12 men, who would be paid on a sliding scale from around £40,000 to £60,000[53] for a month-long tour, ultimately constituted a mixed side, containing only four players from the Sri Lanka tour but 11 men with Test caps. After Gower, Botham and Willis there were few English players who could make an unanswerable case to improve the line-up, making it something like a half-1st XI, half-2nd XI in strength. As well as undeniable playing qualities, the trio were also self-confident personalities: Botham the gregarious superstar, Gower the laconic genius and Willis the forthright would-be captain.

In their absence the squad was notably characterised by idiosyncrasies and insecurities. For veterans such as Amiss, 38, and Underwood, 36, it was a straightforward opportunity for a pension, but a number of the others were encumbered by curious personal baggage. Boycott's ongoing disagreements with the world at large were now legend. Despite their youth and obvious pedigree Gooch, 28, and Emburey, 29, were haunted by financial insecurity while Taylor, for all his accomplishments in the county championship, was convinced that his miner's background would forever prevent him playing international cricket. Hendrick had recently left his county, Leicestershire, after a row, while Larkins was renowned as talented and erratic in equal measure. Most unusual of all was the veteran wicketkeeper Knott, who many considered the greatest in the game's history but who had not toured with England for years as it kept him from his family. He was surprised to have played international cricket again after his World Series Cricket involvement and turned to prayer for the wisdom of proceeding: 'The Lord knew that I wanted to go and that I thought it was right for me to do so. I prayed that if it wasn't right He would prevent me from going, or that if it wasn't right for the tour to go ahead He would stop it from taking place. I knew that even when we arrived in South Africa the tour could still be called off.'[54]

Seven cricketers – Boycott, Gooch, Amiss, Knott, Emburey, Underwood and Lever – thus boarded the plane to South Africa on 28 February to embark on an unprecedented and still secret expedition. Larkins, Willey and Hendrick, who had been playing in Dubai, would follow the next day while Old and Taylor were already in the republic. All had come to accept the prospect of a private tour just playing cricket. None apparently shared Viv Richards' reservations that 'That kind of money goes to show you that things are not really right.'

1 Lapchick (1976).
2 p 85, Booth (1998).
3 p 99, Booth (1998).
4 29 September 1973. Basil D'Oliveira had been invited to play but was refused permission by SACBOC, for whom he was working as a coach. Pairings were Rhodesia: Mike Procter and Brian Davison; South Africa: Barry Richards and Eddie Barlow; South African Africans: Edmund Ntikinca and Edward Habane; Australia: Greg and Ian Chappell; England: Tony Greig and Frank Hayes; New Zealand: Bev Congdon and Bruce Taylor. Rhodesia won with South African Africans finishing fifth of six. (Back, *Rand Daily Mail*, 1 October 1973). Such double-wicket competitions were popular exhibition exercises around the world but not official international events.
5 p 103, Bose (1994).
6 p 103, Booth (1998). Famously, when the minister for sport Piet Koornhof was asked whether he would object to running tagged as an Englishman, he responded: 'If I was an Englishman I suppose I wouldn't mind.'
7 2, 3, 5, 6 February 1973 at Wanderers Stadium, Johannesburg. South African Invitational XI (387) beat DH Robins' XI (118 & 152) by an innings and 117 runs. Bob Willis recalls, 'We were a sort of England 3rd XI, a mish-mash of promising young players and county stalwarts. From South Africa's point of view it was a big deal, it wasn't a big deal for us and we were totally outplayed against the stronger sides.'
8 20 October 1973 at Moroka-Jabatu Stadium, Soweto. South African African XI (139) lost to DH Robins XI (359) by 220 runs.
9 Anthony 'Tich' Smith, Natal wicketkeeper 1971–84, who would almost certainly have played for South Africa without isolation.
10 8, 9, 10, 12 April 1976 at Kingsmead, Durban. Invitational XI (178 & 269) beat International Wanderers (99 & 226) by 122 runs. Smith and van der Bijl added 75 for the eighth wicket in the first innings having been brought together at 99-7.
11 Front, *The Australian*, 22 July 1986. A similar story is recounted pps 22–3, Francis (1989).
12 p 136, Richards (1978).
13 p 183, Knowles (1995).
14 p 960, in Preston (ed.), *Wisden*, 1975.

15 p 2, *Rand Daily Mail*, 22 October 1973.
16 p 190, Odendaal (2003).
17 p 21, Richards (1978).
18 pp 185–6, Odendaal (2003).
19 p 225, Odendaal (2003).
20 p 76, Nixon (1992).
21 p 58, Thomspon (1975).
22 p 196, Lewis (2003).
23 p 113, Beckles (ed., 1998).
24 p 118, Hartman (2004).
25 The term 'God's forgotten cricketers' is telling as it encapsulates the self-importance and religious martyrdom that the white establishment attached to South African isolation. Of course, their fate was naught compared to that of contemporary non-white cricketers. In the limited exposure enjoyed by leading black players such as Khaya Majola, Edmund Ntikinca and Edward Habane against white opposition they were often found wanting, which was hardly a surprise considering the disadvantages endured under apartheid. When the great West Indian Rohan Kanhai spent a season in the SACBOC league in 1973–74, he expressed surprise at the high standard but stressed a 'crying need' for turf wickets and practice facilities if the standards were to improve.' (p 218, Odendaal, 2003) However, within white South Africa they were ignored and derided – in cricket as other spheres.
26 p 249, Odendaal (ed., 1977).
27 pp 24–25, 123, Richards (1978).
28 p 11, *The Times*, 11 March 1977.
29 p 17, Haigh (2007).
30 p 579, Harte with Whimpress (2003).
31 p 125, Haigh (2007).
32 India were the only major cricket nation not represented. Sunil Gavaskar and Bishen Bedi were rumoured at one stage to be signing up but the development never materialised. Mihir Bose remarks in his *A History of Indian Cricket*, 'Gavaskar's flirtation with Packer – it was little more – remains the most obscure subject in Indian cricket.' (p 202 Haigh 2007).
33 p 30, Imran Khan (1988).
34 p 75, Garner (1988).
35 p 292, Haigh (2007).

36 Preface, Haigh (2007).
37 p 48, *Sunday Express*, 7 March 1982. The unpublished excerpt was revealed by Denis Compton, an iconic former England player who championed South Africa's case in his *Express* columns and elsewhere.
38 p 175, Hartman (2004).
39 p 177, Hartman (2004).
40 p 176, Hartman (2004).
41 p 139, Lister (2007).
42 pp 124–5, McDonald (1984).
43 p 221, Boycott (1987).
44 p 86, Boycott (1981).
45 *Wisden* later reported: 'It was considered elsewhere in the Caribbean to have been largely a reprisal for Lord Avebury's adverse report on election-rigging in Guyana.' (pp 195–6, Moss, ed., *Wisden*, 2006).
46 Roger Fieldhouse writes, 'AAM rather gloomily concluded at the end of 1983 that "any sober assessment of the International Year of Mobilisation for Sanctions against South Africa … cannot give rise to optimism. Instead of being a period during which South Africa was increasingly isolated, as a result of the policies of the Reagan and Thatcher Administrations South Africa continues to enjoy close economic links with most Western countries.' (p 75, Fieldhouse 2004).
47 p 221, Boycott (1987).
48 p 165, Odendaal (ed., 1977).
49 This victory was by no means a blessing. Simon Barnes later wrote: 'There is a case for saying that Headingley 1981 is one of the greatest disasters to have hit England's cricket. Certainly, it plunged into a pattern of self-destructiveness as the echoes of that extraordinary year died away. The England team became based around an Inner Ring, with Botham at its heart: Botham, self-justified by his prodigious defeats that unforgettable summer. To be accepted you had to hate the press, hate practice, enjoy a few beers and what have you, and generally be one hell of a good ol' boy.' (p 80, *Wisden* 1991).
50 The book was *In the Fast Lane*, a memoir of the 1980–81 series in the West Indies. The precise wording of his condemnation was: 'I hate apartheid as much as I love South Africa. I detest the system just as I detest Communism; yet I confess I would love to go to Russia or China for a visit.' (p 203, Boycott 1981)

51 pp 7–23, Gooch (1985). The frustration on that tour was felt by a number of England players but opinions on who to blame for the standard of cricket remain a question of viewpoint. Don Mosey, who followed the tour as a journalist, records the Indian authorities as open in their admission that pitches were doctored to eliminate any chance of Indian defeat (pp 108–9, Mosey 1987). But Fletcher was an unimaginative captain and, for the journalist and historian Mihir Bose, England were not up to the challenge of breaking the hosts down (pp 322–3, Bose 2002). How one becomes bored off the field in India is another question altogether.
52 p 227, McKinistry (2005).
53 A good county salary was around £9,000 for the season; international players could more than double this with Test and ODI appearance money but very few England players were sure of their places.
54 p 70, Knott (1985).

# Chapter 3
# This Dirty Dozen

*'The richest, loneliest men in cricket.' – Tony Lewis*

The 'quiet, private tour' got very loud and very public very quickly. Strident opposition poured forth from the worlds of cricket, media and politics, which in turn prompted acrimonious disputes with those who supported their actions. Few sporting ventures had ever matched the volume and ill-feeling of front-page publicity.

In England press disapproval was all but universal. The tourists were denounced as rebels and traitors, pirates and defectors, a cause for national shame, as typified by a *Daily Mirror* editorial: 'The England cricketers selling their talents to South Africa are as contemptible as any mercenary who hires out his gun ... Every run they score will be a blow to someone else's freedom.'[1] *The Times* censured the 'selfish attitude of this touring party', risking a cricket world fractured along racial lines that would 'quite possibly bring about an end to Test cricket as we have known it.'[2]

Fears of a black–white split were widespread, that leading players from 'white' nations would sign up for a 'Packer-style' circus in South Africa with remainder sides left to contest Tests with full-strength India, Pakistan, West Indies and Sri Lanka teams. There were worries that any collapse of international cricket would have a domino effect, wrecking the Olympics, Commonwealth Games and even the football World Cup. Faced with demands in India and Pakistan for the 12 players to be banned, the TCCB denounced the tourists for their deceit and confirmed that all participants had placed their international careers in jeopardy, committee meeting pending.

If media hysteria and displeasure at Lord's had been expected, then top billing in the Houses of Parliament had not. An ill-tempered Prime Minister's Questions was dominated by the topic, where Labour MP Gerald Kaufman declared that the players were 'selling themselves for blood-covered Krugerrands' and another Labour MP, Neil Kinnock, wrote the following day's headlines in reproaching 'this dirty dozen'. The Government reiterated their opposition to apartheid in sport through Neil Macfarlane, Minister for Sport, but Prime Minister Margaret Thatcher's official disapproval was ill-supported by her apparent indifference in person. This was freedom of individual choice in action, and a sizable group among her Conservative Party not only defended the tourists but commended their actions. George Gardiner MP wrote that they deserved 'a medal for helping to create a more just and humane world'[3]. Disapproval in the corridors of power was compounded when a newly published United Nations blacklist condemned each of the 12 rebels, and 115 Britons in total, for their sporting links with South Africa.

Amid the contemptuous exchanges multiplying in sporting, political and media groups around the world, the weight of opinion was decidedly against the rebels. This poignant note was struck by former England captain Tony Lewis when, in *The Sunday Telegraph*, he feared for the impact on relations within and beyond the cricket world, describing the rebels as 'the richest, loneliest men in cricket.'[4]

The eerily quiet eye of the storm was, of course, South Africa, where the establishment adopted these self-styled private individuals as more or less public property. On 1 March 1982 the second story, even in the liberal broadsheet *Rand Daily Mail,* was the greatest crisis of South African government since World War II.[5] Top billing was reserved for the 12 good men and true who would return 'international' cricket to the republic. Those who in the UK were traitors found themselves crusading pioneers. The public were largely able to read between the lines, but the proverbial 'white man in the street' was nevertheless delighted by the prospect of representative cricket and enjoying the discomfort this same prospect caused the rest of the world.

Dennis Amiss recalls: 'We got a tremendous reaction from the South Africans. The people knew we'd put ourselves out to go on the tour, and the people couldn't do enough for us and to make us feel good that what we'd done was for the betterment of sport in South Africa. We all got the phone calls from our wives and girlfriends saying that the press were hammering away back home and in the end one or two of us brought our families out because they were far better off with us than taking all the flak.'

Finally there was a purpose to the perennial question posed when South African cricket fans met: who would make a Springbok XI for a Test match next week? The responsibility for providing an answer fell to Ali Bacher, victorious captain over Bill Lawry 12 years previously and a behind-the-scenes facilitator of the tour. As befitted a man with privileged information, his panel returned their verdict quickly to stoke public anticipation. Mike Procter would captain a side including two fellow survivors of the 1970 team, Graeme Pollock and Barry Richards. Batsmen Jimmy Cook and Peter Kirsten, all-rounder Clive Rice, wicketkeeper Ray Jennings, spinner

Alan Kourie, and fast bowlers Stephen Jefferies, Garth Le Roux and Vince van der Bijl completed the line-up. The squad was reduced to 11 after the 12th man, Allan Lamb, a South African-born batsman who had qualified for England after four years with Northamptonshire, rejected a Springbok cap so as to pursue an official international career.

With gross revenue estimates for the tour touching R2,000,000, South African cricket saw itself entering the big time. Transvaal skipper Rice even went so far as to claim: 'This is the equivalent of Kerry Packer signing up the whole West Indian team.' This was a sentiment few could agree with given that the party included just four players from the recent Sri Lanka tour and that even the best England team of the day were scarcely a match for the world champions. Suggestible newspaper readers would never have known it, though, from analysis pieces discussing Peter Willey in awed tones. There was also the prospect of live international cricket coverage for the first time on South African television, though the powerful Dutch Reformed Church vocally and effectively denounced the broadcast of matches on the Sabbath.

While the white community rejoiced, there was general resentment and disappointment among non-white groups, as the campaigning journalist Percy Qoboza wrote: 'The euphoria accompanying the present cricket tour of South Africa has exposed just how thick-skinned, unashamed and garrulous many South Africans have become. When people take pride that they have beaten the world by smuggling in a cricket team, then it can only be said they have lost their way. The fact that conspiracy is the only way to secure a tour again shows up the extent of South Africa's isolation in sport.'[6]

Speaking for the pro-boycott SACB, Hassan Howa added, 'Bringing the side here was an admission by the South African Cricket Union that they will never be able to do things in a normal way. They are doing the government's propaganda work for them by saying that sport is not political. Sport and politics are rarely inextricable. Bringing out these people is a political act.'[7]

One way to puncture the hysteria in those early days would have been to reveal the shambolic backstage reality. At an opening press conference on 1 March with the seven players who had flown out first, the tourists' reticence to discuss their ambitions in detail was explained easily enough: the team had no name, no captain and no schedule. Dennis Amiss and Alan Knott had not played competitive cricket in six months; Peter Willey, Wayne Larkins and Mike Hendrick had yet to arrive from the UAE; Les Taylor and Chris Old were in transit from Natal; and original leader Geoffrey Boycott remained a divisive figure.

Moreover, once an itinerary was agreed and published the following day, it was a triumph for commercial logic over sporting reality. In their determination to maximise a return on their expensive charges, Peter Cooke and his sponsors had agreed to eight matches with only one free day after each. SACA would not budge on their demand for six 'internationals' against a full-strength South Africa team – three four-day 'Tests' and three 'one-day internationals' – while the players had requested at least two practice matches.

This amounted to 20 days out of 27 on the field with an average 1,000km journey after each match. The prospect of Boycott as captain prompted the spectre of dressing room unrest – some administrations, clearly, were beyond the pale – and Graham Gooch agreed to lead the side. It was a grave misjudgement on his part, making it too easy for press critics to pick out a public enemy number one from the 12.

Gooch's naive decision was just one suggestion that the rebels had misjudged how their actions would be perceived. All the players, and Boycott in particular, dismissed media enquiries with relish and at the opening press conference, in answer to a question on whether he felt any pressure, Gooch responded: 'Not on the cricket side, no.' And what about pressures from anything else? 'I'm not answering on anything else,' he said and stood up to leave. Cooke added hastily: 'This is a cricket tour, so cricket questions only. Nothing political ... We don't care what Fleet Street has to say.'

At this point the *Daily Mail*'s Ian Wooldridge gave voice to English press reservations about the tour manager by demanding to know, 'Who is this bloody clown?' When a pliant South African journalist enquired about the state of local pitches tensions subsided, but the hope that this would prove sufficient for their critics was foolish in the extreme.[8]

Perhaps most significantly the South African squad had been named and SACU had delighted in confirming that all home players would receive Springbok caps in the official record. Yet still Gooch was pushing for Alvin Kallicharran to be signed. The double World Cup-winning West Indies batsman was playing for Transvaal and had made no secret of his enthusiasm for a contract. In Gooch's estimation he would have not only added much-needed batting talent but also undermined South African attempts to brand the matches 'internationals'. Quite right, and so the proposition was pointless. With 'international' cricket imminent in South Africa for the first time in 12 years, there was no intention of allowing an 'England XI' to become 'GA Gooch and Friends'.

Nevertheless, the new captain's urgent request for reinforcements was heeded. With only four specialist batsmen in the party, fortifying the top order was a clear priority. And despite protestations to being a more-or-less full-strength England team, they lacked not only substance but style. Boycott was, of course, a global star, but his patient approach rarely encouraged a timely return to the seats after lunch. Gooch, 28, was a compelling spectacle at the crease, and Knott and Derek Underwood had secured places in English cricket's pantheon. Still, the brutal truth was that at any given time a national team's strength and marketability are reliant on a select few leading players, and with the average age almost 34, among many worthy cricketers there were few stand-out names.

For example, Amiss had played one of the greatest ever England innings, 262 at Kingston in 1973–74, and, like Boycott and Gooch, would finish his career with 100 first-class centuries. But he was 38 in March 1982, and had not played Test cricket since his Packer defection. Underwood had been an outstanding match-winner for over a decade with his slow left-arm and John Emburey was perhaps the best off-spinner in the world, but slow bowling was seldom headline material anywhere, and least of all in South Africa. The inclusion of three such bowlers, including Willey, in a country where spin was rarely influential provided a stark reminder of the team-building process: the XII in South Africa were the XII who had shown up.

As a record producer Cooke might not have put together a perfectly balanced cricket team, but he understood the value of box office pull. Since the tourists' arrival in South Africa Bob Willis, Mike Gatting and David Gower had reiterated their disinterest which left only one A-lister in the sights: that man Botham. Having become so close to signing the all-rounder in Bangalore, further enquiries were made. But Cooke was not the only man who understood image management and on 3 March a column appeared under Ian Botham's name in *The Sun*.

Beneath the headline 'I could never have looked Viv in the eye again', Botham was reported as saying:

> *'I can't deny that the £50,000 tempted me to join the English cricket rebels on their tour of South Africa. But one thought kept flashing across my mind: I could never have looked my mate Viv Richards in the eye this season ... Every player approached by the Springboks had to decide for himself whether it was right to accept. I couldn't say yes. I didn't want to risk my Test career and, quite frankly, I'm surprised that certain others have chosen to do just that. I had to consider my own future, the future of my wife and children, and the future of English cricket itself ... I won't be earning the £50,000 I was promised in South Africa – but at least I will be able to hold my head up when I play county cricket again.'*[9]

As a piece of journalism it was risible, and Botham later insisted that the statement was published without his consent. But it was a public relations masterstroke. England's favourite cricketer had shored up his credentials and the only dissenters were 6,000 miles away.

Boycott was furious, declaring that he would never trust the 'puke-making'[10] Botham again, and for once he was not alone in the dressing room. But fury would not supplement the squad and in any case there was other business to attend to. Something called the South African Breweries English XI were to make their bow.

The SAB XI opened their tour with a two-day match against South African Colts, a national under-25 XI, at the unpretentious Berea Park starting 3rd March. The depth and ferocity of opposition back home had been startling but their reception by home fans in Pretoria heralded a return to the comfort zone: sponsorship boards advertising Benson & Hedges and Leyland, a ring of trees beyond the boundary rope and a raucous flock of autograph hunters.

Anti-apartheid protests, such an inconvenience back in England, were illegal and therefore invisible, though a local election poster outside the ground implored the electorate, 'Stem ons stad weer wit' ('Vote our city white again'). The genial atmosphere was reminiscent of a well-attended county match with an overwhelmingly white crowd heaping praise on the men who would return international cricket to the republic.

That hospitality extended to the toss, where Graham Gooch called incorrectly but was still given first opportunity to bat on a placid surface under cloudless skies. He and Geoffrey Boycott resumed their England opening partnership, met at the crease by a roar of spectator approval and a throng of photographers from the press box and the crowd.

When play belatedly got underway, the chaotic build-up and lack of match practice was immediately apparent as the inexperienced Colts limited the visitors to 152-7 in 66 overs. Boycott, sporting a full and bushy beard that altered his appearance but did little to disguise his identity as a batsman, observed a 40-minute vigil at the crease before getting off the mark. He managed a scratchy 13 from 83 balls before top-edging to square leg, and the Colts captain Adrian Kuiper's lively seam made regular inroads either side of lunch, giving him 5-22.

When Gooch, who had top-scored with 33, declared shortly after tea the decision seemed as much to spare the batting side's blushes as allow his bowlers their own much-needed practice. The hosts were mostly untroubled in reaching 51-1 overnight but lost wickets regularly in taking risks on day two, Kuiper declaring mid-afternoon on 170-8 so that the tourists could bat again. His courtesy was in vain. The visitors' quest for time in the middle was curtailed by a thunderstorm shortly after tea, Boycott left on 11 not out as the innings closed on 32-2 with Gooch and Wayne Larkins each dismissed cheaply. Writing in the *Daily Mail*, Ian Wooldridge described the tourists' batting as 'not only abysmal but a public relations exercise comparable with Neville Chamberlain's "I have here a piece of paper."'[11]

The on-the-hoof organisation was apparent at the post-match press conference in the pavilion ladies' toilets, where Gooch declared that he would 'answer questions only on the cricket', which was tantamount to a vow of silence. In London, match reports of the tour opener took a back seat as the TCCB continued its attempts to end the tour before the 'international' matches could be played. TCCB secretary Donald Carr released the details of his pre-match missive to the players warning that proceeding would endanger their careers and those of fellow professionals. With a full meeting of the board not scheduled for another week there was no way to add substance to the threat before the first 'one-day international', though marketing manager Peter Lush added rather optimistically: 'We are disappointed they have not heeded our appeals. We now appeal to their consciences to abandon the tour.'

While Lord's pondered an international ban for the 12, some county boards were demanding a harder line. Despite the fact that two key players for the club, Wayne Larkins and Peter Willey, were among those at risk, and Allan Lamb was also on their books, Northamptonshire led the call for the rebels to be banned not only from international cricket but at county level too. These sentiments captured the widespread disappointment at the players' secret plotting – and doubtless committee men's outrage at players thinking and acting autonomously – but they might as well have threatened to fire all 12 into the heart of the sun. While facing a fully representative South Africa team could be dealt with at international level to protect English cricket's interests, there was no chance of a blanket ban on all clubs employing South African tourists. It was a blatant restraint of trade. Leicestershire's Mike Turner offered a coded call for calm: 'Northants' proposal is an indication of the depth of feeling about these players. However, all of these matters must be looked at carefully as there are serious legal implications.' Implications to the tune of £200,000, if the Packer case was any guide.

Certainly the counties' threats had little impact on the tourists. Boycott, whose Yorkshire future was in doubt amid a particularly severe bout of banana republicanism at Headingley, would receive offers to stay in South Africa full-time as a coach and Currie Cup player but never seriously considered severing ties with the county. As Dennis Amiss, a veteran of the Packer controversy, explains, while there were worries among his team-mates about a brief international ban, at no stage were they concerned for their county careers: 'We'd already gone through something similar in World Series Cricket and they said we were OK to come back and play county cricket. It did get very messy at one stage but all settled down and we were sure it would again.'

Despite the acres of newsprint devoted to the topic, and fierce opposition campaigning, the die had been cast. Peter Cooke was at pains to remind the players in public and private that they would be in breach of contract should they refuse to complete the tour but the tourists were in any case unmoved. Gooch wrote of calls to turn back: 'Having made the decision, I will stick by it. To the grave. That's me, take it or leave it.'[12] The players had bought fully into the defence that they were merely professionals exercising freedom of choice and were reluctant to accept that there might be consequences. Moreover, not even Gooch and Boycott's fiercest detractors would call them pliant in the face of criticism. Lush's appeal to player consciences, like Alan Knott's wait for divine intervention, would go unfulfilled.

And so attention returned to the Mystery of the Thirteenth Man. Willey, an all-rounder whose 27.96 Test average had been mostly acquired in the lower-middle order, had batted number five at Berea Park. He had been directly followed by Knott and John Emburey, each probably a place higher than they'd have expected in a balanced team, with four specialist bowlers behind them. Expectation in South Africa was growing, and Mike Procter was promising the visitors an authentic Springbok welcome in the 'international' fixtures. It was self-evident that a batting order undone by an under-25s XI would stand little chance in the face of the full national side. Despite the tourists embracing the 'dirty dozen' tag with sardonic resignation, reinforcements were patently required.

After Cooke's remarkable success in arranging the tour in secret, though, it appeared his luck had run out. The tour manager had become increasingly and visibly unsettled by his repeated failure to expand the squad. For three consecutive days he had arranged conferences promising 'sensational' additions only to cancel on each occasion. Geoff Cook had decided to remain in England. Gooch then offered a position to Keith Fletcher, but after 24 hours' consideration the England captain declined. Clive Rice telephoned his Nottinghamshire colleague Derek Randall in Australia, but the most eccentric of all England cricketers was unwilling to join an already eclectic party. That other great fieldsman, once-capped Paul Parker, was also in Australia and offered the same response. Suspicion lingered briefly on Tony Greig, no stranger to South Africa or player power, before moving on to Lord Lucan and Anthony Blunt. Ian Botham was now not merely the biggest prize, he was the only one left worth having. And so, despite his 'I could not look Viv in the eye' column and the apoplexy it had caused Boycott, a final 'name your own price' offer was put to the all-rounder. He again refused and again did so publicly: 'Money is not my prime objective. It is conscience.'[13]

Botham had now become a particular irritation for all parties involved with the tour. The organisers and their backers were severely disappointed that the all-rounder's late withdrawal had denied them his bankable talents while the home team were aware that his absence essentially undermined the matches' claim to international status. There were those, including Procter, who considered David Gower had much to prove, while Bob Willis was now 32 and beset by knee injuries. But by any measure a full England team had to include Botham. The SAB XI tourists, meanwhile, professed their exasperation at his ubiquity although he had withdrawn. His absence was a constant source of interest to the press, and the steady stream of disapproval from Team Botham, three months after his interest in Bangalore, had drawn a withering response in the tourists' camp.

For his part, Botham had declared the matter closed. After rejecting the 'name your own price' offer from a South African retail firm he said, 'It is all becoming a complete nuisance. It is pointless for anyone in South Africa to pursue this idea. All I want for the next few weeks is some peace.'[14] And he had set about that quest as only he knew how, knocking his erstwhile colleagues off the sports pages two days later with a promotion for his forthcoming *Botham's Ashes* video under the headline 'Big Game Shooter' and the same week having his trademark beard shaved off in a publicity event for Braun. The *Daily Express* splashed 'before and after' shots across the front page, tagged with the quote: 'I feel naked without it, but it was worth every minute.'[15]

No doubt. While the rebels were collecting a handsome £1,300 per day, Botham reportedly earned twenty times as much for eight hours with the German firm. In the same week he was reported as signing a new deal with Duncan Fearnley, continued to enjoy lucrative deals with Shredded Wheat and Lyle & Scott knitwear, and cheerfully turned out for Scunthorpe United in the fourth division of the football league. In an environment where discord and accusations of poor judgement abounded, everyone could agree that Alan Herd and Reg Hayter had served their client's best interests by persuading him to stay in the UK. For the SAB XI management, the situation had become desperate. When the *Daily Mirror* correspondent asked Cooke if the Barbados-born England international Roland Butcher was a target, Cooke confirmed his interest – 'Roland's dashing style would certainly go down well with South African crowds' – before asking the journalist for Butcher's phone number.[16]

All calls to England were in vain. The furore had made any potential target wary of the slightest involvement. Instead Cooke was forced to look within the South African bubble and on 6 March, after a week's negotiation and cancelled conferences for 'sensational signings', he unveiled the proud owner of a new SAB XI touring blazer – Warwickshire wicketkeeper-batsman Geoff Humpage. A stout, broad policeman who wielded his bat with robust simplicity, Humpage was a popular figure at Edgbaston and had scored more runs than any member of the 'dirty dozen' during the 1981 county season. He was nobody's idea of a superstar but, wintering with Orange Free State, he was undeniably available. Though only 27 and not far from adding a Test cap to his three ODI appearances against Australia the previous summer, he recalls that he had no hesitation in signing up: 'I was over there earning a living. As a cricketer you couldn't earn money in England in the winter. I had missed out on the India tour – though apparently I was on the shortlist – and I had to work. Someone offered me more money for three weeks' cricket than I got for five months. And that's a difficult thing to turn down. It had nothing to do with the politicians. I could understand it if we were representing the nation but we were private individuals.'

Humpage would provide cover for Knott as well as providing an extra batsman in the squad, but South Africans expressed unguarded disappointment after bullish teasers had pointed to a Botham or a Greig. Aware of the yawning gap between his hyperbolic promotion and the reality, Cooke buoyantly claimed that England players were 'queuing up' to join the touring party. But if Humpage was at the front of the queue, who was at the back?

On Sunday 6th March South Africa greeted a 50-over match with a South African Breweries XI as an authentic return to international cricket. The first 'one-day Test' carried no official status outside the republic, but the crowd at St George's Park in Port Elizabeth, the venue that had hosted the very first Test between South Africa and England in 1889, were gleefully oblivious. The crowd was a handsome 15,000, swelled by around 800 non-white spectators now that the tourists had left overwhelmingly white Pretoria.

Vince van der Bijl recalls: 'The crowd was abuzz; it was completely jam-packed. It reminded me of the stories Graeme Pollock used to tell us about coming to the Wanderers on the first day of a Test match against the Aussies – you'd get here at 8 o'clock because the place was teeming.'

Twelve years on from the rout of Australia, which was completed at Port Elizabeth with a fourth Test win, local hero Pollock was the main attraction. Despite averaging around 80 in Currie Cup cricket he was said to be out of form as age took its toll, but this late unexpected career bonus left joy unconfined as the Springbok flag fluttered once more over a pavilion. For the tourists, Geoff Humpage was introduced immediately to fortify the batting at number seven, beneath Peter Willey and Alan Knott.

Graham Gooch again lost the toss and Mike Procter preferred to chase, allowing the visitors first use of a friendly batting track in fine conditions. Geoffrey Boycott continued to struggle for form, falling in Procter's first spell for five, but Gooch was at his brutish best, taking advantage of a shortened boundary rope, early fielding restrictions and a home attack wracked with tension to hit a 132-ball 114, including 14 fours and four sixes. Garth Le Roux eventually claimed the captain's scalp with a neat caught and bowled, but not before he had borne the brunt of the right-hander's power. That wicket provided a fig leaf to his figures of 1-70 from ten overs while van der Bijl was almost as chastened for his nervous inaccuracy, 1-56 including two towering sixes over mid-wicket. Wayne Larkins appeared to have joined Boycott in the ninth circle of batting hell after falling cheaply again but Dennis Amiss, the best English one-day batsman of his generation, showed few signs of ring-rust in first dropping anchor for Gooch in a partnership worth 138 and then opening up his shoulders to finish unbeaten on 71.

The SAB XI total of 240-5 from 50 overs was an imposing score by the standards of the day, and particularly so against a nation that had never played one-day international cricket. However, with fervent support, the South African openers saw off the dangerous Les Taylor with the new ball and set about the task with vigour. Jimmy Cook (82) and Barry Richards (62) put on

125 for the first wicket and the quick dismissal of Peter Kirsten only hastened Pollock's arrival to a rapturous reception. Brought together at 176-3, he and Clive Rice still needed 60 from ten overs but the left-hander was without apparent nerves or self-doubt on an occasion that had got the better of less experienced team-mates. He was as broad and immovable an object as ever before, unflustered in clubbing 57 not out from 44 balls with a flurry of fours and sixes that thrilled the crowd and secured a seven-wicket victory with 16 balls to spare. It was the perfect denouement for the hosts, Chris Old joining the praise of the local 'Prince of Batsmen', whom world cricket had missed for over a decade: 'His batting certainly brought back memories. I played my first Test against him back in 1970 when he represented the Rest of the World against England at Headingley. He's still as good as he was then.' Gooch, furthering his hard line of press conference solemnity, merely added, 'If he's out of nick, I hope he never gets in it.'

For the SAB XI captain there was the consolation of a R500 prize for top-scoring, which amounted to 20 per cent of his daily fee for the tour, and a growing cult status among South African fans. Gooch's unorthodox but effective aggression had earned him the nickname 'the man who does everything wrong' among the home press, who were quietly relieved to see one English name on the scorecard doing something right. There had been a stark illustration that the home side were better staffed, organised and motivated for the series ahead.

Amiss recalls: 'They played to a very high standard straight away. We weren't surprised – we knew lots of their players because they'd played county cricket, people like Mike Procter and Barry Richards. They'd become a strong side because they'd been able to play abroad despite isolation. Vintcent van der Bijl played for Middlesex and Garth Le Roux, who was really quick on his day, had made a big impression in World Series Cricket. And, of course, they had a wonderful batting side. They were acclimatised, but it took us a little time to acclimatise as it does in hot countries.'

South Africans were jubilant and the high-scoring contest, albeit within a shortened boundary, renewed confidence that the series would be a sporting and commercial success. *The Observer* reported, 'If this is the sort of cricket which the tour is going to produce then it will be a sell-out everywhere.'[17] South African cricket viewed it as a vindication, a triumph for sport over wider considerations, but the notion that sport and politics had somehow been separated was quietly undermined by the presence of one spectator in particular. A delighted ex-Prime Minister BJ Vorster, reviled abroad but also blamed by most South Africans for their sporting isolation, hailed a 'triumph for common sense' to reporters during the game: 'I haven't been to many cricket games in the past ten years but I am enjoying this one. It's one thing I did not want to miss.'[18]

A week into the tour and still short of numbers, the 'pirates' found a 14th man to join their crew. Bob Woolmer, the 33-year-old Kent all-rounder, had been playing and coaching in South Africa for some years, but had been shocked to see on the news some old friends coming through customs at Johannesburg. Peter Cooke made contact a few days later but found Woolmer reluctant to commit due to a foot injury. An offer of £10,000 had more or less convinced Woolmer to sign up subject to his doctor's approval – but Cooke took the wait for medical results as tactical bargaining and promptly doubled it even though Woolmer would not be able to bowl.[19] With a strong record of multi-racial cricket in South Africa behind him, Woolmer felt well within his rights to sign up for the tour, telling the BBC: 'Naturally the financial aspect comes into it – I'm not going to say it doesn't. But at the same time I just feel from the moral point of view that I've done a job with a coloured side out here … I thought that having committed myself to doing that there was no harm in joining the tour already out here.'[20]

He went straight into the XI to play Western Province at Newlands in a final warm-up match. The previous evening Yorkshire had announced that they would be retaining Geoffrey Boycott despite opposition among players and membership, and in celebration he replaced Graham Gooch as captain. When asked about the decision Gooch merely deadpanned: 'It's nothing to do with Yorkshire – we all thought it was the best way of ensuring Geoff bought us a drink out of his captain's expense allowance.' The odd turn of events was crowned by Boycott deciding on Chris Old to open the bowling. Old was his county skipper and prominent among those who would have seen the world's leading run-scorer chased out of Headingley. Even personal politics, it seemed, were anathema to the rebels.

Again, though, the tourists were out of luck. Old's opening partner John Lever managed only two balls on the first morning before retiring for X-rays which revealed a long-standing, unidentified back injury while Mike Hendrick continued to struggle with ankle trouble. The contrast with South Africa's strength in depth was exposed: despite starting poorly – John Emburey reduced the hosts to 25-4 – they would declare on 263-8 before the close. Adrian Kuiper, on the fringes of a full call-up to the national team after leading the Colts with such distinction the previous week, scored a blistering 90 to strengthen further that case.

The Western Province side was the subject of particular scrutiny as they had the best two spinners in the country after the Springboks' first choice Alan Kourie. More than that, one of these was Omar Henry – the only 'coloured' player with a realistic chance of earning selection for South Africa during the tour. Henry was by no means the best non-white player in the country, but he was the best among the few who played with SACU and therefore the leading candidate who would agree to wear a Springbok cap. His lively 33 in support of Kuiper reinforced the view that he was a capable all-round cricketer, but his main rival Denys Hobson, five years on from his Packer exclusion, was a more dangerous bowler. When Hobson's legbreaks claimed 4-57 on day two, he seemed to jump the queue as second spinner behind Kourie in the national pecking order.

Gooch was once again in unforgiving form, hitting 58 in less than an hour with six fours and four savage sixes, but other than Dennis Amiss (52) there was no sign of form from the other batsmen. Woolmer fell to Hobson for just three and no-one else made more than wicketkeeper Alan Knott's 27 in a total of 219 all out. A sporting declaration from Peter Kirsten on the final afternoon set the tourists 249 in three hours plus an extra 20 overs, and Boycott finally found some form in making 95 before calling Amiss for a doomed single and seeing Kirsten execute a direct hit. After a run-a-ball 30 from Amiss, however, there was no other contribution from the SAB XI with Gooch holing out to square leg for a duck. Having lost John Emburey to Cape Town Hospital in the morning session after he broke a finger trying to take a sharp return catch from Kirsten, the ninth-wicket partnership between Lever and Hendrick was effectively the last and they were happy to bat out to avoid a third consecutive defeat.

Emburey would spend the rest of the tour with a hand in plaster, fulfilling his playing contract as assistant tour manager. His absence had caused a further embarrassment for the tourists during the game: when no player could be found to field as 12th man Cooke himself had to step into the breach, much to the amusement of the attendant fans who enquired how much extra money the player-manager earned for stepping out onto the pitch. The South African Breweries' XI were beginning to resemble a true pub team.

After being thoroughly outplayed for three consecutive matches, batsmen struggling for form and bowlers convalescing in transit, the credibility of the tour was already creaking ahead of the first 'Test' at Wanderers. Even the players themselves appeared to be questioning the value of the contests, when the stricken Mike Hendrick lamented: 'Unless you play in the matches, you cannot get match fit. And the nature of this tour is such that we will have to play in the big games despite not being ready.'

In the Johannesburg build-up the respective messages laid bare the gulf between views inside and outside the South African bubble. Graham Gooch, intent on minimising or even avoiding an international ban as the TCCB considered their options, adamantly stuck to the tour position that these were private individuals engaged in private business. 'It is just another game,' he said. 'Of course it's important to us all but no-one thinks for a minute we're starting a Test series.'

Five minutes later the same journalists were told by his opposite number Mike Procter: 'The three four-day games are being billed as Test matches because that's exactly what they are. We're fielding our best team. I also believe that, with the exception of Ian Botham, we're also facing just about the best team from England.'

To the great surprise and dismay of home players and administrators, the Johannesburg public inclined towards the Gooch view. A crowd of just 8,759, at a stadium with 30,000 seats in a city of more than two million, turned up to watch a one-sided first day at the 'Test'. The rebels lost a fourth successive toss and, despite being invited to bowl first on a green wicket that looked a nightmare for batsmen, found the South African welcome mat emphatically withdrawn.

The day's play was bisected by a single wicket, Barry Richards chipping a simple catch to Dennis Amiss from Derek Underwood after a typically fluent 66. Jimmy Cook and Peter Kirsten then put on an unbroken 160, closing on 277-1. For the 28-year-old Cook it was a tumultuous experience. Dropped at the wicket by Knott on 5, and then in the slips on 27 (Old), 46 (Gooch) and 64 (Old again), he had suffered in comparison to Richards and would later recall: 'I could not believe we were facing the same bowlers. He was playing as if they were throwing the ball at him underarm and I kept saying to myself, "Why are they bowling so fast to me and so slowly to him?"'[21]

Yet, unbeaten overnight on 114, he was anointed by the home authorities as the first South African to score a Test century in 12 years – and the first ever to do so on debut. A leading player in the generation of cricketers denied official Test cricket, Cook still takes great personal satisfaction in the recognition of his abilities. 'I had never played for South Africa before so it was a fantastic thing for me to come out having achieved something I'd worked for all my life. It did not worry me too much that the matches were not official – it was all that was available to me at the time so I did what I could.'

The tourists had been little more than bystanders at the parade, the dispiriting sight of repeated dropped catches exacerbated by an over rate that barely touched 13. They made some amends early on day two in front of a crowd that had swelled to nearly 20,000, Les Taylor removing Cook and Kirsten first thing in the morning. But Graeme Pollock, 64 not out, was an impenetrable barrier in guiding the home side to a declaration on 400-7. While South Africa's top four had all made major contributions, SAB remained too reliant on Gooch and too vulnerable to the giant Vince van der Bijl, who started with a wide but overcame his nerves to deliver a brilliant performance. Geoffrey Boycott and Wayne Larkins once again fell cheaply and when the captain became the third dismissal in 16 balls, albeit after a brisk 30, a first-innings reply of 42-3 told its own story. Amiss continued to defy the years and the South African bowlers but was the only recognisable batsman to survive to the close at 90-5, still 161 short of avoiding the follow-on.

The third day brought belated hope for the tourists, though Amiss was first left stranded on 66 not out as five partners fell for 60 runs in the morning session, van der Bijl finishing with 5-25. Procter forced his guests to bat again but was met with a spirited rearguard action. Gooch and Boycott put on 119 for the first wicket and closed on 169-1, the furious veteran on the wrong end of a poor lbw decision to van der Bijl and his captain peppering the cover boundary for 104 not out. But when Gooch fell early on day four, the rebels reverted to type. Amiss and Peter Willey top-scored on 24 as nine wickets cost just 110 in a collapse to 283 all out with van der Bijl acclaimed as the third South African to take ten wickets in a Test on debut. Even though Procter's knee limited him to off-spin in the second innings and Clive Rice could not bowl at all due to neck pain, this set a gentle 34 for victory, and Kirsten hooked and pulled John Lever for sixes to bring up an eight-wicket win.

If the quality of South African cricket during isolation looked as impressive as promised, then fears over the umpiring standard had also been confirmed: four lbw decisions from Barrie Smith went against SAB XI on day four as well as Procter claiming a catch to Amiss that the batsman hotly disputed. If nothing else, these controversies provided the sparse crowd and dwindling television audience with reasons to believe that the match was competitive.

SACU were alarmed by the gate receipts – 18,000 and 4,000 had turned up for the latter two days, meaning that fewer than half of the tickets had been sold. Joe Pamensky immediately became converted to the Dutch Reformed Church and demanded that television coverage of the matches be ended to boost attendances. It was an irksome time for the sponsors, too. If co-operation between the government and South African Breweries was at this stage hardly a secret, then the news had not filtered through to the traffic police who set up breathalyser roadblocks near the ground.

There was no little irritation in the respective dressing rooms either. John Woodcock, *The Times* correspondent and *Wisden* editor who was with the team in South Africa, announced through his *Wisden* office that the matches would be recorded for historic interest only and not as official internationals. Meanwhile, over the weekend in Trafalgar Square the largest anti-apartheid rally in the UK in a decade had denounced the tourists and featured a notable star cameo. To much eye-rolling in the SAB dressing room, there had been an in absentia message of best wishes from Ian Botham.

The SAB XI had no time to heal injuries or renew spirit ahead of the second 'one-day international' at Kingsmead although uncapped Yorkshire bowler Arnie Sidebottom, a cult figure at Headingley for his dramatic on-field demeanour, who was on a coaching stint with Orange Free State, had been signed. The 'one match on, one day off' schedule hung ever heavier around the tourists' necks – and 500km separated Johannesburg from the hot and humid seaside town of Durban. Les Taylor, who had played the first 'Test' only with the help of cortisone injections, and Chris Old had also succumbed to injury so, with John Emburey a long-term casualty, the SAB party were a dozen once more. Geoff Humpage was the man to miss out and the superior home batting was once again in evidence, Graeme Pollock top-scoring with 41 as contributions throughout the list brought 231-6 from 50 overs on a slow, dull pitch before a 14,000 crowd. In reply Graham Gooch and Geoffrey Boycott started slowly and fell, and only Wayne Larkins (47) and Peter Willey (31) passed 15 in a sorry reply of 152, a thumping 79-run defeat. Larkins had at least found some touch, top-scoring and falling only to an outstanding catch from Ray Jennings off the impressive Stephen Jefferies. But positives were few and far between for the SAB XI, who had again been overwhelmed by Vince van der Bijl's combination of nagging accuracy and alarming bounce. The home side were even afforded the luxury of wrapping up matters with Peter Kirsten's occasional off-breaks.

The gulf in class between the sides was now unmistakable and a lack of meaningful competition translated to unrest among the crowd. Two streakers interrupted the play and there were outbreaks of fighting with unconfirmed reports that 22-year-old Rava Chetty was killed in a disturbance on the terraces. Peter Cooke retreated to his apolitical stance, which was providing ever less protection: 'We realise the implication of a coloured man dying in this way – but only a racist would try to make capital out of it.'[22]

The players barely had time to register the news. They had to set off immediately on a 1300km flight to Cape Town for the second 'Test'. To his great regret Mike Procter, who had been a shadow of his rampaging former self, was forced to withdraw but the home side hardly missed a step. Barry Richards assumed the captaincy while Adrian Kuiper, the all-rounder who had terrorised the SAB XI on arrival at Berea Park and again in Cape Town for Western Province, stepped straight into Procter's shoes.

The home side even enjoyed the luxury of a tactical switch with Denys Hobson finally handed the experience of 'international' cricket ahead of Omar Henry as Garth Le Roux dropped out of the XI. For the tourists, Taylor and Old were at least passed fit to play and Gooch finally called correctly at the toss, only to see questions about the umpires resurfacing after a rain-delayed start. If Geoffrey Boycott held any man in lower esteem than members of the attendant press, that man was Durban-based lawyer Barrie Smith, who had been the subject of SAB ire in Johannesburg. When Boycott was dismissed, caught by Kuiper off Alan Kourie while television replays clearly showed a bump ball, the batsman, whose 16 had taken 80 minutes, was incensed and marched down the wicket to demand: 'Can you tell me how that was out?' This potential flashpoint was doused with further rain, however, and with no play after tea and the SAB on 101-1, a draw already looked inevitable.

The second day was again slow, SAB XI all out for a time-consuming 223 and South Africa a par 74-3. Peter Kirsten's cautious, methodical century on day three afforded the hosts a 12-run first-innings lead and before the close Boycott was out cheaply once again. He was therefore left to watch on the fourth and final day as Gooch took Hobson to task, and Wayne Larkins and Dennis Amiss each helped themselves to big half-centuries. In front of a crowd of fewer than 1,000 with no possibility of a result it could be little more than batting practice, prompting Pollock to break SACU media protocol and vent his frustration: 'I must say the tour has been disappointing from the point of view of the English performances. We've had the whip hand all along. They're only about three players short of being the full England side. Geoff Boycott is struggling. People are a bit disappointed. They ask us why we're winning so easily – and they're particularly surprised because we're not as good a team as when we last played Test cricket in 1970.'[23]

An initially extraordinary expedition was providing all-too-ordinary cricket. South Africa had waited 12 years to test themselves against top opposition and were beginning to realise that the wait would go on. With the SAB XI outclassed and neither money for nor interest from additional recruits, the tour might have been quietly completed and forgotten.

But the dwindling interest in the event was given a wake-up call by events elsewhere. On the afternoon of Saturday 19 March, day one of the rain-ruined second 'Test', the TCCB made public its verdict on the 15 rebels: a three-year ban from international cricket as well as a ban from facing India or Pakistan in tour matches with counties in the forthcoming summer. This would apply equally to high-profile leaders Geoffrey Boycott and Graham Gooch as to Geoff Humpage, who had played only a single match, and Arnie Sidebottom, who had joined less than a week previously on a pay-as-you-play contract.

The Professional Cricketers' Association supported the ban as they ensured the survival of Test series that underpinned the English professional game, secretary Jack Bannister saying, 'Hopefully the 15 will now understand the anxieties and needs of the rest in pursuing their livelihood, which would be affected considerably in the event of a badly disrupted Test programme.' But the South African establishment were predictably less impressed, as Joe Pamensky lamented: 'The English authorities have bowed to political pressure from India and Pakistan.' He vowed to provide financial support for the rebels both during future cricket seasons and in any court case they sought to pursue.

If the cricket was now forgettable then the tour was nevertheless historic, drawing a line under some of the game's most illustrious names. Boycott's 108th Test at Kolkata in January would be his last; the world-record total of 8,114 runs would rise no higher. Derek Underwood, with 297 wickets, just ten short of Fred Trueman in the all-time England list, would have to settle for second best. Alan Knott's career, though near its conclusion, was brought to an abrupt halt on 269 Test dismissals, second only to Rod Marsh of Australia.

And then there was Gooch. After a promising but uneven seven-year Test career, the right-hander had dominated a strong and committed South African attack with negligible support. His broad-bat approach had thrilled the home crowds and united opinion in England and the republic that here was a successor to Boycott as a noteworthy top-order batsman. TCCB executive committee chairman George Mann was even made to comment in his otherwise unapologetic statement: 'Gooch was a tragedy. We did feel anguished. Who could be happy doing a thing like that?'

Keith Fletcher, England captain and friend of Gooch, was equally distressed yet adamant: 'I feel very sad … he had so much to offer. But like everyone else in South Africa, he knew the score and must have expected punishment of some sort.'

The players themselves had resolved not to talk about the incident in public, but there was a deep sense of shock and dismay. Contrary to Fletcher's assessment, the players had convinced themselves – perhaps with some encouragement from those who had tempted them to South Africa – that not only had they done nothing wrong but that they remained out of the reach of anything more than a nominal one-Test or one-summer ban. Gooch has often recalled his surprise in Cape Town upon hearing the news on the BBC World Service: 'It struck home like a thunderbolt. Three years. Perhaps now I know how a prisoner feels, standing in the dock convinced of his own innocence but hearing the judge pass sentence, sending him to jail.'[24] Contemporaries Emburey and Larkins were equally upset.

Underwood was more philosophical, declaring: 'We went into this with our eyes open.' But that was highly questionable given the reaction of a fellow veteran. Boycott was visibly shell-shocked by his exclusion, staring wordlessly from a sofa in the hotel foyer for half an hour, oblivious to the enquiring gentlemen of the press. He had become used to unpopularity at Headingley and England but had previously waited out problems. It was apparent that there was no such option on this occasion.

For the TCCB, it was mission accomplished. India and Pakistan indicated that the ruling would ensure their participation in the summer's forthcoming Test series and the future of English professional cricket was therefore secure. There would be no 'black–white' split in international cricket, and limited consequences for other events such as the Commonwealth Games in Brisbane. The future of the 15 men who had travelled a different path was also clearer but much less inviting. The isolation feared by Tony Lewis a fortnight earlier was all but absolute.

This unanticipated blow to morale compounding their multiple injuries, the tourists digested the news on the 1,200km flight from Cape Town to their penultimate date: the third 'one-day international' at the Wanderers. Interest had now thinned even among the South African press, with the SAB XI slipping off the front pages for the first time since their arrival in the republic. Attention on the tour had fallen away after first uncompetitive visitors, then poor umpiring and finally bleak weather had variously put paid to scheduled contests. The tourists had resolved to ignore their long-term fate until after the tour and focus on a strong performance in their remaining two matches, but it was now the turn of the rule book to undermine the occasion.

South Africa batted first in Johannesburg and despite brief rain delays used their full 50 overs. Clive Rice, who had rejected a Buckingham Palace reception with his Nottinghamshire team-mates to play in the match, justified his decision with a first half-century of the series. The star of the show though was Adrian Kuiper, who looked every inch an international-class all-rounder in the buccaneering Botham mould with 54 from 57 balls. The total of 243-5 set the highest victory target of the one-day series.

The SAB XI had nevertheless looked in control after a solid opening stand of 60 before the star pair found themselves at the same end when running a single. Geoffrey Boycott stood his ground and Graham Gooch departed with the philosophical shrug of a man who had seen it before. Rain interruptions then saw England's target reduced to 112 from 23 overs but with rhythm gone and in a panic to secure victory, three further wickets fell. Still the tourists kept just about in contention, with 21 runs required from two overs and six wickets still in hand. Dennis Amiss launched a lacerating attack on Garth Le Roux to reduce the arrears to four runs with six deliveries remaining but Geoff Humpage played and missed at two balls from Vince van der Bijl before being clean-bowled. A wide and a leg bye from Alan Knott's pads edged the total closer and brought Amiss back on strike but the veteran's high carve down towards third man was claimed spectacularly on the run by wicketkeeper Ray Jennings. Oblivious to the wide, hundreds of spectators invaded the field to celebrate a stylish victory but there was still one chance – one ball – to claim the two runs required for an overdue away win. The new man, Arnie Sidebottom, pushed van der Bijl's delivery down to third man and scampered a single only to be run out returning for a second, leaving the total on 111 and all parties in undisguised confusion.

In accordance with domestic convention, the scorers promptly awarded the SAB XI a first victory of the tour by virtue of a better score after 20 overs. Others declared South Africa the winners for losing fewer wickets but it was the umpires who delivered the final verdict: a home win by better overall run rate, 4.86 to 4.83. It was an outcome to have confused the hardiest among a 13,000 crowd, but 81 minutes after stumps most of these had headed home along with the man who disconnected and stored the public address system. The result was announced by a blazered official circling the outfield and bellowing, 'South Africa wins.'

The Springboks had concluded their first ever 'one-day international' series with a notional 3-0 whitewash, but few had bothered to stick around for it. Van der Bijl recalls, 'I got a wet ball on a sodden outfield and I just bowled a perfect over, probably the best of my life: got a couple of wickets, there was a run out … they had to get two off the last ball and they only got one. But I never regarded it as having won an international, nor did my wife. As I walked up she was sitting in the stand and just said to me, "You couldn't even let them win one game, could you?"'

In bald contrast to the euphoric anticipation of the early 'international' contests, expectations were modest upon the return to Kingsmead for the final rubber. Four defeats in five matches – including those by margins of seven wickets, eight wickets and 79 runs – had outweighed any amount of promotional bluster from Peter Cooke,

Joe Pamensky and the South African press. The South African stars had not really fired either: Graeme Pollock had faded after an electric start, Mike Procter had withdrawn with injury before the halfway stage and Barry Richards had struggled to revive his 1970s magic amid enduring disillusionment. The stand-out performer for the home side had been Vince van der Bijl, with the team's consistency and strength in all three departments suffocating the opposition even though in Gooch they boasted the outstanding individual of the series. As stand-in captain, Richards had become a spokesperson for the visitors as much as for his own men, claiming that the Wanderers debacle – the SAB had lost three wickets in an over chasing just four to win – had shown a team 'getting its act together'.

His team were sufficiently indifferent, deciding to forego any pre-match practice in Durban. Apparently conducting press conferences on autopilot to the bitter end, Gooch was adamant that a victory was a huge incentive and it certainly represented his best chance of the tour. The players were finally something near match fit, the South Africans were now struggling to motivate themselves and the subtropical Durban offered encouragement for SAB XI's swing and seam bowlers.

In such circumstances it was a helpful toss to win and the English bowlers belatedly showed their pedigree. In particular Les Taylor cemented his reputation as the best seamer on tour, bowling with verve and hostility to remove Pollock and Adrian Kuiper in successive deliveries before finishing with 5-61 as the hosts declared on 181-9 just before the close. SAB XI survived the first evening and batted all of day two, seemingly creating an opportunity to win not only the match but also some belated admiration from a lacklustre South African public. But throughout the second day on a lifeless pitch they made only 182 from 82 overs. A particular culprit was Geoffrey Boycott, whose 214-minute, 130-ball 31 drew the jeers of an exasperated crowd. The Yorkshireman was thrust back onto the front pages as South African irritation spilled over, but in England it was widely and wryly observed that if the Springboks wanted a faithful recreation of Test cricket then there was no more authentic experience than hour upon painful hour of Boycottian obduracy.

A Sunday wash-out ensured the match would be a draw, but the authorities resisted the urge to play a one-day international lest this 'undermine the authenticity of the Tests.' Instead Bob Woolmer completed the only century by a tourist other than Gooch and the match tapered out with Alan Knott bowling an over. That did not happen in Test matches. The lack of competitive action was perhaps in keeping with all that observers had come to expect, but a particular regret on all sides was Richards ending his series retired hurt on 17. He had previously admitted his enjoyment in wearing Springbok colours once more. 'These matches have been a real bonus for us. Playing together for the first time in years has given us a real team spirit.' But he now lamented, 'At the age of 37 you can't do what you did when you were 25. You've just got to hang in there.'

Twelve years in the making, the first rebel tour had been revealed, conducted and concluded within a chaotic month. On their return the rebels had to face down photographers and press at Heathrow, but Graham Gooch stonewalled while Arnie Sidebottom simply barked at any photographer blocking his luggage trolley: 'Get out the ****ing way!' These tactics appeared to work until Geoffrey Boycott and his girlfriend Anne Wyatt tried to sneak out incognito into a waiting Black Maria. The *Daily Mirror,* which had been most vocal in its criticism from the start, gleefully reported Boycott's bizarre return:

'He wore a baseball cap pulled low over his eyes [and] sprinted into Customs as if he were in danger of being run out.'[25]

It provided a suitably confused conclusion from the tour's erstwhile leader and did nothing to repair the rebels' reputations. Peter Willey lamented: 'I said to him, "We've done nothing wrong. Let's walk through with our heads held high. We haven't broken any laws." But he walked through with hat down and collar up. I told him, "What's the point? They know who you are." I think he made it worse.'[26]

Nor were the South African players immune from the fall-out as Mike Procter, Graeme Pollock and Eddie Barlow, who had been due to play for an Old Rest of the World XI against an Old England XI for the Ken Barrington Memorial Trust at The Oval, were told they would not be welcome following the rebel tour. A furious Procter denounced the decision as 'an insult' and there was no apparent support for the expulsion from the Trust itself. A spokesman for Courage, who were sponsoring the match, said, 'The last thing we want is anything controversial. Our invitations are going to former West Indies, Pakistan, Indian and Australian players and we do not want to offend anyone.' The trio's myriad work in multi-racial cricket had been eclipsed by a 30-day unofficial tour.

SACU acclaimed it a triumph, though the truth was predictably more opaque. Gate receipts of £392,000 would not cover the tourists' wages, much less their travel and accommodation, administrative costs and the match fees of the capped Springboks. Live television coverage and poor weather were blamed for low turnout but inadequate preparation and selection of the visiting team was inescapable.

John Woodcock, who had supported the rebels, wrote in *Wisden*, 'Not only was the tour fiercely controversial;

the cricket itself was disappointing and as an exercise in public relations the whole operation left a lot to be desired.'[27] A 'Packer-style' circus was out of the question and the finances lent a final hollow ring to the words of the South African organisers. Multi-racial cricket, Joe Pamensky had proclaimed, would yield the profits but, in the absence of any, beneficiaries were few and far between. In desegregated stadia there had been low non-white turnout.

For those who had experienced authentic Test cricket, there were no illusions as to the matches' true meaning following the initial euphoria. Neither Mike Procter nor Barry Richards consider themselves to have captained South Africa, as Richards explains: 'It wasn't a substitute in the full sense of the word. It just wasn't something where you could say "this really counts". It was good for us to test ourselves but it wasn't the real thing.'

And the uncapped Vince van der Bijl is similarly keen to keep the matches in perspective: 'I had a Springbok cap on, but I knew this wasn't a Springbok cap. It was a nice hype and just a fantastic experience to be working with some of the best players and see what it would have been like if you had to play for South Africa. But I certainly didn't have any illusions about it. I never considered myself to be playing for South Africa.'

At the same time the initial excitement had been undeniable and the standard of South African cricket reassuringly high in 1-0 and 3-0 series wins. While SACU's pretensions towards authentic international cricket had fallen flat, their ambition to excite domestic cricket had been achieved. Jimmy Cook, a leading player in the generation of cricketers denied official Test cricket, takes great personal satisfaction in the recognition of his abilities: 'For me personally it was a matter of if I was good enough to play for South Africa at the time, whether it was official or unofficial. We did have the teams picked in a proper manner, so I thought to myself,

"Well, I've achieved what I wanted to achieve." I set out my goal to try and play for South Africa and whether they're official or not I've managed to achieve that and that was just wonderful for me. To suddenly have Barry Richards and to have Mike Procter in your own team was absolutely fantastic.'

For South African sport, the awkward stumbling towards multi-racial sport continued with a series of rugby union Tests between South Africa and the South American Jaguars, a team comprised mostly of Argentinians. On the day of the rebels' return, the Argentine supplanted South Africa as the UK's Public Enemy Number One when General Galtieri invaded the Falkland Islands. In the republic, the authorities now turned to arranging bigger and better rebel tours to invigorate their cricket and infuriate the rest of the world.

1 p 2, *Daily Mirror*, 1 March 1982.
2 p 11, *The Times*, 2 March 1982. Press coverage extended beyond the animated cricket world to the unfamiliar surroundings of the *New York Times* (A3, 3 March 1982) and the *Frankfurter Allgemeine* (p 23, 3 March 1982).
3 p 16, *Sunday Express*, 7 March 1982.
4 p 17, *Sunday Telegraph*, 7 March 1982.
5 Front, *Rand Daily Mail*, 1 March 1982. The governmental crisis centred on an impending split in the ruling National Party. Dr Andries Treurnicht, architect of the education policy that prompted the 1976 Soweto riots and a.k.a. 'Dr No' for his absolute opposition to any dilution of the political status quo, led a rebellion against PW Botha's limited reform agenda. On 20 March 1982 Treurnicht and 17 fellow MPs quit the NP to form the Conservative Party, which continued to oppose democratisation to the last. He died in April 1993, exactly a year before the first universal elections in the republic.
6 p 8, *Rand Daily Mail*, 9 March 1982.
7 p 24, *Guardian*, 11 March 1982.
8 p 174, McGlew and Chesterfield (1995).
9 Back, *The Sun*, 3 March 1982.

10 p 231, Boycott biography (1987).
11 p 2, *Daily Mail*, 4 March 1982.
12 p 98, Gooch and Keating (1995).
13 p 18, *Daily Mail*, 6 March 1982.
14 Front, *The Sun*, 6 March 1982.
16 Front, *Daily Express*, 11 March 1982.
16 Back, *Daily Mirror*, 3 March 1982.
17 p 24, *The Observer*, 7 March 1982.
18 p 3, *Daily Express*, 8 March 1982.
19 pp 133–135, Woolmer (1984).
20 BBC Radio, *Rebel Hell*, first broadcast 8 February 2003.
21 p 11, Cook and Cleary (1993).
22 Front, *The Sun*, 19 March 1982.
23 p 21, *News of the World*, 21 March 1982.
24 p 63, Gooch (1986).
25 p 9, *Daily Mirror*, 1 April 1982.
26 p 233, McKinistry (2005).
27 p 1096, *Wisden*, 1983.

## Chapter 4

# Of Caps and Cuckoos

*'There is no law in this country, as there is in some others, which forbids travel abroad.'* – Lord Chalfont

The rebel cricketers left South Africa having been routed on the field and whitewashed in the PR war. The frantic back-room organisation had neglected not only proper playing preparation but also serious appraisal of the reaction the tour would provoke. Peter Cooke, for whom there 'was no moral principle involved at all'[1], had been concerned only with getting the strongest possible squad to travel. And the players had resolved to concentrate entirely on the job in hand and face the consequences upon their return.

Now that they had to do so, the prevailing mood was of neither contrition nor pride but shock: they had not anticipated the severity of public criticism or professional punishment. 'Hindsight,' wrote Graham Gooch of the three-year ban from international cricket, 'dictates that none of us should have been surprised and yet, without exception, we all were.'[2]

One popular analysis suggested that Cooke and Martin Locke had sold the players, emboldened by the Packer precedent, on the freedom to trade without fully acknowledging that a South African tour carried different implications.

But to have accepted this proposal suggests hopeless

naivety or wilful ignorance. Basil D'Oliveira and the 1970 cancellation had established in no uncertain terms the emotions and arguments in the South African debate, and the Jackman affair had made clear that these remained pertinent a decade later. Indeed the tour's clandestine organisation demonstrated a tacit acceptance among the players that they would stir up similar outrage – as David Gower later wrote, 'You don't get paid that sort of money and go around behaving like an MI5 agent without suspecting that there might be a penalty clause.'[3]

The TCCB had warned that players would 'jeopardise' their international careers through association with South Africa, an imprecise but serious threat. A reluctance to think seriously about what the lucrative proposition entailed was evident too in the players' failure to anticipate manipulation into an 'international' series where Springbok caps were awarded.

In fact, a ban from international cricket had been all but inevitable as soon as they had boarded the plane. The tour had threatened relations with India, Pakistan and the West Indies, and thus the stability of English professional cricket, and this ought to have been wholly foreseeable.

The TCCB had changed its constitution since the Packer affair to ensure that it was free to protect English cricket's interests, so a ban on international selection was quite legal. A subsequent vote by the Professional Cricketers' Association confirmed peer support for the rebels' international exclusion while domestic availability remained the responsibility of individual counties.[4]

The rebels were at least justified in questioning the specific three-year length of the ban, which fitted suspiciously well into England's upcoming schedule:

| | |
|---|---|
| 1982 | India and Pakistan in England |
| 1982–83 | England in Australia and New Zealand |
| 1983 | World Cup and New Zealand in England |
| 1983–84 | England in Pakistan |
| 1984 | West Indies and Sri Lanka in England |
| 1984–85 | England in India |

It meant the rebels would miss a run of series against the 'black' countries and be available for the first time against Australia in 1985, which was, to say the least, convenient for the TCCB. Nevertheless a substantial ban had been widely predicted in the press as soon as the news of the tour broke. Had the tour been public knowledge before departure, then the expected punishment would have been too.

The secret organisation had harmed the rebels in avoiding a public debate about the arguments for and against the tour – because there was far greater support for their actions than the blanket newspaper opprobrium suggested. In the UK the bridge-building vs. isolation debate remained polarised, and among the general public there was sympathy as well as disdain.

For one thing, most professional cricketers were not only modestly paid but literally unemployed between October and March.[5] Graham Gooch had taken the decision that as a professional in a free country he ought to be free to ply his trade where he chose, and more than 25 years after the tour this remained his position: 'County contracts began on 1 April and my commitments to the England side ended at the end of February, so I was not contracted to do anything in March. We believed as players we were within our rights as players to go and earn a living as cricketers anywhere in the world and as it transpired we were offered the chance to go on a private tour to South Africa. My only form of earning a living at that time was playing cricket.'[6]

The SAB XI captain had become fond of quoting Lord Chalfont, who had written to *The Times* in support of the tour in its earliest days. His proclamation had been pinned up in Gooch's hotel room throughout the trip: 'It is not reasonable, or indeed tolerable, that citizens of this country should be deprived by harassment, blackmail or threat of their freedom to pursue their sporting activities whether for pleasure or for gain, wherever they wish to do so. There is no law in this country, as there is in some others, which forbids travel abroad.'[7]

Simply put, in a free country governments and other groups do not dictate the individual rights and freedoms of fellow citizens. This fundamental point was hardly disputed beyond a minority – it was unthinkable that the UK government would have confiscated the cricketers' passports or income – and many of the most severe views found voice in newspapers whose stance was staggeringly hypocritical. The *Daily Mirror* had taken particular delight in baiting Geoffrey Boycott throughout the tour and upon his bizarre return to the UK. But on the same day they teased the Yorkshireman for his Heathrow theatre, the newspaper's careers pages sought workers among *Mirror* readers who might pick up 'attractive salaries in a country with a higher standard of living and lower taxation levels … South Africa will provide excellent schooling at all levels, beautiful countryside and scenic holiday resorts, first class sporting and recreational facilities and a world famous climate.'[8]

In addition to the right to individual choice, 'bridge-builders' could call on three further arguments. First, that sport ought not to be a special case when commercial relations were commonplace. Trade agreements between South Africa and the United Kingdom exceeded £1 billion, as Gooch repeatedly pointed out: 'A doctor, a lawyer, these people could go to South Africa and earn a living. In fact the trade between the UK and South Africa was going on freely – and with other countries. That was my way of earning a living and I didn't believe that I was doing anything wrong.'[9]

Secondly, the tourists and their supporters could argue that it was illogical and indefensible to continue sporting relations with regimes such as the Soviet Union and Uganda yet suspend them with South Africa. For many in the UK apartheid was insufficient to make the republic a particularly unpalatable regime, reflecting prevailing ideology. Many Conservatives, including Prime Minister Thatcher, who had declined to denounce the cricketers in 1982, had two years previously espoused a British boycott of the Moscow Olympics. 'Now just supposing the Russians played cricket…' wrote the Tory MP George Gardiner in an argument that had been heard vocally ever since 1970.[10]

And thirdly, many believed that South African cricket was now multi-racial and further interaction would expedite reform in the republic. At a time when ideological conflict dominated UK politics through the Cold War, the value of individual freedom over collective restriction was not cheaply discounted. This argument, too, had been aired regularly ever since 1970 and was particularly popular within cricket itself. The TCCB had been inclined towards engagement until being outvoted within the ICC, and only Michael Brearley among leading England players had publicly opposed the tour on moral grounds. Even before multi-racial cricket, many in the UK had favoured engagement over isolation, and the argument since 1970 could only have been strengthened by SACU's progress. Among the rebels Bob Woolmer had by far the strongest authority through extensive experience of coaching all over South Africa and was convinced of the value of the 'yes to cricket, no to apartheid' argument.[11]

The coherent counter-points were also typically found some distance from tabloid hysteria and blanket, bilateral accusations of hypocrisy. The argument for making an exception of sport rather than, say, banking or jewel trading was not irrational: the sporting boycott had exerted a unique and significant influence on the National Party regime in the 1970s. As Matthew Engel wrote in the *Guardian*: 'There is no special merit to the sporting boycott except that it works ... The alternatives are advice, which has always been ignored; economic sanctions, which would fail; or war, which would be horrendous ... by a combination of historical accidents sport and politics have become inextricably linked in South Africa ... and the politics is more important.'[12]

This argument did not justify irrefutably the inconsistency, but explained why sport had been singled out. Anti-apartheid leader Desmond Tutu explained his position thus: 'I didn't mind the apparent inconsistency or hypocrisy ... It was something the so-called man or woman in the street – the white man or woman in the street who supported apartheid – understood. They wanted to be able to play rugby against the All Blacks, the Wallabies – you name it. When it wasn't happening even the dullest among them realised that the world was taking this thing seriously.'[13]

Even within sport, the boycott was far from universal. Individual sports remained more or less exempt, with South African golfers and tennis players plying their trades worldwide and many from those sports visiting the republic without punishment. And rugby union continued to exempt itself from the boycott; in 1980 Bill Beaumont had captained a British and Irish Lions tour to the republic and was the following year awarded the MBE.

Many aggrieved South African cricket figures had therefore bemoaned the international protest movement's ignorance in targeting 'the wrong sport'. But the anomaly was explained easily enough: the elite rugby world, All

Black Maoris excepted, was almost universally white and the cricket world, in per capita terms, overwhelmingly non-white. The boycott was felt most forcibly in cricket not because the protestors had ignorantly chosen the wrong sport – this was the sport where most leverage could be exerted.

On the second issue – ought tyrannies to be dealt with differently? – the obvious answer was again that of Engel: South Africa's sporting culture and geopolitical status made it vulnerable to a boycott in a way that the Soviet Union or Uganda simply were not. Moreover, as Mike Brearley wrote in *The Sunday Times*, the republic was a special case: 'The answer is, I think, that the system of government of these countries is not designed to oppress people on the basis of birth or race. South Africa's is.'[14]

While opposition from India, Pakistan and the West Indies was routinely dismissed by pro-engagement groups as infantile and hypocritical, it is interesting to consider whether the same people would have supported sporting links with any country that treated whites as apartheid did blacks. Apartheid was an issue of far greater importance in India, Pakistan and the West Indies because in those countries, as across the world, people were overwhelmingly not white.

Thirdly, the issue that South African cricket was multi-racial and SACU ought to have been rewarded for their accomplishments was highly subjective. As Brearley wrote, 'I am reminded of the rosy accounts of Stalin's Russia that some Fabians brought back. It is hard to know the true significance of changes in South African sport. My personal response is that we should require more positive indications from the oppressed in that country, that we should lean over to lend our psychological support to the black majority rather than the whites.'[15]

The question of canvassing black opinion was complicated by the repeated claim that black South Africans did not seriously play cricket. Even the left-leaning *Observer* in London was happy to argue: 'Cricket is not really an African game ... Perhaps it is too slow to suit the African temperament. One does not hear of notable Nigerian or Ghanaian cricketers. The West Indians are the only people of African ancestry to have taken to it.'[16] Certainly the *Guardian* writer John Arlott was in no doubt as to the true value of multi-racial cricket. He wrote, 'The coloured people are taken into the vaunted multiracial teams as a propaganda move. Neither they nor their children have remotely equal opportunities with the whites ... Critically, the "integrated" coloured players are still barred from social contact with their "white team-mates". That is not the fault of the South African cricketers, but of their Government which needs the cricketers as propaganda.'[17]

Thus, while the balance of opinion in India, Pakistan and the West Indies was emphatic this was not the case in the UK. Objective judgement of the arguments was complicated by a shortage of reliable information and vagaries of personal bias. While Ian Wooldridge was castigating the tourists with acerbic gusto in Johannesburg, a poll of his *Daily Mail* readers found only a small minority to condemn them.[18] If the anti-tour response to that was straightforward – no-one ever went bust underestimating the intelligence of the general public – then there were also better informed and more respected voices behind the tourists.

*Wisden Cricketers' Almanack* is known as the cricket bible, and often with good reason. It is all things to all cricket people: a treasure trove of statistics and stories; a home for the best of cricket writing; and, its adherents would hope, a source of sound and intelligent judgement on the issues affecting the game. For a decade from the mid-1970s, *Wisden* was a repeated proponent of increased engagement with South Africa. The editor John Woodcock had defended the tourists from 'the hysterical reactions of people who should know better' in his role as *The Times* cricket correspondent[19], and in successive *Wisdens* he published lengthy contributions espousing bridge-building. The first of these, by New Zealand Cricket Council president Walter Hadlee, proclaimed, 'With the goodwill and support of all cricketers, greater influence will be possible, and will demonstrate that cricket knows no barriers and sets the highest example of integrated sport, so providing the closer co-operation in the wider spheres of everyday life embracing social, cultural and economic activities.'

A year later Graham Johnson of Kent, who had toured the republic with the Derrick Robins XI and then become a coach in SACU's multi-racial set-up, wrote, 'There has been an honest and sincere effort by the South African cricket authorities to overcome deep-seated internal problems and prejudices. They have challenged the laws of the land so that their belief in non-racial sport may be realised.'[20]

This support for increased engagement was strengthened as the boycott bred further inconsistencies. While Gooch was banned for the 1982–83 Ashes, England called up the South African batsman Allan Lamb, who had played Currie Cup cricket every winter since joining Northamptonshire and rejected a chance to play for the Springboks against the SAB XI to avail himself of this career opportunity; he and Gooch effectively swapped places as the Essex batsman wintered with Western Province, Lamb's domestic side. And the ban itself represented a breach of the proposition accepted by the vast majority during the D'Oliveira and Jackman affairs: the pressure exerted by India, Pakistan and the West

Indies had apparently led to the three-year exclusion, and so Mad Hatterism was apparently alive and well in cricket administration. 'If that was not hypocritical, what is?' wrote John Woodcock in *Wisden*.[21]

What was clear was that the stigma fell unevenly. For those in the party at peace with retirement such as Dennis Amiss and Alan Knott, the ban was a decidedly peripheral concern. But for others, notably Gooch, whose name had become synonymous with the rebels, it was a blight. The dishonour attached to rebel status made the punishment a double jeopardy: while even the likes of Geoffrey Boycott and Derek Underwood, who might have played on for a season or two to further their formidable Test legacies, could quietly take their money into semi-retirement, Gooch would bear the costs of the team carrying his name for years to come. He was lampooned at county grounds as a 'traitor' and successfully sued *The Sun* for the fabrication of quotes that he 'didn't care about England any more'.[22]

On his return to England colours after three years he was faced by a hostile reception on a first tour of the West Indies alongside Ian Botham and David Gower, both of whom had rejected the tour on financial rather than moral grounds.[23]

Ultimately the tour's validity rested on value judgements and each individual had to be free to reach their own conclusion. Gooch and Lord Chalfont were quite right: it was impossible for the UK government or any group to prevent the tourists travelling by 'harassment, blackmail or threat'. However, this freedom did not guarantee immunity from criticism for, or consequences of, their actions. It was telling that the players did not seek to address opposing arguments but merely reiterated that no-one could stop them when, in fact, no-one had tried.[24]

Any 'threats' made against the rebels were from an extreme minority and certainly not supported by the

Anti-Apartheid Movement while 'blackmail' was an ungenerous assessment of the TCCB's entirely foreseeable and legally defensible three-year ban.

The argument continued to rest on the relative merits of engagement versus isolation. Certainly the tour itself could claim little in this regard – hopeful claims to visiting and coaching in non-white areas had disappeared from the schedule back in the earliest days. More than that, the rebels could make no credible claim to understanding the reality of South African life after a luxurious month inside the bubble. Black leaders who disputed any government policy, never mind the tour, were often in prison or in exile and any opposition to the tour kept from the players by laws restricting protest and media coverage. Many of the blacks staffing the tourists' hotels and restaurants were no more visible.

Did engagement with South Africa equate to collusion with apartheid? Was the sporting boycott significantly more effective than one on commerce? Did multi-racial cricket represent genuine progress or a propagandistic diversion? If the boycott had wrought serious change then might it not yield more improvements if maintained?

In an environment of mixed information and ideological obfuscation, the tourists were not necessarily damned by the answers, yet they had not addressed themselves to the questions. This 'three wise monkeys' approach, fortified only by the occasional insistence that all the rebels opposed apartheid, left them open to repeated criticism. Asif Iqbal wrote in *The Cricketer* that it was 'the height of hypocrisy to condemn apartheid [with whatever degree of sincerity], but to have no qualms about fraternising with those who perpetrate it.' And the reluctance to acknowledge any argument, for or against the tour, beyond individual freedom was satirised by the poet Kit Wright in 'I Found South African Breweries Most Hospitable':

*Meat smell of blood in locked rooms I cannot smell it,*
*Screams of the brave in torture loges I never heard or heard of*
*Apartheid I wouldn't know how to spell it,*
*None of these things am I paid to believe a word of*
*For I am a stranger to cant and contumely.*
*I am a professional cricketer.*
*My only consideration is my family.*
...
*They keep falling out of the window they must be clumsy*
*And unprofessional not that anyone told me,*
*Spare me your wittering spare me your whimsy,*
*Sixty thousand pounds is what they sold me*
*And I have no brain. I am an anomaly.*
*I am a professional cricketer.*
*My only consideration is my family.*[25]

Despite his long-standing friendship with Geoffrey Boycott, journalist Michael Parkinson was similarly scathing of this studied indifference: 'They frankly neither know, nor care, nor can be bothered to find out about the politics of whichever country their job takes them to nor, as has just been proven, do they give a tuppenny damn about the eventual price to be paid by their colleagues at home.'[26]

In particular one question went almost wholly unasked: how were the largely amateur South African Cricket Union able to afford such lucrative compensation for bridge-builders?

One of the few men who knew the answer was Ali Bacher, who a decade after the end of his playing career was leading South African cricket once again. In the late 1970s he had given up medical practice to become one of the few full-time cricket administrators in the country, a persuasive salesman whose shrewd analytical and negotiating skills proved as applicable to leadership off the field as on it. At Transvaal Cricket Council, first as director of cricket and then managing director, he overhauled an essentially amateur operation by pursuing an agenda of professionalism and competitiveness.

Under Bacher's leadership Transvaal became the leading province in the domestic game, dominating the media agenda through a combination of on-field success and skilled promotion. They built a formidable team under the aggressive captaincy of Clive Rice, adding to a core of local players, which included Jimmy Cook, Alan Kourie and Kevin McKenzie, by attracting the best of their rivals. Leading Springboks Graeme Pollock and Vince van der Bijl and successful provincial players such as Henry Fotheringham and Rupert Hanley signed from Eastern Province and Natal. In 1981–82 they had strengthened further with the double World Cup winning batsman Alvin Kallicharran, the first West Indian to sign for SACU, who received an immediate ban from cricket in the Caribbean.

Transvaal became a rival to Barbados as the strongest provincial team in the world; as Van der Bijl says, 'I think the Transvaal team of that year could have taken on almost any national team – I mean our team was: Cook, Fotheringham, Kallicharran, Pollock, McKenzie, Rice, Kourie, Ray Jennings, 'Spook' Hanley, Neal Radford and myself. We were strong.'

But their success and attention had attracted resentment among rival provinces – such as the New York Yankees do in baseball or Manchester United in football. The team's nickname 'the Mean Machine' reflected a capacity to subdue opponents mercilessly which was also reflected in a ruthless off-field organisation. This success, and the single-minded pursuit of it in the face of criticism, made Bacher's value to SACU obvious and he now became an influential voice in the organisation alongside Joe Pamensky and Geoff Dakin.

Although all three men professed opposition to apartheid, SACU's mission statement remained the protection and promotion of South African cricket without undue concern for the wider context of life in the republic. Politics in South Africa was both shambolic and vicious. The ruling government under PW Botha was instituting limited 'power-sharing' reforms at a glacial pace while typically excluding black people and their leaders from decision-making. Even Botha's pitiful concessions provoked ire in the National Party and reforms were watered down once again, and so while pro-engagement groups cited progress in the republic's social affairs the results were often hollow. At a beach in Durban, for example, a black lifeguard was employed, but as the Chairman of the Durban Ratepayers' Association pointed out, 'I cannot see for the life of me what good he is. In terms of Section 37 of the by-laws he is not allowed into the water.'[27]

The power struggle between such extreme elements had disastrous results. Bacher's biographer Rodney Hartman wrote, 'In this theoretical climate of reform in South Africa, the reality was that Botha's security forces became a law unto themselves and more atrocities against anti-apartheid activists were perpetrated than at any other time. Most white South Africans would not have known at this time, but they must have known that they were being governed by desperate people who were uncompromising in their ruthless subjugation of blacks.'[28] Botha masked this subjugation with the creation of a tiny black middle class, perpetuating the illusion of reform to whites and outsiders alike.

Feeling impotent to the barbarity of apartheid, Bacher considered his responsibility to South African cricket – and with no expectation of international cricket in his lifetime in the republic, renegade action was necessary. It was a position that placed him at odds with the anti-apartheid movement, inviting allegations of government collaboration. Hassan Howa continued to voice SACB's opposition, to question the funding sources and to highlight the importance of maintaining the international boycott. But his protests invariably went under-reported in the South African press and SACU ridiculed suggestions of government funding. Transvaal board member Mark Henning later said, 'What we lacked was a powerful liberal voice to say, "Listen, chaps, you're not thinking this through properly." We were good guys, we had respect for human dignity but...' Hartman added, 'The unspoken part was a common problem among white South Africans: an insensitivity based on lack of understanding in the bubble they had created on the southern tip of Africa; and their reluctance to understand, perhaps the fear of finding out.'[29]

Bacher had played only a peripheral role in the organisation of the English tour, but echoed the reaction of his players. 'It was an emotional time,' he said, 'but after the initial excitement, that feeling disappeared as the tour progressed. It just wasn't the real thing.'[30] The limitations of that venture suggested that any future organisation ought to be brought in-house. He now became recruiter-in-chief for future rebel tours and concluded that the demise of the English tour had resulted not only from last-minute organisation but also the limited appeal of the tourists.

After discussions with Kallicharran, he began arranging a West Indian tour, visiting England during the 1982 county championship season to speak to world-class cricketers including Desmond Haynes, Malcolm Marshall and Sylvester Clarke. West Indians, and leading West Indians at that, would change the rebel tour picture; as Bacher later said, 'We had never had any involvement with West Indian cricketers. We held them in very high regard … they played a form of cricket that was highly attractive and most importantly the fact that they were black. They could come to South Africa and show white conservatives that black people can play cricket at the highest level.'[31]

The South African authorities knew that while public and political opposition to apartheid was far stronger in the Caribbean than in the UK, the attraction of a lucrative cricket tour would also appeal to poorly paid cricketers: you cannot eat international caps. Clarke put Bacher in touch with former West Indies fast bowler Gregory Armstrong, who began co-ordinating the acquisition of more Caribbean cricketers. Having already begun preliminary negotiations with contacts in Australia, Bacher was keeping multiple plates spinning when he was contacted by a Sri Lankan, Tony Opatha.

A player-coach working in Sri Lanka and the Netherlands, Opatha was interested in organising a rebel tour by Sri Lankan players. Sri Lanka was a fledgling cricket nation, only a few months into Test status, but had competed at both the 1975 and 1979 World Cup, and even defeated India in the second of these. The talent within Sri Lankan cricket had remained largely unrealised with an amateur system and little experience. A cautiously curious Bacher was taken aback on asking Opatha how much each player expected to be paid.

'$30,000.'

'You say thirty thousand dollars? You're in cuckoo land.'

'Okay,' said Opatha. 'How many cuckoos to the dollar?'[32]

On 14th October SACU's Joe Pamensky confirmed that a secret planned tour of the republic by Sri Lankan cricketers had been called off after the prospective tourists' government had become aware of the scheme. Although commercial operations were commonplace between the two nations – South Africa imported almost R10 million worth of tea alone in each of 1981 and 1982 – the prevailing public and political attitudes were wholly different to the UK. The sporting boycott remained a priority political issue and fears that the Sri Lankan government might intervene led Pamensky to betray a weak grasp of irony: 'I don't want to be derogatory about other countries but, with respect, there are some places where they act first and ask about the law later.'[33]

The misdirection worked. Two days later a key Sri Lankan domestic clash between Ceylon Tobacco and Mercantile at Bloomfield was delayed because the home side were missing three key men: captain Bandula Warnapura, Mahes Goonatilleke and Bernard Perera. Along with Opatha and ten other Sri Lankan cricketers they were at the airport receiving tickets from a SACU official. Boarding planes without cricket kit so as to avoid attention, they flew to Hong Kong and then Johannesburg, arriving 21st October to be met by Piet Kellerman from the Department of National Education. As 'honorary whites' the newcomers would require constant protection against the petty official enforcers of apartheid, but Kellerman assured reporters he would ensure 'everything goes smoothly.'[34]

In Sri Lanka, the reaction was fevered as race betrayal became the central issue. 'The lepers who are surreptitiously worming their way to South Africa must understand that they are not playing fair by the coloured world,' said cabinet minister Gamini Dissanayake. And internationally the taboo of non-whites visiting South Africa attracted similar affront, as Sam Ramsamy of SANROC said, 'It is disgusting that black people can succumb like this to financial inducements and undermine the anti-apartheid movement. They should be banned from playing in their own country. They should realise that South Africa makes its money from exploiting black people but these players are cashing in on Sri Lanka's new Test status.'[35]

Hassan Howa and the SACB were equally unforgiving, distributing 16,000 pamphlets in the townships calling for a boycott of the matches and threatening punitive action against any player from the body attending the games. When the Board of Control for Cricket in Sri Lanka (BCCSL) rapidly handed out 25-year bans to all 14 rebels, Ramsamy was still unsatisfied: 'We don't think a 25-year ban from cricket is enough. If we can get positive action we will fly to Sri Lanka to consult with the government and legal experts.

'Either the rebel players have been so cruelly fooled by the South Africans or they are so blinded by greed for Krugerrands that they don't realise the scale of the anger they have caused in Asia. They will never be forgiven for the way they have abused Sri Lankan cricket. But their compromise with apartheid is their greatest crime.'

The 25-year ban, with no confiscation of income, would stand.

There was no doubt that without Test status the Sri Lankan cricketers would not have been invited to South Africa but this recent promotion allowed SACU to perpetuate the 'international' theme. Since an inaugural Test against England in February, Sri Lanka had played four more matches without victory and quite reasonably needed more time to develop into a competitive international force. Moreover, the team arranged by Opatha was by no means the strongest Sri Lanka could field, even if the South African public were not being told as much.

Warnapura, who had captained in four Tests to date including that inaugural match against England, would lead the side and Goonatilleke had played in all five as wicketkeeper. But there were only three other capped players in the party: batsman Anura Ranasinghe, a former teen prodigy who had played for Sri Lanka at the 1975 World Cup; the off-spinner Lalith Kaluperuma, who had also played two Tests; and left-arm spinner Ajit de Silva, who had played in both World Cups and was considered the nation's best bowler.

Beyond these there were others, including Opatha, who had represented Sri Lanka before ascendency to Test status but none of the men who had most impressed in official internationals. The three men to have scored a Test century for Sri Lanka – Roy Dias, Duleep Mendis, and Siddath Wettimuny[36] – were all absent, which did not bode well against a Springbok attack that had proven too much for the all-time Test run-scorer.

Playing with their national red lion emblem under the name Arosa Sri Lanka[37], the tourists were unequivocal when it came to motivation. Although opposed to apartheid they made no pretence at breaking down barriers; they were in it for the money. Pay for even Sri Lankan internationals was very low and for all the differences between Sri Lankan and UK attitudes to apartheid, at least one constant remained: professional dissatisfaction with the authorities. Warnapura later said, 'It was the pressure I was under from some of the senior BCCSL members. I was not sure if I was wanted in the side. They were gunning for me. So, after some hesitation, I decided to secure my future.'[38]

Despite the bans, the Arosa Sri Lankans began their 15-match tour with low-key matches against provincial opposition and, in a return to the anticipation of the SAB XI's earliest days, the media offered optimistic appraisals. The visitors from the Asian subcontinent approached the game in an altogether different way to South Africans, relying almost exclusively on slow bowling and batting deep in the crease with an emphasis on soft-handed shot-making. Each seemed to offer a distinct challenge to home players unaccustomed to anything but the hard-and-fast South African norm, and purely in terms of cricketing technique isolation's impact on white cricketers was unusually apparent. Their batsmen, characterised by the exuberant Anura Ranasinghe, exerted a fascination on those attending the early games while off-spinner Lalith Kaluperuma impressed particularly with changes of flight and speed. Politely ignored were the travails of Ajit de Silva. Rated as the visitors' star player and a leading exponent of left-arm spin, he was apparently bewildered. His opening spells were characterised by a total absence of confidence, full tosses and double-bouncing balls bearing no relation to the reputation that had preceded him.

As the tour matches progressed the threat proved illusory. The pressure on the Sri Lankans was readily apparent as before even the first international Tony Opatha had begun to blame poor pitches and officiating for his side's defeat to Boland from the Currie Cup B section. With de Silva misfiring and pitches a world away from those on the Asian subcontinent, the much-heralded spin bowling attack was treated with disdain by provincial batsmen. There was not a single bowler in the party pushing Lanthra Fernando's medium-fast and the few wickets that came their way typically did so as collateral damage in a frenzy of boundaries. Their batting also began to fray on pitches that aided faster bowlers and, though charitable observers felt that the heavy bans and international scrutiny had placed severe mental challenges on the tourists, the indications for the forthcoming 'internationals' were inauspicious.

Even more so when for the one-day series the Springboks left out fit-again Mike Procter for the first time since 1966, Western Province all-rounder Adrian

Kuiper keeping the berth he had first inherited during the English tour. Six of the Transvaal 'Mean Machine' were present and correct but it was Peter Kirsten, enjoying success leading Western Province, who was surprisingly announced ahead of Clive Rice as the permanent successor to Procter as captain – the first Springbok skipper of the post-1970 generation. The long-dormant Springbok brand was evidently an attractive commercial prospect and individual sponsorships mushroomed: in the 'Test' series, Graeme Pollock would earn R15 a run, Ray Jennings R1,000 for a catch and R2,000 for a stumping with the same amount knocked off his winnings for each missed opportunity, and Vince van der Bijl R450 for a wicket against a R10 loss for each run conceded.

The sponsors' liabilities were large. Ahead of the first 'one-day international', Rodney Hartman wrote in the *Rand Daily Mail* that the Red Lions had 'as much chance of victory as they have of being given a tickertape welcome when they return to Sri Lanka next month.'[39] The fears proved correct in a 189-run hammering that raised immediate doubts about the value on offer and it was not only the paying public who had concerns. Jimmy Cook and Barry Richards had added 150 for the opening wicket when the veteran Richards walked down the wicket to his partner and said, 'Enjoy the rest of your innings.' He calmly hit Ranasinghe to Jerry Woutersz at mid-off for 71, leaving a gobsmacked Cook at the crease. Even in Springbok colours Richards could not contain his disdain for inferior opposition.

Sri Lanka had impressed with their application and enthusiasm in the field but been found horribly wanting. Cook, who scored a century at the Wanderers and another in a 109-run victory in the second 'one-day international' at Berea Park, recalls, 'It was quite strange because they came out and didn't have a very strong side. But playing against them you've still got to do your thing. You can't just say, "Ah, these guys are weak so the runs don't mean anything." So I just took the attitude of "Look, if they're not up to it, well, bad luck for them." We just played it as normal games – we were playing for our country and we were going to do as well as we could.'

After the first 55-over game Kirsten and his team were offering the Sri Lankans advice on how to improve. However, as much as cricket coaching they needed physiology and psychology experts. De Silva was complaining of a nervous condition which provoked severe sweating in his bowling hand, implying a failure to come to terms with the pressure of the venture. Having played in four Tests and two World Cups, as well as claiming the scalp of Kirsten when Derbyshire played Sri Lanka three years previously, hopes had been high. Yet now he cut a distressed and distressing figure.

By the first 'Test' at Wanderers in mid-November the Springboks had added an eight-wicket win at Kingsmead to lead the one-day series 3-0. Warnapura went into the four-day game admitting that defeat was a certainty and spectators seemed to agree as the crowd barely exceeded 1,000 on day one. In that context the tourists acquitted themselves moderately well. After winning the toss they made 213 at a quick rate and claimed the wicket of the increasingly indifferent Richards before the close. But the Saturday, in front of barely 2,000, was a day of hard toil as nightwatchman Stephen Jefferies was as assured as Pollock in making 45, Cook prospered again with a century and the 29-year-old de Silva suffered something close to a breakdown, leaving the field unable to bowl despite admitting he carried no specific injury.

Kirsten had said upon his appointment that motivating this Springbok side was unnecessary, but he was forced to eat his words as the first 'Test' reached a woefully premature conclusion. South Africa resumed on 302-5 on the third morning but were bowled out for 378 as normally adhesive lower-order battlers Alan Kourie, Jennings and Garth Le Roux carelessly lost their wickets. They nevertheless bowled out the Sri Lankans in four hours for 141 to claim victory by an innings and 24 runs inside three days despite having lost part of day two to rain. Kourie, an unheralded member of the Springbok team, came to the fore with a five-wicket haul from his subtly varied slow left-arm.

The Sri Lankan visit was rapidly becoming an embarrassment and SACU even attempted to sign three further members of the official team as they ended a tour in neighbouring Zimbabwe. But the would-be rebels demanded a full-tour payment despite ten of the 15-match schedule having been completed and, facing significant financial losses in any case, Joe Pamensky conceded that the measure would be too little, too late.[40]

Richards then captained two Natal teams in facile wins over the tourists, sustaining a back injury requiring emergency hospital treatment that would keep him out of the remainder of the series. As the English XI had discovered earlier in the year, there was no shortage of takers when a Springbok cap was up for grabs and Lawrence Seeff was chosen to fill the coveted opener's slot alongside Cook.

The fourteen tourists, meanwhile, were mentally and physically shot as a demanding schedule had put Fernando and Woutersz on the injury list. De Silva had to be left out completely after refusing requests to bowl against Natal while batting number 11.

Some face was saved in the fourth and final 'one-day international', Ranasinghe making the tourists' first century in setting a competitive 277 to win but again the Sri Lankan bowling was impotent. Debutant Seeff and Kirsten made a century apiece as the Springboks eased to a six-wicket win with 13 balls to spare. The same week those bowlers could take only a single wicket in an innings defeat to Transvaal.

For the tour finale, the second 'Test' at Newlands, a changing of the Springbok guard was apparent. With Procter already excluded, another star of the 1970s in Vintcent van der Bijl dropped out with a thigh injury while Richards remained on the sidelines. As injuries and apathy took hold there was a danger that the precious Springbok cap was becoming too widely available. When Kourie suffered a groin strain in the build-up, Denys Hobson returned to the side and Omar Henry edged closer to his own piece of history as 12th man.

With school holidays in full swing, only 1,500 turned out for the first day, the Sri Lankans managing 282 on a pitch whose batsman-friendliness became fully apparent only on day two. The Springboks compiled 437-3 with ease, Seeff reflecting on his 188 with the frank admission: 'You can never equate this with real Test cricket.' He was promptly fined his match fee by SACU for breaking the strict media protocols in place to maintain their product promotion. Cook had scored his fourth century against the Red Lions and the only other batsman out during the day was Kirsten – after a freak run-out when Ranasinghe deflected a Graeme Pollock drive onto the non-striker's stumps. The reaction was one of embarrassed relief – relief that such a match would not be recorded as an official Test, where Seeff would have been acknowledged as the highest ever South African score on debut while his partnership with Cook fell just ten short of the national record. Rather than 'never before', the motto was 'never again': SACU simply had to arrange better opposition than this if the rebel tour concept was to have any enduring justification.

South Africa were ruthless in finishing the match off, Pollock thumping 197, with 17 fours and five sixes, in a total of 663-6 and though the Lions offered a spirited defence, they were bowled out for 281 early on day four despite a defiant century from the diminutive Bernard Perera. When Jennings stumped the hapless de Silva he sealed an innings victory and took his total sponsorship winnings to R23,000.

Short of any meaningful praise, some sections of the South African press took to criticising the organisers – and even the Springboks themselves. 'One had to pinch oneself regularly to believe that this match was billed as an unofficial Test,' wrote Michael Owen-Smith in the *Cape Argus*.[41] And Ted Partridge for the *Sunday Times* claimed, 'The third day of the so-called Test became a day of shame for South African cricket' under the headline 'Kirsten's bully boys humiliate Arosans.'[42]

Cook insists that he and his team-mates had no choice but to maintain their professional standards: 'You know, I'm playing for South Africa so I'm going to try and get as many runs as I can. I didn't care who was bowling to me, I just wanted to be successful. And there was a thing that we took out of the Transvaal 'Mean Machine' – we tried to win every game as convincingly as we could. In other words if we were playing a side in a one-day fixture, we wanted to win that game by a hundred runs or eight wickets. If we won by five runs against a weak team we weren't very chuffed with ourselves. So we had that killer instinct and that pride, and I carried that through to playing for South Africa because I wanted to win every game as convincingly as we could.'

Joe Pamensky took to calling the Arosa visit the 'Cuckooland tour' and when asked what they recall of it, the answer from Mike Procter and Vince van der Bijl is identical: 'Not a lot.' Barry Richards adds only, 'The team that Sri Lanka sent out were a club side as far as we were concerned, so for me that was no incentive at all. I'd rather not have played them, and that's with due respect to the players that came on the tour. They just weren't up to an international standard.'

Rather than adding to the cricket knowledge of the country, the tourists had at times taken coaching sessions with Alvin Kallicharran and Ali Bacher, and received team talks from opposing captain Peter Kirsten. Financially, too, the tour had been a disaster with supporter interest minimal. The newspapers projected losses in excess of R1 million[43] though SACU later would admit to only R600,000.[44]

After the stuttering English tour earlier in the year, the imperative had been to identify and attract better opposition. Even after the SAB XI's moderate performances, though, the only significant change wrought by Tony Opatha's team had been improved over rates. The player-manager continued to blame poor umpiring for his side's struggles, but Richards is reluctant to concede the point: 'If the umpiring was better? I tell you what; if there had been no umpires they wouldn't have given us a run! There was just no way they were competitive.'

Although the series was a mockery, South African self-regard had been strengthened again by a moderate Ashes series in which Allan Lamb, for England, and Kepler Wessels, for Australia, had both distinguished themselves. Journalists and former players, including Hugh Tayfield, predicted that the Boks would massacre either side in an Ashes series 'turning to embers'.[45] Graham Gooch, in the Cape with Western Province, begged to differ: 'Good as they are, when you compare the various qualities of the teams, you can give the Boks no more than a 50-50 chance against Australia.'[46]

South African cricket's desire to test itself remained clear. Bacher was working industriously to that end and would begin serious negotiations with the Australia squad at the World Cup the following year. Before that, however, he had arranged something even more remarkable. If the Sri Lankan tour had served any purpose whatsoever, it was to experiment with hosting 'honorary white' visitors in PW Botha's South Africa. Shepherded by a senior government official throughout, the Sri Lankans had kept out of harm's way. Within a month, a team from the West Indies would hope to do the same.

1 Quoted p 18, *Daily Mail*, 5 March 1982. Mihir Bose, who interviewed Peter Cooke for *Sporting Colours*, wrote, 'While in principle, like the majority of English speaking whites, he was against apartheid (though as an English passport holder he did not even have the vote) Cooke could see nothing wrong in accepting all the economic, social and legal advantages of apartheid, and cocooned in this distorting world felt that it was almost his moral right to try to organize a tour of English players who would provide the South Africans with some international competition.' (p 124, Bose 1994).
2 p 58, Gooch (1986). Some players even claimed that the criticism had affected their form on tour, leading to the poor competitive spectacle.
3 p 26, Gower (1992).
4 An outright sacking of a player by a county was almost certainly illegal and none took serious steps along this route. However, there were minor repercussions. Peter Willey remained at odds with Northamptonshire over their strong condemnation – his team-mate Allan Lamb was now an England player – and after two seasons joined Leicestershire; John Emburey was denied the Middlesex captaincy that had appeared in his gift. The rebels did not play for their counties in tour matches against India in 1982 but, while still banned from international cricket, did face New Zealand (1983) and the West Indies (1984) for their counties.
5 This insecurity was demonstrated by Keith Fletcher's story. In March 1982 he turned down an SAB XI contract to continue as England captain but by the next series he had been replaced by Bob Willis. After rejecting the South African offer he never again played for England, as captain or not.
6 *Out of the Wilderness: Part II*, British Sky Broadcasting, first broadcast 19 July 2008.
7 p 11, *The Times*, 3 March 1982.

8 p 26, *Daily Mirror*, 1 April 1982. Such advertisements were commonplace for newspapers who took great delight in bashing the tourists. *The Sun*, who had also struck a condemnatory note and would later libel Gooch from the supposed moral high ground, never ran a 'Free Nelson Mandela' campaign; they did, however, find space for a 'Free Deirdre Rachid' campaign some years later.
9 *Out of the Wilderness: Part II*, British Sky Broadcasting, first broadcast 19 July 2008.
10 p 16, *Sunday Express*, 7 March 1982. Of course, the Soviet Union did play football at club and international level: Aston Villa had beaten Dynamo Kiev in the European Cup quarter-finals during the rebel tour and the USSR reached the second round of the FIFA World Cup some months later. These were not overtly political although successive Olympics, Moscow 1980 and Los Angeles 1984, were both marked by substantial politicisation.
11 pp 109–16, Woolmer (1984).
12 p 15, *Guardian*, 19 March 1982.
13 BBC Radio, *Rebel Hell*, first broadcast 8 February 2003.
14 p 28, *The Sunday Times*, 7 March 1982.
15 p 28, *The Sunday Times*, 7 March 1982.
16 p 8, *Observer*, 7 March 1982. As Odendaal (2003) shows, this was a fabrication of the apartheid system. In cricket, as wider social life, the black population was largely ignored.
17 p 21, *Guardian*, 9 March 1982.
18 The NOP poll results were reported p 2, *Daily Mail*, 4 March 1982: Do you approve or disapprove of the cricketers' action, or are you not concerned by it? Approved 47%; disapproved 21%; not concerned 29%; don't know 3%. Do sporting links with South Africa help the apartheid system or do they help black South Africans? Sporting links support apartheid 19%; sporting links help blacks 47%; don't know 34%. Predictably the results were splashed prominently across all South African newspapers in the early days of the tour.
19 p 19, *The Times*, 2 March 1982.
20 pp 106–8, *Wisden* 1982; pp 104-5, *Wisden* 1983. Note that *Wisden* is published in the spring of each year with the result that although the 1982 edition was published after the rebels arrived in South Africa, it had been written and printed some time in advance. Thus, the 1983 edition included relevant coverage of the rebel tour (pp 1096–1102) and 1981–82 seasons

in Australia, India, New Zealand, Pakistan, South Africa and the West Indies.

21 p 81, *Wisden* 1983.

22 p 34, Gooch (1986).

23 Botham's decision process has been covered in Chapters 2 and 3; for Gower, see p 26, Gower (1992): 'I make no bones about my own reasons for not going. I was advised that it was likely to be commercially unfavourable for me.' Manley (2002) repeatedly references Gooch's South Africa connections when reporting his visits to the West Indies and suggests that he was a singularly unpopular figure in the Caribbean. But it is noticeable that these soften over time, and by 1990, when Gooch is both England captain and among the world's very best batsmen, he is respected rather than resented.

24 This would almost certainly not have been the case if the tour had been prior public knowledge. Given the outcry upon their arrival, a STST-style attempt to impede the tourists' departure might well have occurred but it is difficult to see how it could have succeeded in stymieing international travel indefinitely.

25 'I Found South African Breweries Most Hospitable' by Kit Wright, excerpt repeated pp 250–1, Rae (2001). The title was said to originate in an assessment of the tour made by Gooch in an interview. *Hoping It Might Be So: Poems 1974–2000* (Leviathan 2000).

26 p 29, *The Sunday Times*, 7 March 1982.

27 pp 101-2, Booth (1998).

28 p 179, Hartman (2004).

29 p 177, Hartman (2004).

30 p 181, Hartman (2004).

31 *Out of the Wilderness: Part II*, British Sky Broadcasting, first broadcast 19 July 2008.

32 p 182, Hartman (2004).

33 Front, *Rand Daily Mail*, 15 October 1982. Of course, SACU's arch enemy Hassan Howa was among the many apartheid opponents forbidden from leaving the country to make his case to an international audience. The evidence that Sri Lanka would have impinged on its citizens' rights in the same way is weak.

34 Front, *Cape Argus*, 22 October 1982.

35 Front, *Daily News* (Colombo), 19 October 1982. With the outrage on the Asian subcontinent Warnapura immediately resigned his role as a factory personnel manager for Ceylon Tobacco to

save his employers embarrassment.

36 Warnapura later insisted that Duleep Mendis and Roy Dias had been integral to the organisation of the tour alongside Opatha. He said that Mendis and Dias backed out under pressure from Dissanayake. 'Had he spoken to a few others and given some assurances like he gave Duleep and Roy, the tour would never have taken place. Duleep and Roy were made captain and vice-captain respectively for two years when the Sri Lankan Board policy was to make such decisions on a series by series basis.' (*Indian Express* Online, 22 August 1997).

37 Modestly, the player-manager Anthony Ralph Opatha appended his initials with those of South Africa to create the Arosa moniker.

38 *Indian Express* Online, 22 August 1997.

39 Front, *Rand Daily Mail*, 6 November 1982.

40 This was the information publicly accepted at the time. On Warnapura's later account, the reinforcements would have joined the tour except the team manager confiscated their passports. (*Indian Express* Online, 22 August 1997).

41 p 30, *Cape Argus*, 10 December 1982.

42 p 44 *Sunday Times* (SA), 12 December 1982.

43 Back, *Sunday Times* (SA), 24 November 1982.

44 Front, *Rand Daily Mail*, 14 January 1983.

45 p 43, *Sunday Times* (SA), 21 November 1982.

46 p 44, *Sunday Times* (SA), 28 November 1982.

Chapter 5

# Mercenaries and Missionaries

*'The betrayal is extreme ... Apartheid points like a dagger at the throat of black self-worth in every corner occupied by the descendants of Africa.' – Michael Manley*

Seventeen West Indian rebels had followed a familiar pattern before landing at Jan Smuts Airport in January 1983. Like the English and Sri Lankan tourists before them, the new arrivals had negotiated their contracts in secret across crackling international phone lines, deploying amateur espionage techniques to disguise their intentions; they had reinforced these misdirections with lies where necessary and arrived by circuitous air travel routes so as to further befuddle their opponents; and they had made clear their absolute opposition to apartheid while feeling this did not prevent them touring. Yet for all the extraordinary circumstances surrounding the previous two tours, the arrival of a West Indian team in South Africa represented the greatest coup and the deepest affront.

In cricketing terms, the West Indies stood alone. They had enjoyed six years of global dominance, twice winning the World Cup and rising to Test match pre-eminence with a phenomenal strength and breadth of on-field weaponry. A succession of brilliant strokemakers headed by Viv Richards, Gordon Greenidge and Clive Lloyd had humbled opponents around the world. And as captain Lloyd had harnessed an unprecedented strength in fast bowling to redefine the greatest challenge a batsman could face. Able to call upon Michael Holding, Malcolm Marshall, Joel Garner, Vanburn Holder, Colin Croft, Andy Roberts, Wayne Daniel and Sylvester Clarke, the West Indies could almost invariably field four bowlers who offered speed, accuracy and aggression, but no respite. Allied to the best fielding of any international team, the West Indies were brilliant, stylish, ruthless; iconic.

But not even SACU would pretend that their latest attraction was purely about cricket. The official West Indies team was itself a political symbol, a statement of excellence and liberation for a region populated by slave descendants and emerging from colonialism. 'West Indians crowding into Test match venues,' wrote CLR James, 'bring with them the whole past history and future hopes of the region.'[1] Only in 1960, after 30 years as a Test playing nation, had they appointed a first full-time black captain, Frank Worrell. And the rich success enjoyed by West Indian cricketers, from George Headley and Learie Constantine through Worrell, Everton Weekes and Clyde Walcott to the all-conquering Lloyd side, had made standard bearers of those in maroon caps.

Even their great glories came laden with political baggage. Many commentators summed up their innovation and aggression under the term 'Calypso cricket', something Lloyd in particular abhorred as a racist simplification suggesting happy-go-lucky indolence rather than hard-won success forged in adversity. Their greatest weapon, the four-pronged pace attack, was denounced as a bullying tactic exploiting size and strength at the expense of more refined opponents. And, of course, South Africa represented a particular taboo: 'a museum piece in our time, a hangover from the dark past of mankind'[2], where the legacies of African slavery were not receding but all too present. The West Indies had never played in South Africa and even outside the republic the issue was pertinent. When in 1976 England's Cape Province-born captain Tony Greig had pledged to make the touring West Indians 'grovel' it was taken as a declaration of war, inviting annihilation of the hosts.[3]

The prospect of West Indians, and among them once great West Indian cricketers, being hired to break international collective action against white South Africa was horrific. As former Jamaica Prime Minister Michael Manley wrote in his definitive *History of West Indies Cricket*, 'The betrayal is extreme. The Caribbean is 90% black. Accordingly, the anti-apartheid struggle is both principled and visceral … Apartheid points like a dagger at the throat of black self-worth in every corner occupied by the descendants of Africa.'[4]

Across the Caribbean islands, the sorrow and anger were acute. The news broke while the rebels were en route and before they had landed the rage found many voices. Lloyd denounced the venture as 'an affront to the black man throughout the world … the South Africans can now sit back and feel proud that they have removed virtually all of the things we have put in their path.'[5] His colleague Holding added, 'These men are selling themselves. If they were offered enough money they would probably agree to wear chains.'[6]

The West Indies are a multi-national coalition and the difficulty uniting disparate identities and cultures had been evident in brokering the Gleneagles Agreement. Nevertheless, the governments now spoke with one voice in response. Barbados Minister for Sports Vic Johnson said, 'There is no price for which self-respect or human integrity can ever be bought. Those who did not go upheld the honour of the whole region and signalled to the rest of the world that human dignity is not a commodity to be traded in the market place of expediency.'[7] Trinidad condemned the rebels as 'mercenaries fighting the cause of apartheid' making money 'on the backs and blood of the black people of South Africa' while St Kitts & Nevis lamented 'a degrading act of adventurism'. Grenada urged their neighbours to confiscate the tourists' pay and donate it to the African National Congress. Former West Indies player and Guyanese Minister for Sport Roy Fredericks went further still and said that the rebels ought not to return but should instead settle in the republic 'and not cause further discomfort to the West Indian population by attempting to live among us.'[8]

Despite unmistakable anger, there was greater sympathy in the press. The *Daily Nation* of Barbados published a powerful editorial: 'Perhaps, as they make their long journey to Johannesburg, the players can reflect on the fact that, had they been born in Soweto and not St Peter, Cape Town and not Spanish Town, their sporting talent would never have seen the light of day.'[9] This disappointment was compounded by the rebels' deceit. In early January, a tour featuring Lawrence Rowe, Colin Croft, Richard Austin and Everton Mattis was rumoured to be imminent but Joe Pamensky dismissed the prospect, saying plans had been cancelled. At a West Indies Cricket Board of Control function president Allan Rae commended Croft and Rowe for their loyalty; a few days later Austin and Mattis told reporters at an airport that they were visiting Florida on a short shopping trip and would represent Jamaica in the Shell Shield the following Friday. Within a week, via Miami and Madrid, all four were in the arrivals hall at Jan Smuts Airport.

Yet there was also a degree of understanding. Though disapproving, *Jamaica News* columnist Tony Becca reflected that the decision had been made out of economic need: 'Here in Jamaica there have been many sad stories of our outstanding sportsmen of the past, men who walk the street punch drunk and without assistance ... with nothing but the memories of bright lights and cheering crowds ... Lawrence Rowe, Richard Austin and Everton Mattis see these sad figures as constant reminders, and anyone with a little conscience should understand if nothing else their fears of the tomorrows to come after serving their country.'[10]

Becca was acknowledging an uncomfortable truth: the betrayal was extreme, but not unexpected. The established dressing room under Lloyd were committed and content, but outside the elite group it was a different story. Some players felt slighted at not being in the side; others simply could not see themselves as regular internationals against such strong opposition. For all the West Indies' success, even the greatest among them did not find it easy to make a full-time living out of the game. The Caribbean region was not wealthy and their ruling boards were no less short-sighted than those elsewhere when it came to player loyalty.

Kerry Packer had recruited the world champions almost wholesale with the help of Lloyd and Alvin Kallicharran in 1977 and rumours of an approach by the South African authorities, for whom the political and financial benefits of a star-studded West Indian touring party were obvious, had scarcely abated since. Kallicharran had become the first West Indian on the SACU's books in 1981 and returned the following year. In the aftermath of the English rebel tour, Lloyd had warned the WICBC that Caribbean players would inevitably follow suit. His suggestion of centrally contracting 20 to 25 leading West Indian cricketers on healthy salaries to eliminate the threat was not taken up[11] – but in any case it was perhaps too late.

As Clive Lloyd feared, Ali Bacher had paved the way for the visit of a West Indian squad in signing Alvin Kallicharran for Transvaal. The Guyanese became an instant hit with colleagues and fans alike, a diminutive batsman with the fullest range of shots. He had also shown potential recruiters that politics were not a prominent concern.

Though living as an 'honorary white' in a flat arranged by Bacher, when asked to leave all-white areas at the Rosebank Hotel and a Wimpy restaurant he would do so uncomplainingly, saying, 'I was wrong to go there.'[12]

While the nucleus of the West Indian team had ruled out the possibility of visiting South Africa, there were many others who would consider an offer from Bacher, like that from Packer, too good to turn down. The former South Africa captain was busy throughout the 1982 county championship season, arranging secret negotiations with Viv Richards, Gordon Greenidge, Desmond Haynes, Colin Croft, Malcolm Marshall and Sylvester Clarke.

Richards and Greenidge were hostile to the offer and Bacher rapidly withdrew them from consideration but the remaining quartet indicated serious interest while Marshall was also mulling an offer to join Kallicharran as a cog in the Transvaal 'Mean Machine'. Clarke discussed this offer with former West Indian fast bowler Gregory Armstrong and found Bacher a willing tour manager and Caribbean contact. Over the next few months the pair put together a team in code over the telephone.

With a number of leading West Indian players out of the picture, Bacher was at a disadvantage. He was forbidden from entering the Caribbean and, in the absence of television coverage, he had never seen Shell Shield cricket. He was left to rely on Armstrong's recommendations and book research, admitting later, 'I approved a team by studying the *Wisden Cricketers' Almanack* ... I could look up all the details and statistics on all these players – the matches they played, what they scored against which bowlers, how many wickets they took against which batsmen. I was then able to get an idea of each player's strength; although it was hardly the ideal way to select a team.'[13]

Haynes, an outstanding opening batsman, and Marshall, an even more distinguished fast bowler, had been expected to join the party but withdrew days before the tour was due to start.[14] This absence of two elite players was a big blow to signing the 'West Indies' but the party announced was evidently strong. It was comparable to the English squad from ten months previously insofar as it included a handful of established internationals and leading players now past their best, fortified by a larger group of peripheral names. But such was the comparative strength of cricket in the Caribbean that they would present South Africa with a far sterner challenge.

The captain, Lawrence Rowe, had been a particularly distinguished batsman even by West Indian standards in the 1970s, earning from Michael Manley the accolade that he was more talented than Viv Richards.[15] Having marked his debut with an unprecedented double century and century against New Zealand in 1972 he scored 302 against England in 1974, becoming only the second West Indian to post a triple century after Garry Sobers. To some he had been better still in making 175 at the World Series Cricket in Melbourne, an innings that later led Rowe to claim, 'There was no shot I couldn't play.'[16]

For all of the discord that his visit to South Africa would cause, few among even his harshest critics would dispute that fact, but doubts around his commitment had been commonplace. In addition to his fair share of conventional injuries, Rowe suffered from eye problems and, improbably for a cricketer, hay fever. He had lost his place in the Windies team in 1980 and not regained it amid further doubts by Clive Lloyd that he possessed the necessary mental fortitude. Feeling forgotten and then ignored, he had little hope left of resuming his international career and upon accepting Armstrong's advances gave the West Indian rebels a leader with pedigree.

Rowe had long enjoyed a friendship with Kallicharran, whose 4,399 Test runs placed him fifth in the West Indies' all-time list. Although both past 30, they were still young enough to merit serious respect, while in all-rounder Collis King the tourists also had the 'box office' entertainer their English predecessors lacked. The Barbadian was a peripheral player at Test level but his clinical shot-making had clinched the 1979 World Cup final, and he completed a middle-order line-up that represented a serious proposition for opponents and promoters alike.

As with Lloyd's official team, however, the media and opposition were preoccupied with the West Indian trademark: fast bowlers. The inclusion of Croft, who in a five-year career had taken 125 Test wickets, appeared a particular coup but his back troubles belied his 29 years, and he would spend more time with Bacher's medical specialist than on the field.

Instead it was Clarke who would prove SACU's greatest signing, a giant fast bowler who revelled in the threat he posed to batsmen. He had won only 12 caps over four years, and some of those because Packer had deprived the Windies of their first choice attack, yet he would soon rank alongside the most fearsome bowlers the Caribbean islands had produced. With the veteran Bernard Julien, who brought the total number of World Cup winners in the party to four, Ezra Moseley and the enormous Franklyn Stephenson, Rowe would not be able to match the relentless speed and accuracy of Lloyd's four-pronged 'Panzer' attack but promised a far greater threat than the Sri Lankans.

Thereafter the squad inevitably tapered away into the shallow end of the talent pool. The South African media made much of the 200-plus Test caps between 17 men as they sought to establish a link between the unofficial team and the dual World Cup winners. But almost three-quarters of these belonged to Kallicharran, Rowe, Croft and Julien. A good number of the remainder had been earned by the likes of Richard Austin and Alvin Greenidge when Lloyd's men were at World Series Cricket, though the off-spinner Derick Parry and wicketkeeper David Murray had each toured regularly without becoming established in the first-choice XI. If these and others were good cricketers, then the West Indians, like the English before them, would find that the hyperbole demanded big names and bold feats – particularly against opponents ecstatic at the unprecedented, hitherto unthinkable opportunity.

By the time Rowe had held a first press conference, life bans for all members of the party were already a formality. It was unclear whether they would even be allowed to re-enter their home countries. Rowe admitted he and his side were 'obviously a little jittery' at both the controversy their actions would cause and the reception they would receive in the republic. He told the inaugural press conference, 'We hope you will treat us and love us in the manner we would like.'

Within the bubble, they would have no worries on this account. As 'honorary whites' the West Indian players would be spared the indignities of apartheid and only three daring protestors had greeted them on arrival. Tickets to the tour opener, a one-day match against Western Province less than 48 hours after landing, had sold out Newlands' 16,000 capacity as quickly as the cash register would allow and the following day their opening practice was repeatedly interrupted by autograph hunters.

Among many non-whites, however, the disillusionment was boundless. The West Indies had been the international team of choice for the vast majority of black African cricket fans, and nowhere more than South Africa. To see a team in that name, which featured at least three great owners of a maroon cap in Rowe, Kallicharran and Croft, co-operating with the white establishment caused great offence. Norman Arendse, who played under Hassan Howa's SACB before becoming a leading administrator, recalls, 'The feeling was that these guys were betraying us – and they were. Instead of helping us to unshackle from apartheid, they were tightening the shackles. Because by them coming out as black cricketers they were proving or supporting one of the theories that underpinned apartheid – that we can play together in harmony even though we are separate communities.'

In the white media the prospect of the Springboks facing West Indians was billed as the 'dream' series. For many in the republic, as in the Caribbean, it was quite the opposite.

As with Sri Lanka, the other-worldly nature of black West Indians to white South Africa was compounded by a contrast in styles. The promotional hyperbole around the tour predictably leaned heavily on the 'Calypso cricket' cliché, but the West Indians did constitute an altogether different proposition to the Sri Lankans. The wristy virtuoso Alvin Kallicharran had already proven an eye-opener to cricketers schooled in the hard, fast and often attritional South African scene. Jimmy Cook recalls of his Transvaal team-mate: 'He was absolutely brilliant to bat with. He was just so unorthodox, hit balls in different areas to what we were used to, so quick on his feet and had such a good eye. Just fantastic.'

And, unlike Bandula Warnapura, Lawrence Rowe had the players to make his side's approach count. He and Kallicharran would provide a range of shot-making that perhaps only Barry Richards among the South Africans could match but it was West Indian fast bowling, discussed in fearful tones, that had really captured the imagination. Of Marshall, Holding and Garner there was no sign but Colin Croft had the name and Sylvester Clarke the game to present South African cricket with an unprecedented challenge. In reddish caps bearing a badge as close to the official WICBC logo as SACU dared, there was no mistaking the allusion being made.

The hallmarks of hasty organisation were once again present when a number of tourists arrived for their opening tour match at Newlands wearing blazers with a price tag still hanging from a sleeve but the lack of preparation and a back injury to Croft, who was able to bowl only five overs, did not prevent them administering a 21-run defeat to Western Province, the double South African champions.

The atmosphere was fraught, as Franklyn Stephenson later recalled: 'The majority of the fans were white; the blacks were mainly cleaning the stands. When we walked out on to the field to defend 204, I remember the guys talking about having nine slips because nobody wanted to stand near the boundary. We feared we would get objects thrown at us, maybe get beaten up. I was very tense because I had been asked to field at third man. Then a little white kid ran on to the ground and offered me a Coke. I refused. He came back at the end of the next over and I thought, OK, let me try. I took the bottle, had a little sip and gave it back to him. You should have seen the sight at the end of the next over. There must have been about 15 kids around me, offering me drinks. It was so touching.'[17]

Even in the earliest days of the tour, flamboyant batting by Rowe and King was eclipsed by the fast bowlers, headed by the enormous Clarke. In the second tour match Border could manage only 100-8 in 50 overs against the West Indian attack, with umpires imposing a limit of two bouncers per over to curb the aerial bombardment. Despite these official restrictions, the West Indian pace barrage continued to scare the life out of South African batsmen. A confident 85-run win over Eastern Province was built on the middle-order foundation of Rowe (41), Kallicharran (65) and Collis King (71 from just 36 balls), but again it was the bowling that provoked alarm. Croft, performing at well below his distressing best, was proving impossible to get away and Clarke was a terrifying sight: a gigantic bowler whose stock delivery was dug in short of a length before it honed in on the batsman's chest, which he varied with a wicket-taking away-swinger still short of a good length and a brilliantly disguised slower ball.

The strength in depth of West Indian cricket – and the insularity of South African cricketing culture – was pronounced. Franklyn Stephenson and Ezra Moseley were exerting life and pace from pitches where none had previously existed, and neither had a Test cap to his name.

Barry Richards says, 'They were much better than some of the weaker Test teams. I mean Sylvester Clarke is one of the great all-time bowlers. And then there was Ezra Moseley and Franklyn Stephenson – they had a serious attack. They would have been competitive with any side apart from probably the Michael Holdings, Joel Garners and Andy Robertses, who were playing for the West Indies at the time. They would have given any Test side a very good run for their money.'

After three warm-ups, the first 'Test' at Newlands

was upon the tourists less than a week after they had arrived; a further four-day match and six 'one-day internationals' had also been squeezed into a four-week trip. They remained an outrageous curiosity, dominating the front pages as well as the back to the extent that when SACU appealed to businesses to allow employees to take impromptu unpaid leave to watch the match, Minister for National Education Gerrit Viljoen offered cautious support.[18]

'Today ends a barren 13 years for Test cricket,' declared the *Cape Argus* on the dawn of the first 'Test', apparently joining those outside the republic in their appraisal of the English and Sri Lankan series. The Springboks were wary at the prospect of West Indian fast bowling, recalling the experienced Richards at the expense of Lawrence Seef and practising with a specially arranged bowling machine at full throttle. Kevin McKenzie, a consistently successful batsman with Transvaal noted for his back-foot play against fast bowling, was handed a first cap at the age of 34 while their own attack of Vince van der Bijl, Garth Le Roux, Stephen Jefferies and Alan Kourie remained unchanged.

No-one had worked harder in the build-up than the ground staff, taking a heavy roller to the Newlands pitch in the hope of blunting Clarke and co. The joke around the ground in the build-up was that the track would be sunk inches into the square, so wary were the home side. The groundsmen, however, did their job, and after Peter Kirsten won an important toss his side batted through a rain-affected day in mostly commanding fashion, Graeme Pollock striking a 56th first-class century before a mini-collapse in the final session reduced the Springboks from 264-3 to 276-6. Even so it proved a culture shock. Jimmy Cook continued a career-long policy of not wearing a helmet and was captured in a photo evading a Moseley bouncer like a puppet on a string: 18 inches off the ground, limbs stretched in every direction but the trajectory of the ball.

Cook remembers that facing the West Indian attack posed an unprecedented test for a batsman previously restricted to South African tactics. 'I think at first we got a bit of a shock – they were pretty sharp and bowled quite short. At the first 'Test' at Newlands Barry (Richards) came to me and said, "Listen, it's very important for us to put on a good partnership here, and to stand up to these guys so that we can show everybody that these guys can be played." And we put on about 80-odd in that very first 'Test'. I nearly got killed – there's that lovely photograph of Ezra Moseley nearly killing me – but we stuck around and put on about 80 together, and I think it was a good calming influence on the rest of the guys in the dressing room. They could see, "These guys are really quick with the new ball but, hey, our blokes have coped."'

The Springbok recklessness when batting against the Sri Lankans was erased in the face of their greatest challenge to date and Kourie, Le Roux and Jefferies all made considerable contributions on the second morning in guiding the home team to a commanding 449 all out. The West Indians responded in the promised fashion, aggressively addressing the South African attack despite losing Alvin Greenidge and Everton Mattis before the total was in double figures. Number four Kallicharran promptly hit Jefferies out of the attack with three consecutive boundaries before being bowled by van der Bijl for 21. The buccaneering King was more incautious still. Brought to the crease at 66-4 he hit three fours and a six to reach 19 from just 11 balls. Kirsten reintroduced van der Bijl and the batsman did not see fit to waste time on sizing up the new bowler, attempting to hit the very first ball back over his head but instead edging behind to Ray Jennings.

The tourists had reason to thank opener Richard

Austin, who had struggled for form and taken more than three hours to reach 63, for guiding them to 157-7 by the close. Van der Bijl, no longer given use of the new ball and on the one ground where spectacular success had eluded him in Currie Cup cricket, had distinguished himself at 34 with overnight figures of 3-22.

Entering a Sunday rest day 142 short of the follow-on score, the West Indians were not the only ones under pressure. SACU had finally hit on a winning formula to attract the South African cricket public but were now facing a result inside three days with the subsequent loss of revenue from day four. So officials took a quite extraordinary action: at the end of the second day they entered the Springbok dressing room and announced that the 150-run follow-on rule no longer applied. The senior players vehemently refused, citing the most basic of sporting principles that the rules of a game cannot be changed mid-way. As a consequence the 'Test' proceeded under the established guidelines and without the news becoming public, but behind the scenes it only compounded questions over the credibility of the matches and that of the series.

If SACU found the Springboks hostile to their idea, their guests appeared no more interested in prolonging the life of the 'Test'. The West Indians renewed their assault on Monday, the giant all-rounder Stephenson resuming unbeaten on 13. He hit a further 43 all around the wicket at nearly a run a ball while Austin edged along in support. The partnership was worth 83 when Stephenson underestimated the fielding of Le Roux at mid-wicket and ran himself out. While Austin battled on to 93 he had minimal support from Moseley and Clarke and the West Indians were bundled out for 246, 53 shy of the follow-on total linked to SACU's bottom line.

Kirsten ruthlessly put the opposition in to bat again

and despite making a decent start Austin, Greenidge and Mattis were removed for 23, 23 and 19 respectively. Visiting hopes now rested on Kallicharran and Rowe, individually great batsmen and also partners in a record-breaking 198 fourth-wicket partnership against Australia in 1974–75. An effort of that magnitude was not to be discounted as the two eased to a 50 partnership in 65 minutes when the captain was given out lbw to Jefferies. It was a decision that prompted derisive mutterings from the terraces and universal disapproval in the press box. The culpable umpire, Barrie Smith, had attracted some choice language from Geoffrey Boycott ten months previously and while Rowe was stoical in his post-match media conference, SACU accountants were doubtless less restrained as the tourists entered the final day on 136-4 without their best batsman.

Attempts to subvert the match proved as unnecessary as they were unjustifiable. Kallicharran batted beyond lunch before the beguiling Kourie had him stumped by Jennings for 89 and contributions throughout the lower order carried the tourists to 309 before Parry and Stephenson fell to Jefferies in the same over. Fifteen minutes before tea, this set the Springboks an apparently straightforward 107 from 38 overs but Clarke and Moseley were in no mood to give up the game just yet. After his first-innings experience Cook was moved to wear a helmet for the first time, but he and Richards were out before the score reached 20. When Pollock survived a committed caught-behind appeal off Moseley to his very first ball the nerves around Newlands were palpable but the veteran and Kirsten steadied the ship with a 47-run stand.

Even then the match remained in the balance. Kirsten fell for 13, followed quickly by Rice (six) and McKenzie (0) and the score was 85-5 as the West Indian bowlers threw themselves into every delivery and every marginal appeal with gusto. This competitive rancour added further spice to an absorbing contest but the veteran Pollock was unmovable and would reach 43 in edging the winning runs through the slips at 5.45 p.m. with a drawn match in sight.

Despite the behaviour of their officials, the South African players were delighted. Their greatest victory since 1970 was celebrated in heavy style – though again without the men in blazers. Cook later recalled: 'Celebratory drinks flowed freely in the Springbok dressing room. Normally after a team has done well its dressing room is soon filled with well-wishers, but, strange to relate, on this occasion not a single South African official came in to congratulate us for at least half an hour ... It transpired that our board members had gone into the West Indies [*sic*] dressing room to commiserate with them on their defeat and had promised to produce a wicket that would suit them in the next 'Test' at the Wanderers in Johannesburg.'[19]

The sense of injustice was compounded by the Newlands crowd, who, in contrast to the heavily partisan Currie Cup atmosphere, had cheered the tourists as loudly as the Springboks. Bacher later admitted, 'It was the first time we had ever seen West Indians in South Africa and obviously everyone got caught up in the euphoria.'[20]

As ever, it was impossible for the match to be viewed entirely on its own merits. Michael Holding, playing with Tasmania, revealed in the *Hobart Mercury* that Rowe had telephoned to offer $250,000 for two tour games. Holding recalls, 'I told him it was not something I could do. I don't think he understood my viewpoint. He just couldn't understand what I was saying. He was in South Africa and saying that he saw black people in positions of authority. He did not appreciate what apartheid was. When you get someone like that it is best to let them get on with it.'

Instead a less heralded son of Kingston, Ray Wynter, flew in as cover for the stricken Croft. Meanwhile eyes in Cape Town had been trained particularly keenly on David Murray after Australian Prime Minister Malcolm Fraser announced on the first day of the 'Test' that the rebel tourists would be forbidden from entering the country. Murray lived in South Australia with his Australian wife Kerry, who was expecting their first child. His sub-standard performance was easily understood as he and his wife were facing expulsion from their respective homelands, and Murray announced he was considering moving to South Africa. It said something that he thought the transition desirable for a black man, white woman and their child.

After the apolitical stance taken by the cricket bible, *Wisden* magazine in February added its voice to those denouncing rebel tours. Jonathan Rice wrote, 'Apartheid lives on as an increasingly disregarded law, but as long as it exists, and the vicious inequalities of the South African government's policies continue, it cannot be overturned. It is quite true that the South African sports authorities have complied with all the preconditions laid down for their re-entry into international sport but this is no longer enough. Now that sport and politics are so inextricably entwined, there is no hope of South Africa's readmission to the world's stadia until the principle of perpetual white government is abandoned. Or until the 12th of never, and that's a long, long time.'[21]

Inside the bubble, approval was only growing. After a two-day break, the second 'Test' was due to begin at pace-friendly Wanderers and the second day was already a sell-out. The South African anticipation remained rooted in 'Calypso cricket' and the promoters could have had no better ambassador for their promotional pitch than Collis King. After Peter Kirsten had won the toss he had no hesitation in giving his bowlers first use of the Wanderers green top and inside the first hour Richard Austin and Everton Mattis fell cheaply while Lawrence Rowe inside-edged Vince van der Bijl onto his stumps for a three-ball duck. With opener Alvin Greenidge off the field with tonsillitis, King was brought to the crease at 39-3. Two and a quarter hours later he was raising his bat to salute an audacious, apparently effortless 114-ball century that had included 15 fours and a six. 'Coll is King' declared a banner after seeing the right-hander execute a series of bludgeoning hits over the South African field. The West Indian total was still only 185-5 and the very next ball Alan Kourie trapped the centurion's back leg in front of the wicket before having Franklyn Stephenson caught first ball by Graeme Pollock at slip. Greenidge returned to guide the West Indians to 267 with the help of Sylvester Clarke, and the giant bowler ended the day on a high by removing Richards for a duck.

A 29,000 sell-out filled Wanderers on day two, a Saturday, when SACU's juggling of commercial return and cricketing spectacle appeared initially justified. If the crowd had come expecting explosive West Indian pace they were not disappointed, Stephenson and Clarke removing Jimmy Cook and nightwatchman Ray Jennings for ducks in the opening exchanges to leave the Springboks at 8-3. As in Cape Town the previous week, it was the battle-hardened duo of Kirsten (56) and Pollock (73) who guided the home team to safer ground with an obdurate century partnership. After their failures in the first 'Test' Clive Rice and Kevin McKenzie were keen to make amends and advanced the score to 199-5 before Ray Wynter's slingshot action claimed 2-2 in precipitating another mini-collapse. Kourie and Stephen Jefferies were left with the unenviable challenge of facing Clarke in the Johannesburg dusk and when the light was offered with more than an hour's play still scheduled the pair accepted with undisguised relief. The sell-out crowd were unimpressed, as were many observers.

Charles Fortune, the voice of South African cricket, proclaimed that the public had been denied an hour of cricket and the implication that a soft offer had been made to the batsmen to ensure a full four days' play was widespread. At the very least the cricket the crowd had seen had been hugely competitive, the exaggerated appeals that had caused bad blood in Cape Town persisting as both sides clawed desperately for victory. Kirsten certainly was energised by a captain's back-to-the-wall innings: 'It was the biggest pressure I have ever encountered – the nearest thing to real Test cricket that we have ever experienced.'

The 'Test' at Wanderers had certainly begun to exhibit all of the qualities that aficionados look for in on-field endeavour: after King's exhilarating innings there had developed an even battle between bat and ball, a physical and mental test of players' limits, and by the end of day three all outcomes remained viable. Clarke, with 5-66, had finished off the Springboks in the morning session for 233 to establish a slender visiting lead but the West Indians' brittle batting line-up was soon cracking under a brilliant fielding and bowling performance. Van der Bijl struck first, capturing the wicket of Austin before lunch but it was after the restart when things fell apart. Jefferies bowled Mattis and then Rowe to give the captain his first-ever pair in first-class cricket while van der Bijl did for Alvin Kallicharran.

Three wickets had fallen in an hour and the tourists were 57-4. Their first-innings saviour King was confined to the dressing room with muscle cramps and, with only Greenidge offering more than token resistance, wickets fell regularly, drawing King from the physio's bench at 105-8. Their last hopes doped up for cramps and tonsillitis, the West Indians appeared doomed but both men batted through obvious discomfort to put on 71 for the ninth wicket and, after both were out in quick succession just before the close, South Africa need 211 to win on the final day.

On the fourth morning, the white South African media made no apologies for making the impending drama their main focus. The Springboks perhaps had a marginal advantage as Kirsten pledged: 'We're in a good position but the first hour of the final day will be crucial. We cannot afford to lose early wickets.' On a Wanderers' green top against bowlers who had proven the best many batsmen had faced and scared the life out of them to boot, no assumptions were made in the home dressing room. The Springboks batted with due caution and reached lunch at 82 without loss on a pitch betraying few of the supposed demons. In the pavilion the South Africans were confident and Clarke declared the match out of sight; after a heavy morning's work for no reward, he retired to the dressing room to change his boots for trainers. The vice-captain Kallicharran approached him and asked for one last effort before giving the series up as a bad job and in return received one of the greatest bowling performances the Wanderers stadium had ever seen.

After a pulsating three and a half days in which both sides had enjoyed then relinquished the whip hand on multiple occasions, the 14,000 Wanderers crowd were for the first time confident of a famous home victory. Instead in five overs after lunch they saw a brilliant spell from Clarke remove Cook, Kirsten, Pollock and Rice for the cost of eight runs. The South African batsmen were exposed not so much by pace as length against a gigantic bowler whose height precipitated alarming bounce into the batsman while his away-swinger deceived and bettered the Springboks time and again. With Richards out playing a loose drive to Parry at the other end,

South Africa were 111-5. McKenzie provided some stoic resistance but the giant Clarke was now in frenzied form, having the often stubborn Kourie and Jennings caught at the wicket while King trapped Le Roux lbw. In the afternoon session the Springboks had lost eight wickets for 37 runs and though McKenzie and Jefferies made a brief stand after tea the bowler was run out and van der Bijl was clean bowled by Clarke, whose 7-34 in the second innings gave him match figures of 12-100 in a 29-run victory.

Kirsten was left bewildered by the collapse, telling reporters, 'We lost it – they didn't win it. Barry Richards got out when he shouldn't have and I guess we just froze a bit. All I can say is that we batted badly and Clarke bowled cleverly.'[22] In the West Indian dressing room the delight was tangible as an infamous, much-derided team celebrated a dramatic victory over a side rated among the best in the world. Despite his pair, Rowe enthused: 'This victory is probably the sweetest I've been involved in. It's so important for our image back home. Some of our countrymen described us as a second-rate side but we disproved that today.'

The rebel tours had moved into new territory: first-class competitive cricket, full stadia, unprecedented opposition and Springbok defeat. Nevertheless some constants remained and the schedule was punishing for either side. Having spent 11 of the previous 18 days in the field the West Indians now faced a one-day practice match against Natal followed by a six-rubber 'one-day international' series in 11 days; the last three matches to be played consecutively. During the second 'Test' they had added Jamaican batsman Herbert Chang, a consistent performer in the Shell Shield and recipient of a Test cap during World Series Cricket, to their side but even the local media struggled to make that front-page news.

Cracks had also begun to appear in the edifice of South African self-confidence for the first time, with newspapers directing 'Dad's Army' jibes at a top five that included Graeme Pollock, 38; Barry Richards, 37; and Clive Rice, 33. While victories had been greeted with self-congratulatory eulogies and generous comparisons with both sides in the contemporaneous Ashes series, defeats were met with doom-laden misery as the technical and mental weaknesses of the insular Springbok set-up were exposed. This instability was only exacerbated by the established pattern of provincialism in the South African game as captain Kirsten was booed by Transvaal fans on his visits to Wanderers and whispers persisted that dressing room rivalries between Johannesburg and Cape Town were resurfacing in the face of unanticipated setbacks. The media was becoming complicit in the instability. After a decade-long lament that the Springboks had been denied their rightful place at the top of world cricket, it was a sign of how brittle and volatile South African self-confidence was.

The public's fickle relationship with the players, and particularly so the enigmatic Richards, was exemplified in the opening one-day match. The maestro had not recovered in the public perception for his admission that he was no longer committed to the game and some thought they perceived indifference throughout the Sri Lankan and West Indian series. Though rarely if ever troubled by the opposing bowling, he had repeatedly got out to apparently careless shots but by lunch in the first 'ODI' he was a genius once more after a stylish century. Though far from his best, benefitting from three dropped catches between 50 and 100, he and Pollock (66) underpinned a South African total of 250 and 'Dad's Army' were the 'Golden Oldies' once more. Despite Rowe's bullish pre-match talk none of his batsmen bettered Alvin Greenidge's 32 while King and Croft were each patently carrying injuries as the intelligent Alan Kourie led the way in dismissing the visitors for 159.

That set the tone for an underwhelming series in which the tourists never managed to reach 200 in six 50-over attempts. Their batting and fielding were poor as fatigue, injuries to Croft and King, and a lack of obvious incentive limited their impact. The Springboks won the second and third 'ODIs' at Newlands and Berea Park after setting totals of 194 and 179-9 such that the home side could not lose the series before the three-match finale. The West Indians reduced the arrears in the first of a Johannesburg double-header, a fine all-round bowling performance skittling the hosts for 139, which even their batsmen were able to chase down. Although an aberration in the Springboks' series dominance, the fans were at their most demanding as Peter Kirsten was jeered for his brief innings. The home skipper had the dubious distinction of being the first man to have a golden duck next to his name on the new Wanderers scoreboard after being beaten for pace by Clarke.

The following day Kirsten was jeered again when out for 16 even though the home side set 229 to win and bowled out the West Indians for 171, new cap Rupert Hanley claiming a hat-trick on his home ground. At 4-1 the series success had been secured and that perhaps contributed to a shambolic final defeat when they were bowled out for 71 in response to the visitors' 155. Fatigue had set in on both sides but despite their success, South African self-doubt persisted and in particular questions continued to circulate about Kirsten's captaincy. So long isolated from international cricket, the Springboks had seemingly forgotten the maxim 'you can't win 'em all'.

This low-key conclusion represented an unjust yet consistent end to two careers eclipsed by the international ban. Richards and Vince van der Bijl both wound up their first-class careers at the end of the 1982–83 season, destined to be underrepresented whenever the records of the game are examined. For Richards, it was simply time to call it a day after more than a decade of frustrated ambition. He says, 'The rebel matches didn't matter to me either way. I thought Natal–Transvaal, or Natal–Western Province games were just as intense as a rebel match. It might have generated a bit more interest internationally but for me the intensity was no different to Currie Cup. We had some tremendously talented cricketers and some of those players will never be properly recognised. Vince van der Bijl is one outstanding example of somebody who would have been a wonderful international player.'

Van der Bijl remains free of bitterness, reflecting, 'Graeme Pollock, Barry Richards, Mike Procter – these guys were geniuses, by right they should have been walking the stadiums and arenas of the world, whereas I always felt it was a privilege to play because I was a workhorse. Everything I achieved was always way beyond my expectation – not my dreams, but my expectation. So, there wasn't devastation in my life in any way at all, and there was a deep-seated feeling that the isolation was right. It made white South Africans realise just what other nations felt about us. It gave us a hard mirror to look into. For myself – I can't talk for the other players.'

After two misfiring rebel tours, an eventful month-long West Indian visit had been a triumph for SACU. Despite the enormous costs – $50,000 per tour was quoted as the basic salary, though pay was differentiated around this median sum as per the English tour – and heavy schedule they had turned a profit for the first time. Fans had not suffered the same waning enthusiasm as players, and the second 'Test' at least had produced exhilarating cricket, albeit with a little help from the pitch. The West Indian XI may not have been full of Test regulars but such was the strength of cricket in the Caribbean that other Test nations might have taken half the visiting side.

Furthermore the boycott had been shattered: black men playing and beating the best South Africa had to offer. This novelty was difficult to overestimate. During one match Franklyn Stephenson had been captured by television cameras signing autographs on the fine leg fence, an attractive blonde woman among the throng of children. SATV commentator Trevor Quirk said, 'I see Stephenson is kept busy signing autographs', to which colleague David Dyer responded, 'And I'm sure picking up a few phone numbers.' The broadcaster was inundated with viewer complaints at the very suggestion.[23]

'When the dust of the whistle stop Windies tour has settled … it was worth the cost,' declared the *Rand Daily Mail*, reflecting the establishment line.[24] But this considered only the implications for SACU. The consequences for the West Indians required a more complex equation. None would be welcomed in their home countries, which for some would have a devastating long-term impact.

Outside of the bubble, opinions remained entrenched. Bacher had focused on West Indians in part because he saw black cricketers as a force for good, and there was a widespread assumption in the white media that their visit could only have been of benefit to non-white cricket. It was an indication of the degree to which the white establishment misunderstood, and neglected to listen to, those communities they professed to help. For young black cricketers in the republic, equipment, facilities and coaching would have done rather more for their development. And those campaigning for 'no normal sport in an abnormal society' saw a setback rather than progress; for many the early sense of betrayal had not gone away.

Gerald Majola, who played and administrated within the SACB before becoming chief executive of post-apartheid Cricket South Africa, said: 'It was the saddest moment in my career because I always looked up to the West Indians … We were trying to emulate the Viv Richards of this world. And unfortunately Lawrence Rowe led a team that came to South Africa. Here were people we idolised. And also doing exactly what we really resent, coming to South Africa and supporting the apartheid regime.'[25]

In the Caribbean the controversy also remained, although some nations would forgive more quickly than others. Tony Cozier wrote in his *Wisden* review of the West Indian season that 'the public at large expressed some sympathy for the players' positions in view of the fees they were earning.'[26] But the verdict from Michael Manley, on trenchantly opposed Jamaica, was unflinching: 'Rowe, Kallicharran and Croft had all brought shame on the West Indies, disgrace upon themselves and the premature close of their careers when they succumbed to temptation.'

Yet the tourists remained defiant. At a casual, beer-fuelled benefit for Rice and Richards at the Rovers Club before departing, the West Indians were mobbed by pitch-invading autograph hunters at every break in play. Rowe also repeated the SAB XI's lack of remorse: 'We have no regrets about going whatsoever. We expected the West Indies cricket authorities to ban us for life. I can't see any chance of the authorities changing their mind but that doesn't bother me at all.'

And after being vehemently denounced by Clive Lloyd and Michael Holding, Rowe felt confident enough to launch a broadside at his former colleagues: 'Holding described us as playing cricket in chains in South Africa. And Lloyd criticised us for throwing away our principles merely to make some extra money. My answer to them is that it is funny that two players who were heavily involved in signing West Indian cricketers to play in Kerry Packer's World Series Cricket now appear to have forgotten that was all about money. Lloyd was the main person to recruit players behind the back of our Cricket Board of Control, and I wonder where his principles were at that time.'[27]

In response to this popular cry of hypocrisy, Holding says: 'Anybody who can't see the difference between World Series Cricket and playing in South Africa doesn't know the history. I can't help him.'

The rebels received an airport send-off from 15 protestors but police quickly broke up the group for harassment. Those returning to their homelands could expect a similar welcome and many preferred to head to the United States or England. The veteran *Daily Nation* journalist Al Gilkes, the only writer from the Caribbean to cover the tour, wrote sympathetically on their departure: 'Lawrence Rowe and his rebel team had become not the mercenaries they were being labelled outside South Africa, but 18 black missionaries converting and baptising thousands and thousands of whites to the religion of black acceptance and respect from Cape Town to Johannesburg, from Durban and right into the throne room of Afrikanerdom itself, Pretoria ... The 18 sad faces that boarded the aircraft at Jan Smuts airport when it was all over were glum, not because they were leaving South Africa, but because they knew that the world outside, having not been there to witness their miracle, would never believe or understand.'[28]

On the day they flew out the MCC rejected a new proposal from some members to send a touring party to South Africa. But SACU no longer needed Lord's to rubber-stamp its international cricket. A second, improved West Indian tour was already on the horizon.

1 p 100, Beckles (ed., 1998).
2 Albert Luthuli, Nobel Peace Prize address, 1961 replicated p 85, Booth (1998).
3 Tossell (2007) provides an excellent account of this extraordinary series. Already covered in Chapter 2 of this volume were the West Indian demands on excluding South African players during World Series Cricket.
4 pp 304–5, Manley (2002).
5 p 16, *Guyana Chronicle*, 12 January 1983.
6 p 118, Holding and Cozier (1993).
7 p 117, Beckles (ed., 1998).
8 p 5, *Guyana Chronicle*, 18 January 1983. Respectively, Trinidad Foreign Minister Basil Ince and St Kitts & Nevis premier Kennedy Simmonds.
9 *Daily Nation*, 12 January 1983.
10 p 7, *Jamaica News*, 12 January 1983.
11 pp 191–3, McDonald (1986).
12 p 126, McDonald (1984).
13 pp 187–8, Hartman (2004).
14 The details of this withdrawal are unclear. Bacher has said that Haynes and Marshall had committed to the tour but a leak in a Melbourne newspaper (the pair were playing Australian league cricket at the time) scared them off (p 136, Bose 1994; p 188, Hartman 2004). Marshall instead wrote that he accepted an initial offer of $100,000 in shock and temptation but thought better of it; a year later Bacher returned with a $1,000,000 offer for the second tour which he turned down outright (pp 107–119, Marshall 1988). Both Haynes and Marshall did go to South Africa after the boycott ended, contributing considerably to the development of young players including Herschelle Gibbs and Shaun Pollock.
15 p 398, Manley (2002).
16 *Cricinfo*, 1 February 2008, http://content.cricinfo.com/magazine/content/story/334541.html.
17 Siddhartha Vaidyanathan, *The Unforgiven*, *Cricinfo*, 2 August 2007, http://content.cricinfo.com/westindies/content/story/286356.html
18 Front, *Rand Daily Mail*, 19 January 1983.
19 pp 30–31, Cook and Cleary (1993).
20 p 189, Hartman (2004).
21 *Wisden Cricketer*, February 1983.
22 Front, *Cape Times*, 2 February 1983.

23 p 169, van der Bijl (1984).
24 p 22, *Rand Daily Mail*, 15 February 1983.
25 *Out of the Wilderness: Part II*, British Sky Broadcasting, first broadcast 19 July 2008.
26 p 1060, *Wisden*, 1984.
27 In a bizarre final twist to the tour, Rowe was later quoted as saying that Lloyd 'wasn't worried about taking money from Kerry Packer. He not only signed West Indian players but also took ten per cent of their wages.' The article, which clearly compromised Lloyd's credentials as a captain and professional, appeared in both the *Daily Express* and *The Sun*. Lloyd sued the newspapers, who apologised and paid compensation, at the High Court in Manchester, UK on 15 June 1983 and 12 July 1983 respectively. No action was taken against Rowe personally. See pp 202–3, Scott (1989).
28 p 117, Beckles (ed., 1998) and pp 183–5, van der Bijl (1984).

## Chapter 6

# A Memorable Series

*'Nobody has forgotten it still.' –*
*Franklyn Stephenson*

In November 1983 the West Indians became the first rebel tourists to return to the republic. In doing so they also travelled as the first team whose arrival was prior public knowledge and, divested of shock value, the reception was notably dull. In the Caribbean the regret remained but there was nothing new to add; the tourists had chosen their path.

Even in South Africa the public appeared open to other distractions. It was announced that the early tour matches would not be televised – cameras instead would cover Severiano Ballesteros and Nick Faldo duelling in The Sun City Million Dollar Golf Challenge. More salaciously than golf, perhaps even more so than West Indian cricketers, there were rumours that the black American heavyweight champion Larry Holmes might be tempted to Sun City to fight the white South African Gerry Coetzee. At a time of ongoing civil unrest in the republic this was by any measure an extraordinarily bad idea, and it was to wide relief that opposition in the US dissuaded Holmes from pursuing the offer.

The West Indians lacked both the intimidation and originality they had exuded a year previously but the comparative lack of off-field excitement created an environment, however superficial, of a routine cricket tour. Sylvester Clarke had been playing for Transvaal with Alvin Kallicharran, enjoying huge success against still terrified batsmen, and he would have a new partner for the West Indians in Hartley Alleyne. Another genuinely fast Barbadian, Alleyne had shown explosive talent in the Shell Shield before persistent mutterings about his action had unsettled his rapid development. He was one of three newcomers – Faoud Bacchus and Monte Lynch had been drafted in to fortify the flimsy batting line-up. Richard Austin, Herbert Chang and Ray Wynter were paid up but not retained for the second year.

More so than any previous party, the tourists were rested and acclimatised. Banned from all levels of cricket in the Caribbean, David Murray and Collis King were playing for clubs in Johannesburg, although those who had not been in the republic had hardly played at all – Lawrence Rowe admitted to hardly picking up a bat in the intervening nine months. The tourists appeared relaxed and ready, placing the focus on a ten-match international series and after the success in 1982–83 local expectations remained high; in newspapers comparing glances were already being made to the 'other West Indies', who were playing India under Clive Lloyd. SACU, television channel TV2/3 and SA Breweries announced a competition to find the 'South African Sylvester Clarke' by rewarding the fastest black bowler in Soweto with R1,000 on a show in which Clarke himself sat as a judge.

An environment of incremental change was widely championed. Since the first West Indian tour the Botha Government had made its greatest concessions to date, the introduction of a tricameral parliament, a new constitutional arrangement whereby white, coloured and Indian racial groups had their own assemblies with responsibility for their own affairs – and a predictable division of power and funding. The whites maintained an effective veto on the coloured and Indian assemblies while there was no provision whatsoever for black groups. Proponents of engagement saw evidence of a changing republic but sceptics were moved to ask, 'How can you reform apartheid? Apartheid is not acceptable in any form. It can only be abolished.'

The reforms were a revival of the 'multi-national' policies that had been tried within sport in the 1970s and their limitations were swiftly illustrated. Colin Croft was travelling on a local Cape Town train on Monday 29 November when the conductor ordered him from the whites-only carriage. Croft had entered the 'net blankes' section unawares and agreed to move so as to avoid fuss but a fellow traveller, Raymond Roos, protested. After a brief stand-off Croft and Roos moved to the non-whites carriage in line with the laws of the country.[1]

The news took three days to reach the South African newspapers, but when it did the embarrassment was widespread. 'It is a pity in this day and age when our country has come such a long way in creating a positive image for change that such an embarrassing situation should arise,' thundered Joe Pamensky on behalf of SACU. The government, architects of the 'positive image' and promoting it forcefully abroad, were apologetic though hardly supine. The problem would never have occurred, explained a spokesman, if Croft had not boarded a train without the West Indian party's pre-assigned 'special liaison'.

For those opposed to the tours, it showed the degree to which West Indian tourists were sheltered from the reality. While PW Botha's reforms stalled and stumbled, security forces continued to apply the existing laws with great zeal and little accountability. As Colin Eglin of the Progressive Federal Party said: 'It is important for us to realise that Croft's humiliation on this single incident is suffered thousands of times over by the coloured citizens of the Peninsula as they travel in segregated trains to their segregated areas.'

But others saw evidence of engagement. Peter Cooke, working with SACU in promotion of the tour, was convinced that Croft's was a deliberate provocation: 'He tested the system on purpose, he was a highly intelligent man and things were being exposed, the window dressing was going, the shop was now starting to crumble.'[2]

Croft later recalled: 'I had inadvertently gone into a carriage supposed to be for whites only. They didn't throw me off the train, they pulled me out of the carriage and I went because there would probably have been a big situation. But I remember Pik Botha, the foreign minister, saying that he needed the Colin Croft incident like a hole in the head. Because he was trying to sell South Africa's case in New York.'[3]

The following week Croft was sponsored at R300 a wicket by the Dazzle Video company 'in recognition of his remarkable courage in overcoming a back injury last year.'[4]

Back inside the bubble, South African cricket remained in a state of anxiety. The superiority complex built up through the 1970s, and apparently confirmed with convincing wins over English and Sri Lankan XIs, had been undone by defeats to a West Indian second string and the end of a golden generation was nigh. Barry Richards and Vince van der Bijl had retired while Graeme Pollock confirmed his willingness to continue for the Springboks once the season was under way. Former Springbok great and selector Jackie McGlew insisted that 'a herd of young players' were competing for caps but all were untested outside of South African cricket. Those South Africans who had gained experience abroad were not inclined to return. Chris Smith had joined Allan Lamb in playing for England while Kepler Wessels was now a fixture in the Australian Test team.

Transvaal batsman Henry Fotheringham was identified as the man to replace Richards, extending his collaboration with Jimmy Cook after a prolific partnership in the now fearsome 'Mean Machine'. A largely unknown figure outside the republic, the stout, barrel-chested Fotheringham was an ideal foil for Cook, a tall and orthodox batsman who scored most of his runs in the V. Just a year earlier when Lawrence Seef had been chosen as Richards' understudy, Fotheringham had been dropped to the Transvaal B team but after a century in a tour match against the Sri Lankans he was partnered with Cook at the top of the order and had never looked back.

Significantly for the provincial tensions said to pervade the Springbok dressing room, Fotheringham's call-up took the Transvaal contingent to seven in a 12-man squad. Outside Transvaal there were rumblings that the powerful Johannesburg press had sought to have Transvaal captain Clive Rice elevated to Springbok skipper after Peter Kirsten's imperfect record during his first season. Those calls were in vain but attempted signs of unity were not helped when Rice and Kirsten exchanged strong words before the 'blood match' between Transvaal and Western Province. The strength and seriousness of McGlew's herd, meanwhile, was brought into question by the recall of 37-year-old Mike Procter after a century against the tourists for Natal. Kirsten, at the age of 28, was the second youngest member of his own side.

While the South African media and administration found themselves at odds over the Springbok team they were united in their admiration of the West Indians. Partly this was born of commercial necessity: the hugely expensive visitors had to be paid for at the gate and the usual hyperbolic previews and player profiles for men with sometimes modest records were par for the course. They also undoubtedly felt a need to repay their visitors with vocal as well as financial support since the lives of the tourists were hardly easy. But there was a genuine fascination bordering on infatuation with these unprecedented visitors playing a previously unimagined brand of cricket.

Ali Bacher in particular had been his usual effervescent self in promoting the matches, encouraging wide circulation of the record-breaking gate revenues that his West Indian coup was providing. 'South Africa will see genuine Test cricket for the first time since 1970,' enthused *The Star*, the third occasion in as many seasons that the claim had been made. 'The West Indies side brought to this country for the 1983–84 series against the Springboks is a very different cup of tea from the side Lawrence Rowe had at his command last season. There are three major reasons for this. The first is that this is no rush job; the players have had time to prepare both mentally and physically. Secondly, the political pressure of January 1983 simply no longer exists. Thirdly, the three newcomers – Hartley Alleyne, Faoud Bacchus and Monte Lynch – are going to strengthen the team in critical areas.'[5] After the Springboks had complained at the disproportionate attention heaped on the visitors in their first tour, their pride was still clearly hurt as McGlew publicly ticked off the media. 'Don't sell us short,' he pleaded.

The South African anxiety was well-founded as their opponents were markedly stronger than the previous year. Bacchus had been part of the 1983 West Indian World Cup squad and, though out to his first ball of the tour, had added steel to a previously brittle batting line-up, the highlight being 88 against Natal. Born in Guyana, Lynch had played county cricket for a number of years as England-qualified and his solid record with Surrey promised a solution at number three. Alleyne offered Lawrence Rowe a fourth fast bowler, and one of undoubted potential; Geoffrey Boycott was among those who considered that he 'would command a place in most Test sides.'[6]

Despite finding favour with public opinion, the West Indians were not having it all their own way. During the five tour matches before the first 'one-day international' at Wanderers, they lodged repeated complaints with SACU over umpiring. They felt local officials protected opposing batsmen by too readily labelling short-pitched balls bouncers, effectively ensuring at least four balls up to the bat in every over. The itinerary also brought the West Indians to each major centre on three occasions, and even before the first of ten international matches Rowe was complaining that too much travel was required.

The international series – six 'one-day internationals' and four 'Tests' – began with a one-dayer at Johannesburg the first Wednesday in December when it became apparent that West Indian unrest went far deeper than paternalistic umpiring. Where the Springbok batsmen took the field in Packer-inspired green-and-gold outfits, the fieldsmen wore inconsistent whites with no sign of the touring party insignia. And once the match got under way after an unexplained delay, acrimony was in the air. The West Indians continued to push the limits of how much short bowling might be allowed, repeatedly showing dissent when penalised, and there was a series of unsightly stand-offs between players.

Kirsten, already under pressure in the Transvaal heartland, was targeted with a bumper barrage by the tourists and when David Murray attempted a stumping with the batsman plainly in his ground, he turned and kicked the uprooted stump in the wicketkeeper's direction. Despite the captain top-scoring with 55, this prompted boos from the crowd and a stand-off between the pair while Colin Croft and Garth Le Roux also exchanged heated words after the Springbok felt impeded in running for a quick single. The West Indian fast bowlers directed their ill-temper at their South African opposite numbers, Clarke rattling Procter's helmet with a bouncer, and Clive Rice and Garth Le Roux had to show resolve as the final nine overs were delivered almost exclusively short of a length. They did so to add 39 runs from the final 30 balls.

Whereas in the first series the South African fans had cheered for the visitors, the partisan atmosphere was now fully restored in Johannesburg; the stadium known as 'the bullring' eschewed the reticence of previous rebel tours. In an atmosphere of unguarded hostility the West Indians, who had scored between 151 and 171 in each of their six 'ODI' innings the previous year, were set 234 to win. Bacchus and Lynch both fell early, the former initially refusing to walk on a caught-behind dismissal, but Alvin Kallicharran and Collis King, driven to win a viscerally competitive match, added 65 before King suffered a relapse of his cramps and had to be carried from the field. Kallicharran made 80 from 98 balls but without support so that when the Guyanese was eighth man out it was King, unbeaten on 24, who hobbled back to the crease. He exhibited remarkable resolve, batting more or less on one leg for an unbeaten 63 as the target was reached when his partner Murray struck a boundary with four balls to spare.

'Funny game out there,' said Kirsten. 'There were lots of things going on that nobody knows about.' Explanation for the undignified scenes became apparent soon afterwards as Rowe hinted that the tour might be abandoned unless the players and SACU could 'come to an agreement'. It emerged that at 5 a.m. on the morning of the match Gregory Armstrong had telephoned Bacher to say that the tourists were aware of the record-breaking gate receipts for the match and the tour, and were demanding a greater cut. The SACU impresario's promotional showmanship had rebounded on him.

In a heated meeting in the visitors' dressing room before the start of play, Joe Pamensky had engaged in a fierce row with Rowe and other senior players. SACU told the West Indians that they ought to honour their contracts, with even the South African lawyer representing the West Indians, Paul Weiner, coming in for criticism: 'Call yourself a South African? Where's your patriotism?'

The West Indians agreed to play only after taking legal advice from Weiner and receiving confirmation from Bacher that their terms would be improved. As Geoff Dakin later said, 'SACU had no choice but to pay up because they had us over a barrel.'[7] The absence of maroon uniforms on the field was therefore explained, as well as naked hostility and aggression. Rowe certainly had no intention of stepping back as ahead of the next tour game the captain warned reporters, 'I am still not sure we are going to Bloemfontein for Saturday's match.'

Ultimately the tour was saved but as Rodney Hartman wrote in the *Rand Daily Mail*, 'The show will probably go on – but it'll never be quite the same again. All the goodwill attached to the West Indies XI tour appears to have gone down the drain amid one of the worst episodes in South African cricket history.'[8]

And go on the tour did, for the same reason that it had occurred in the first place. Joe Pamensky was able to secure R250,000 extra sponsorship from Yellow Pages, whose marketing manager Dave du Preez told reporters, 'As a South African company we deal with virtually every business in South Africa. We feel we have a moral obligation to give something back to the businessmen and the individuals who support us.' A deal with electronics company Panasonic would generate similar income during the 'Test' series. The money for the one-day series would be split between players and SACU, prompting Armstrong to make a straight-faced apology: 'Cricket is our objective. The public is supporting us and we want to go out and play cricket for them.'

Yet those words were not fully backed by action. Despite playing at Bloemfontein and then in a three-day match against Eastern Province, Lawrence Rowe continued to use press conferences to agitate for money. The R250,000 was divided into R80,000 worth of bonuses across the series[9] with the remaining R170,000 ear-marked by SACU to pay off some of their considerable incurred expenses. It made the matches among the most lucrative since World Series Cricket, yet still Rowe was unimpressed.

'Gregory Armstrong and myself would like to see this issue go to sleep,' declared Pamensky. 'If Lawrence Rowe wants to continue it, he can do so by himself.'

Asked whether he was happy with the deal, Rowe replied: 'There is nothing to be happy about.'

But with Ali Bacher and Pamensky unyielding to further demands, by Saturday 17th December peace broke out, 'misunderstandings' were regretted and the tour was set fair to continue. There followed a first West Indian defeat against a Transvaal team featuring familiar faces and then resumption of the so-called 'Super Series' with back-to-back Tests over Christmas and New Year. For the first of these at Kingsmead, South Africa paired spinners in Durban for the first time since facing Australia in 1949–50. Denys Hobson had become a wicket-taking threat around the Currie Cup grounds while Alan Kourie had enjoyed considerable success in each of the previous rebel tours. In preparing a pitch that suited slow bowling, South Africa were subverting expectations at the Kingsmead ground while addressing their enduring phobia of West Indian fast bowlers. New boy Hartley Alleyne had been observed with great nervousness during the tour matches before falling ill and though Croft was once again laid up with a back complaint the threat posed by the giants Sylvester Clarke and Franklyn Stephenson and the deceptive Ezra Moseley was ever-present in South African minds.

Peter Kirsten had shown great confidence in responding to the Wanderers crisis, the former Western Province fly-half laughing off the stump-kicking incident: 'I was just practising my kicking for the new rugby season.' After the criticism that incident had attracted South African support had fallen squarely behind the Springboks as the mood of the tour showed a marked change from a year previously. The West Indian protests over money had coincided with crowds for the Transvaal tour game and the Kingsmead 'Test' registering in low numbers, and there was a growing sense of single-minded purpose to the events.

Only 5,000 therefore saw a good-tempered, even-handed first day at the 'Test' in Durban. Despite the selectors' emphasis on spin it was the seamers who enjoyed the humid seaside conditions most, Garth Le Roux and Clive Rice claiming a wicket apiece while Faoud Bacchus retired hurt with a fractured, bleeding finger. The West Indians were effectively 87-4, therefore, when Alvin Kallicharran and Rowe were brought together, but the old partnership retained much of its lustre as 154 runs were added across three sessions. Kallicharran fell eventually for 103 to Hobson's magnificent running catch down at fine leg off Le Roux and the tourists closed on 250-4 with their captain unbeaten on 66.

Rowe began day two, Christmas Eve, with a minimum target of 350 but the pitch, rolled to within an inch of its life out of fear of the West Indian pace battery, was benign once the early morning humidity had cleared. The captain himself made 157 while each man below him in the order passed 30 before a declaration on 529-7. After years of three-day Currie Cup cricket in South Africa, only Pollock among the Springboks had ever spent close to the 580 minutes in the field. The only possibility of a result now hinged on Sylvester Clarke and his colleagues extracting more life from the pitch than their counterparts had managed, but it was quickly a forlorn task. Henry Fotheringham marked his debut with a golden duck, caught at the wicket off Clarke, but Jimmy Cook and Kirsten guided the home side to 61-1 overnight.

After a Christmas Day break, the duo extended their partnership to 130 on a rain-interrupted third day and, with more than four hours lost to poor weather and bad light, the result was a foregone conclusion. The sparse crowd which attended the final day could not see a result but were rewarded with a duel to linger in the memory: Clarke bombarding Graeme Pollock with short bowling and the veteran batsman, though apparently unsure of himself, persisting with the belief that attack was the best form of defence, bludgeoning the ball through the covers before falling to Derick Parry on 62. Bernard Julien spoke for the cricket world in commenting afterwards: 'How I wish I could have seen GP ten years ago.' There was a brief flurry of excitement when Clarke precipitated a collapse around Pollock from 219-2 to 333 all out, allowing Rowe to enforce the follow-on. But few among the final day crowd of 1,100 were moved to complain when the match was abandoned with a positive result still some days off.

Despite claiming what Rowe called a 'moral victory' in dominating the drawn first 'Test', the West Indians could not easily carry the momentum into the second match which started two days later. Bacchus was a non-starter after Le Roux had broken his finger at Kingsmead and just as Graham Gooch and Dennis Amiss had lacked for meaningful support for much of the English tour, so Rowe and Kallicharran needed help. In particular Bacchus' withdrawal revisted the problems of the previous year: the lack of a substantial opening batsman. The choice was now again between Alvin Greenidge, dropped three weeks previously after 147 runs from ten innings, and Everton Mattis, a middle-order specialist whose only sign of form had been a half-century against Transvaal. An injury to Moseley let in Julien and further weakened the visitors' options.

The pressure on Rowe was evident in the pre-match build-up as he criticised the Newlands staff for shearing bald an already spin-friendly surface, and those fears proved well grounded as Kourie and the Cape Town wind combined to put the Springboks back in control of the series on day one. In his first four overs the burly left-armer recorded figures of 4-9 to leave the visitors reeling at 49-5 but in an echo of the 1982–83 Newlands 'Test', when the West Indians had recovered from 89-6 to 246, the tourists rallied. King was his usual ebullient self. Apparently deaf to the match situation, he hit a half-century at a run a ball including 36 in boundaries. When he was out for 83 the West Indian tail again proved its mettle as Julien (33 not out) and Parry (30) carried the tourists to an apparently respectable 252.

That was put into perspective on the second morning by a more accomplished batting line-up. Cook and Fotheringham continued to look short of confidence and both fell after making a start but they had the perfect model for self-improvement in their captain. Kirsten, who had cut a harassed figure a year previously when Clarke had sensed his insecurity against short, fast bowling, was now a study in resilience and strength. He withstood the best that Clarke and Franklyn Stephenson could manage on an admittedly kind wicket and batted for more than four hours in compiling 88. His partner, Pollock, in many ways the physical and stylistic opposite to Kirsten, took advantage of his foil to strike 18 fours and a six in reaching 102. Their 183 partnership appeared to set the home side fair for a huge total even if both fell before the close.

Clarke resumed his torment of the home side on day three, taking a five-wicket haul for the second consecutive innings, as the home side slipped from 315-4 to 404 all out. Transvaaler Rice was the unlikely star of the show at the Western Province citadel, remaining scoreless for almost an hour and being hit full on the head by a Stephenson beamer that drew a preposterous lbw appeal from the bowler and a flurry of forthright opinion from the batsman. The needle between the sides resurfacing, Rice unleashed a barrage of boundaries including two hooked sixes in an over from Stephenson. He reached his 50 by hitting back over the giant Barbadian and struck a fourth six from Clarke before being stranded on 71 not out. His final five partners mustered only 22 between them to leave a 152-run lead looking somehow short but when the tourists' makeshift top three again fell away to 89-4 overnight there appeared little between the Springboks and reclaimed superiority.

And so it proved. Kourie took his match total to eight wickets as the West Indians again relied on Parry and David Murray to get them even to 268 while Le Roux and Jefferies turned their own fury on the West Indian batsmen. Clarke and Stephenson had been relentless in their examination of top order and tail-enders alike and there was undisguised pleasure in redressing the balance. More importantly Cook and Fotheringham brought the 117 required for victory in just over 20 overs with more than an hour to spare. For Fotheringham in particular it was a joyous moment. He was facing replacement by

Northern Transvaal's Mandy Yachad when the one-day series resumed and had developed a slapstick habit against West Indian pace of getting struck by the ball wherever it pitched. The bruised right-hander's 71 from 83 balls, with 14 fours including successive boundaries to secure victory, seemingly put those doubts to rest and tightened the Transvaal stranglehold on the Springbok team.

Eyebrows were raised at the announcement of the South African one-day party with suspicions that commercial goals were taking precedence over cricket. Rupert Hanley, the Transvaal fast bowler, had been 12th man for each of the two 'Tests' and bowled very well in the one-day series the previous year, yet he found himself dropped for Kenny Watson for the second 'one-day international' at St George's Park. The most popular explanation was that as an Eastern Province bowler, Watson might do more for the gate in Port Elizabeth. Similarly Mike Procter dropped out of the first 'ODI' squad for Adrian Kuiper but was widely expected to be recalled on his home ground in Natal, where the crowd had been so poor for the first 'Test'. Most curiously of all, Peter Kirsten was appointed captain for three matches only. For the West Indians, Hartley Alleyne had at least recovered from chickenpox but the keenest eyes were now on the tourists' application in pursuit of the improved prize money and an extension of their 1-0 series lead.

The unorthodoxy of the visitors continued to delight as Emmerson Trotman hit the first three balls of the second 'ODI' to the boundary but they still needed the tail to wag through David Murray (32), Ezra Moseley (63) and Sylvester Clarke (34) to turn 77-5 into 260. At the small St George's Park ground that was never enough and the home side let rip at the second-string bowling of Collis King and Albert Padmore in reaching their target with some four overs to spare. Graeme Pollock, Ken McEwan and Kuiper scored at around a run a ball and the *Rand Daily Mail* rejoiced that their men now 'had the measure of the much-vaunted West Indian bowlers – and that this series is very definitely heading South Africa's way.'[10]

The established pattern of South African volatility, lauding the team one minute and castigating them the next, gave the lie to this enthusiasm. If nothing else, of 11 sixes hit in the second 'ODI' more than half had been from the unthreatening off-spin of ageing player-manager Padmore.

The rebel rhythm was now in full swing – match, rest, match, rest – and 48 hours after the second 'ODI' the teams met again at Kingsmead. Rowe marked his 35th birthday with an unbeaten 45 in guiding his side to a victory by virtue of higher scoring rate after bad light stopped play. The R1,000 man of the match cheque was also his. For South Africa's part it was obvious that sustaining their high level of performance, not to mention fan expectation, with matches coming so thick and fast was a problem. Kirsten lamented his men's fielding as 'the worst I have seen from a Springbok team.'

He had to expand that verdict to his team's batting two days later as a capitulation to 149 all out in 41.2 overs allowed the West Indians to take an unbeatable 3-1 lead in the six-rubber series even without Rowe, who was stricken with gastric flu. Trotman scored 94 of the tourists' runs as they knocked off the total to claim another R10,000 match-winning fee as well as piling the pressure onto Kirsten, whose innings had lasted only two deliveries in front of a 14,000 crowd. At the close of play the selectors announced that Rice would be replacing Kirsten as captain with immediate effect.

The decision reinvigorated the old provincial rivalries in South African cricket. Kirsten, it was darkly implied, had received less than full support from all his team-mates, but Jimmy Cook is dismissive of those rumours: 'We all got on so well together and actually gelled as a team. Having not done it for so many years you would have thought that there would have been a bit of provincialism involved, but there was anything but that. The guys all got stuck into it. We were all professional in our attitudes and got on fantastically well.'

Probably Kirsten had been made captain too early thanks to a successful season with Western Province in 1981–82. At 28 he was leading a battle-hardened team including the stars of his own childhood in Graeme Pollock, Barry Richards and Mike Procter, and for a quiet man it had been difficult to stamp his authority on a team dominated by Transvaal. In 1982–83 the 'Mean Machine' had completed a five-trophy grand slam to strengthen Rice's claims and, though more complex than his public caricature indicated, he was a tough competitor who relished provoking public opinion.

For the *Rand Daily Mail* and other Johannesburg outlets, 'Rice's rescue mission' was the flavour of the coverage ahead of the third 'Test' at Wanderers. They had seemingly forgotten that with two matches to play the home side were leading the 'Test' series 1-0.

While the South African dressing room might have been divided on some issues, they remained united in being wary of opposition bowling. After successive defeats in the 'one-day internationals', the last place even Transvaal captain Clive Rice would have chosen to lead South Africa for the first time was the Wanderers, a lively, green surface that had helped Sylvester Clarke to a record-breaking haul in domestic cricket and which had hosted the remarkable West Indian 'Test' comeback a year previously. Denys Hobson, disappointing at Durban and then on his home Cape Town ground while fellow spinner Alan Kourie wreaked havoc, was replaced by

Transvaal's Rupert Hanley. As off-spinner Derick Parry struggled with an injury, the West Indians took the chance to mimic their official counterparts in naming a fourth seamer for the first time: Clarke, Ezra Moseley, Hartley Alleyne and Franklyn Stephenson might not have been a match for Clive Lloyd's quartet but they compared favourably with other nations' attacks and certainly that of South Africa missing Garth Le Roux, who was injured, and Stephen Jefferies, out of form.

The West Indians' aggressive strategy, all the more precarious with key batsmen Faoud Bacchus and Lawrence Rowe still absent, was rewarded. In his first 'Test', Alleyne picked up four front-line batsmen and Moseley mopped up the tail as Rice's brave new world began with his side bowled out for 160. Only Peter Kirsten (67) and Graeme Pollock (41) were able to provide even basic resistance. The enduring weakness at the top of the visitors' batting was exposed as a makeshift home attack put the Springboks back in the game at 23-3 only for Collis King to enter the fray. At Wanderers 11 months previously he had turned the second 'Test' around with a quick-fire century when most players would have battened down the hatches. Arriving at the crease with only an hour until the close and his team listing he reproduced those fireworks, hooking his first ball from Rice for four, one of five boundaries in his first eight balls. His eleventh delivery was hit off the home captain over extra cover for six and he passed his half-century in 34 balls as if in a rush to reach the landmark before the end of play. Coll was still King.

Rice had promised before the match that the single-minded aggression of his Transvaal and Nottinghamshire teams would be replicated for South Africa and he had the right weapon in Pollock. After Kenny Watson had removed King in the first over of the third morning, Adrian Kuiper had rattled through the tail for a five-wicket haul such that the visitors were grateful for a first-innings lead of 33. With Jimmy Cook and Henry Fotheringham's still having problems with the West Indian attack, Pollock was called to the crease with South Africa on 44-2. But he saw only an opportunity to match King's power-hitting. The left-hander smashed 46 from 33 balls in an innings that belied his advancing years in power and judgement. With the truculent Kirsten (61) reiterating his case to have been retained as captain, South Africa were able to reach 169-6 at the close and set the scene for a second successive Wanderers 'Test' to provide excellent entertainment.

Twenty-six wickets had fallen in two days, seven of those to Alleyne. Two had come in the final two balls of play on the second day to set up a hat-trick ball against Ken McEwan, whom Rice had earmarked as essential in his plan to set 250 to win. The first ball the new batsman faced zipped past the bat; the second caught an edge and was scooped up by Stephenson to give Alleyne three wickets in four balls and the West Indians the advantage once more. Rice was able to move from 21 to 47 before falling to Clarke, and Kourie provided a characteristically dogged 31, but there was a sense that a second-innings total of 236 by mid-afternoon, which gave the West Indians a target of 204, was not quite enough with another day to play.

With the West Indian batting line-up so brittle, however, hope was rarely lost. Greenidge (43) and Mattis (32) made amends for previous shortcomings in a second-wicket partnership of 68 but their departure triggered a collapse from 72-1 to 99-6 as the South African seamers enjoyed themselves on a still lively Wanderers surface. Even King was moved to temper his aggression as the day drew to an end but the loss of Moseley (14) left the West Indians on 172-8 with new batsman Clarke still having one over to survive until the close. The giant bowler swung like a lumberjack at the first and missed, swiped the second through cover for two, pulled the third for a mighty four and nicked a single past Pollock's outstretched hand at second slip. Closing on 180-8, 24 short of the target, it was clear that the Wanderers would not be needed for all of the fourth day's scheduled play.

The final morning was indeed short, but still attracted 3,000 spectators and eclipsed the previous Johannesburg 'Test' for drama. King and Clarke began in circumspect fashion, taking ten runs from four overs, but then they matched that return in a single over from Kenny Watson and victory was in reach. King decided to finish things in style and hit Rice towards long-off only for the 12th man Jefferies to race around and on the run scoop a fine catch above his head. The batsmen had crossed in the process, which saved the new man Alleyne from facing, but Clarke's anxiety to protect the number 11 almost backfired. From the final ball of Rice's over he chanced a single to Kirsten, perhaps the best cover fielder in the world. The former captain made a remarkable stop, turn and throw in the blink of an eye but the ball whistled past the stumps. The following over Clarke pulled Watson to the square leg boundary to secure a one-wicket victory, square the 'Test' series 1-1 and heighten his legend in South Africa.

With unfortunate timing the fourth and final 'Test' would have to wait until the completion of the already dead one-day series. In Johannesburg South Africa happily dominated the first of two 'internationals', debutant Mandy Yachad replacing the dropped Henry Fotheringham and carrying his bat for an unbeaten 123 in a total of 279-3 only for the West Indians to be awarded the match on 208-7 when it was curtailed for bad light. The decision, made on the basis of a faster scoring rate, was generous indeed with no recognised batsman left in the ranks. That result gifted the tourists a 4-1 lead before the final game at Berea Park, where even the keenly fought-for prize money was insufficient to generate a strong effort from the tourists. Set an achievable 228 to win in 50 overs they were skittled out for 54 in 20 overs and one delivery, with Rupert Hanley bowling ten off the reel for a six-wicket haul. Echoing the perennial problems of captains in official and unofficial tours alike, Rowe shrugged: 'After two and a half months on tour it was always going to be difficult to motivate the fellows properly for this last match.'

There would be no such problems for the fourth 'Test' at St George's Park; over the two tours South Africa and the West Indian XI were tied 6-6 in 'one-day internationals' and 2-2 in 'Tests'. The occasion was given added poignancy as the announced finale of Graeme Pollock, on his home ground in Port Elizabeth, 23 years after his first first-class century for Eastern Province. The Springboks also made a surprise selection in omitting veteran wicketkeeper Ray Jennings for the rising star Dave Richardson, and retained Yachad ahead of Fotheringham. A number of the West Indian players were carrying injuries but they pledged a big effort to complete the series and Lawrence Rowe returned to lead them.

Clive Rice won the toss for the first time as Springbok captain and elected to bat on a pitch billed as milk and honey for batsmen. From their arrival 13 months previously, though, the West Indian bowling attack had shown that South African rules of pitch appraisal did not always apply. Clarke, Moseley and Stephenson reduced the South Africans to an alarming 117-6, Clarke in particular excelling with spells of 8-2-13-2, 6-2-9-1 and 6-2-12-0. The bounce and speed the bowlers enjoyed left batsmen unsure whether to defend their fingers, their skulls or their stumps. Wicketkeeper David Murray caught five of the first six wickets to fall while only Ken McEwan among the top seven offered meaningful resistance. His 120, supplemented by a streaky unbeaten 60 from Alan Kourie, dropped in his first 15 minutes at the crease, allowed a patched-up 267-8 by the close.

The second day followed a remarkably similar pattern: the West Indians on top until the middle of the afternoon whereupon a Springbok rearguard brought them back in front as marginal favourites. Clarke dealt with Kenny Watson and Hanley in double-quick time, claiming 5-36 to leave South Africa on 277 before Faoud Bacchus (66) and Emmerson Trotman (43) put together 83, the most impressive opening stand of the West Indian tour. But no-one else reached 20 as Watson removed Collis King and Alvin Kallicharran in a single over and Murray made the mistake of chancing a quick single to Kirsten, run out by yards rather than inches. In the final over Rowe was given out lbw to Adrian Kuiper in a decision that might have prompted serious questions about the umpiring, particularly when Moseley arrived, hit his second ball to the boundary and then was promptly out swiping again to leave the tourists 97 in arrears at 180-8. But Rowe was philosophical at the change of fortunes, lamenting his own side's infuriating inconsistency: 'In future I'm going to instruct the top order to continue failing so that our middle and lower order can continue to rescue us as they have so often in the past.'

Over the Sunday rest day, with 18 wickets down in the match and two days to play, Rice made the draw the overwhelming favourite result but pledged to push for a victory if at all possible. On the third morning his bowlers did their part for the captain in allowing the West Indians to add only 19 runs to their overnight total. But the home team's heralded batsmen were once again humbled by the West Indian bowling attack. Cook continued to struggle to the short-pitched ball on his legs, turning another catch behind to Murray; Kirsten responded to a rap on the hand by Clarke with an attempted cover drive but succeeded only in chopping the ball onto his stumps; Pollock's resistance was ended when he misjudged an Alleyne bouncer for pace, caught the ball full on the ear and retired to hospital for four stitches. Cook later wrote, 'If Graeme could be hit, everyone wondered, how could they possibly cope?'[11] In the face of such hostility the South Africans lost their nerve. McEwan (0), Rice (12), Kuiper (14) and Kourie (4) were all out playing loose shots in a futile attempt to reassert their authority. When Pollock returned for a tenth-wicket stand with Watson, the South African total was 124, and after three runs and three balls he edged a vicious in-swinger from Clarke behind to Murray, whose ten catches in the match equalled the record in official Test cricket.[12]

Clarke once again claimed the headlines, completing match figures of 10-68, but the praise ought to have been spread wider as Stephenson bowled an entire afternoon session unchanged and Alleyne did his part in relief spells for the spearhead as well as pole-axing the iconic Pollock. Buoyed by the change of momentum, and their own belated success in the first innings, Bacchus and Trotman went after the demoralised Boks at almost a run a ball. By the end of play they were halfway towards their 206 victory target from only 18 overs.

During a six-'Test' series over two tours there had been plenty of unforeseen drama, but there was no final chapter. Kallicharran and King were the men to finally bring a conclusion in time for lunch on day four – clinching a six-wicket victory and a 2-1 series success after they had been behind. A delighted Rowe declared: 'I wouldn't be too critical of the Springboks. Their problem is not one of technique but rather the pressures of facing four genuinely fast bowlers. I do believe it's the first time this country has seen such a thing.'

It had been a pulsating four-'Test' series, although the Springbok defeats pointed to a South African game in demise. Without the experienced Peter Kirsten and Graeme Pollock, the margins of defeat would have been spectacular. It had been a chastening experience for the Springbok batsmen, as Jimmy Cook recalls: 'It was a tough series, I must admit. After the second year of their series, certainly a couple of our batsmen were pretty relieved that it was all over and that we could now get back to some, let's call it slightly easier bowling rather than having the ball whizz around your ears every day. So there was quite a relief amongst a few of the guys that they'd had two years of it and that was now enough.'

After the Colin Croft incident the veneer of off-field normality had been maintained and SACU could acclaim a second success despite the very public row over sponsorship dividends. It had been a notably commercial tour with remarkable exposure granted to the sponsors Panasonic and Yellow Pages. An endless stream of female models in branded T-shirts had gripped artificial cricket bats with a provocative eye, while on and off the field the players were rarely without a logo. For the amateur South African game, the era of coloured clothing, big prize money and floodlit cricket had arrived.

For the West Indians, too, it ought to have been a great triumph. Only in Cape Town had they been outplayed, although pitches elsewhere had again proved more suited to their strengths than might have been expected in a genuine Test series. Even without their biggest name, Colin Croft – a fading force before his 30th birthday – they had performed impressively. Lawrence Rowe's 157 at Kingsmead was the last big innings of his career, and the pace quartet of Sylvester Clarke, Ezra Moseley, Franklyn Stephenson and Hartley Alleyne had shown themselves worthy of greater recognition than they would receive at provincial level. For players who had enjoyed limited opportunities to play international cricket, it had been a series of high achievement: Emmerson Trotman and Collis King had shown batting flair and David Murray proved himself a wicketkeeper of high calibre.

Of course, the routine cricket environment, maintained for longer than previously, could not remain indefinitely. 'No joy could be had in these achievements,' wrote Michael Manley, 'because they were all part of a grave betrayal of ethnic solidarity. Indeed, they compromised a cause, which, deeper than ethnicity, went to the very heart of human values.'[13]

In England, their rebel tourists' trespasses had been forgotten quickly enough; in parts of the Caribbean, it was impossible. There was minimal support for defences of individual freedom or advancing South African reform. Only the straightforward economic argument that players could not turn down such a windfall carried any weight, and naturally this elicited very little public sympathy.

Life for the returning tourists was harsh, notably for the three who had been jettisoned after the first tour. Of these, Richard Austin and Herbert Chang would both endure difficult lives on their return to Jamaica, suffering drug problems in the face of social alienation.[14] 'I do not believe the Jamaicans either thought of the long-term repercussions or were properly advised,' wrote Michael Holding.

'[They] should have known that their lives would change completely once they chose to go to South Africa. They would not be able to get any jobs, could play no cricket at any level and would have few friends left [...] Unfortunately the rebel Jamaicans did not seem to think further than the mandatory West Indies Cricket Board ban that put them out of Test and regional cricket forever. Life turned out to be hell for those who remained at home.'[15]

Ali Bacher later admitted that he regretted cancelling those deals: 'Players who were released from the first tour felt we had let them down because they had made the initial sacrifice, were banned from playing in the West Indies and were even ostracised by their own communities. Although we did pay them the second tour contract fee, I believe now we should have been more accommodating.'[16]

But it was not only the first-time tourists who found life difficult. David Murray, son of Everton Weekes, lived in Australia until 1990 but also became a drug addict on his return to Barbados, hounded in the street with cries of 'You sold your soul, man.' Bernard Julien would also endure a difficult return and most of the rebels preferred to settle elsewhere. Croft and Rowe moved to the United States while Alvin Kallicharran lived between Johannesburg and Birmingham, where he continued playing for Warwickshire. Clarke and Trotman remained in South Africa for further seasons while Clarke, Stephenson and Alleyne played county cricket. Back with Surrey and England-qualified, Monte Lynch even found himself playing three one-day internationals against the West Indies in the chaotic summer of 1988.[17]

Ezra Moseley had the unique distinction of playing for the West Indies although a South African rebel. In 1989 the ICC rescinded the ban, and while Jamaica still refused to select its rebels, considering them unworthy representatives of the island, elsewhere the reaction was softer. Moseley was recalled by Barbados, where performances earned an international call-up aged 32 to face England at Port of Spain in 1990. He immediately made an impression on two fellow visitors to South Africa, removing Wayne Larkins with a sharp lifter and breaking Graham Gooch's arm to rule the England captain out for the series. He retained his place on home turf in Bridgetown, but that would prove to be his second and final cap.[18] Irrespective of political concerns, Moseley was simply not a viable long-term prospect for the West Indian selectors, and nor was he alone. Rowe and Kallicharran were past their fortieth birthdays; Clarke, King and Croft not far behind. The five-year ban had ended most careers.

The outstanding exception was Stephenson, who had joined the first rebel tour at 23 and became one of the best players never to earn Test honours. In county cricket with Nottinghamshire and Sussex he was a consistently outstanding bowling all-rounder, claiming 100 wickets and 1,000 runs at Trent Bridge in 1988. He has always maintained that he has no regrets over the decision, and more than two decades on remained under no illusions as to why his international ambitions remained unfulfilled: 'It's all because of '83. Nobody has forgotten it still.'[19]

Stephenson also believed that the tours, which had seen black cricketers ultimately overcome a 'multi-racial' Springbok side yet to include a non-white player, had served a positive purpose: 'I felt we started the change of thinking that we were a lower form of animal.'[20]And Croft agreed: 'I don't know that I betrayed anybody. I might have done something good for the cricket in South Africa. I may have allowed people in South Africa to see black people play properly rather than thinking that black people couldn't do well. When we went to the games in South Africa there were at least 50 per cent black crowds. There was never anything about that written.'[21]

The tour was obviously different from those previously as the West Indians had a marked impact among non-white South Africans. Some observers agreed that the tour had indeed fostered interest among young blacks, as David Dyer wrote in *World Cricket Digest*: 'One thing is certain: the interest which the tour generated is immeasurable. Take a drive past any school and you'll see children not playing their traditional game, soccer, but cricket – taking turns to be Collis, Sylvester or Franklyn.'[22]

Others, however, saw the opposite. The West Indian academic Hilary Beckles wrote that the tourists were rejected by the townships, 'hailed as "villains", and graffiti saying "West Indies traitors go home" was common enough. Their presence was interpreted as part of a strategic political move by the state to counter mounting global criticisms of apartheid.'[23] And his colleague Alan Cobley agreed: 'These, and subsequent, rebel tours did little or nothing to develop black cricket in South Africa, and may in fact have harmed the development of the game among blacks by further alienating potential players and supporters, since cricket was now seen to be linked politically and ideologically to the defence of apartheid.'[24]

Judgements and justifications remained beholden to individual standpoints. In drawing a line under the most painful episode in West Indian cricket history, Sir Vivian Richards made the point thus: 'I talked to some of the West Indians who went on that tour to South Africa, and some not only felt humiliated but were utterly ashamed of themselves.

'I can accept that people do make mistakes; and there were also others who claimed that they were able to work wonders for the people of the townships. That is looking on the positive side, and I have no reason to doubt their honesty. There may have been positives that came out of their tour. Those who went have to live with themselves and decide whether they were right or wrong. They will know it every time they look in the mirror, whether they were black or white players.'[25]

1 The Croft incident occurred shortly after a referendum among whites on desegregating public transport. First elections for Soweto town council were also held in the first week of December with a dismal turnout. Inevitably anti-reform whites proclaimed this as 'proof' that blacks were not interested in political representation but this was a continuation of the 'multi-national' policy of the 1970s (see Chapter 2): apartheid re-branded and doomed to fail.
2 p 137, Bose (1994).
3 *Out of the Wilderness: Part II*, British Sky Broadcasting, first broadcast 19 July 2008.
4 p 22, *Rand Daily Mail*, 6 December 1983.
5 p 28, *The Star*, 17 November 1983.
6 p 99, Boycott (1981).
7 Eyewitness quotes here are taken from pp 190–191, Hartman (2004). However the episode as recounted there is placed between the fourth and fifth 'ODIs' in the first WI tour in 1982–83. To the best of my research this is wrong. All other evidence across newspaper reports, player biographies and eye witness accounts place the stand-off on 7 December 1983. See also p 203, McGlew and Chesterfield (1995).
8 p 18, *Rand Daily Mail*, 9 December 1983.
9 R10,000 to winners of each game, R3,000 to losers, R1,000 to each man of the match, R5,000 to man of the series, R500 for a century, five wickets or five catches.
10 p 14, *Rand Daily Mail*, 7 January 1984.
11 p 35, Cook and Cleary (1993).
12 RW Taylor, India v England at Mumbai, 15–19 February 1980.
13 p 406, Manley (2002).
14 For Richard Austin, see Michael Atherton, *The Times*, 5 February 2009, at http://www.timesonline.co.uk/tol/sport/columnists/mike_atherton/article5662856.ece. For Austin, Herbert Chang and David Murray see Robert Craddock, *The Herald Sun*, 14 April 2007 at http://www.news.com.au/heraldsun/story/0,21985,21552339-11088,00.html.
15 p 120, Holding and Cozier (1993).
16 p 191, Hartman (2004).
17 Texaco Trophy, May 1988. England captain Mike Gatting ran out Lynch after two balls on debut and he made only six runs in three one-day internationals before being dropped. Gatting was the first of four captains England had in an especially shambolic summer. See Chapter 9.

18 See Chapter 9 for details of the amnesty. The eligibility of the tourists remained a hotly contested issue. Michael Holding wrote: 'Personally, I objected to any West Indian who had been to South Africa being allowed to play for the West Indies again. This is not to say I did not accept the necessity for the ICC ruling, and I had nothing against them playing in the Red Stripe Cup for those individual territories who wanted to include them. Jamaicans who went were not allowed to play for Jamaica because people did not want them and I felt the same thing should have held good for the West Indies team. If you represent the West Indies, you represent everybody in the Caribbean and a lot of people in the Caribbean don't want people like that representing them. I am one of them' (pp 122–3, Holding and Cozier 1993). Michael Manley explained Moseley's subsequent exclusion 'presumably because he had toured South Africa in breach of the strictest of all protocols governing West Indian cricket at the time' (pp 393, Manley 2002). However, there were plenty of mitigating factors: his age; a record of six wickets at 43.50 in his two Tests; and most importantly the quality of alternatives. In nine of the ten Tests after dropping Moseley the West Indies picked four of Malcolm Marshall, Curtly Ambrose, Ian Bishop, Patrick Patterson and Courtney Walsh. Although now past its peak, the strength of West Indian fast bowling remained such that the great Walsh, who would become the all-time Test wicket-taker, only graduated to the new ball nine years after his 1984 debut.
19 Vaidyanathan, ibid.
20 Craddock, ibid.
21 *Out of the Wilderness: Part II*, British Sky Broadcasting, first broadcast 19 July 2008.
22 Vaidyanathan, ibid.
23 p 118, Beckles (ed., 1998).
24 p 135, Beckles (ed., 1998).
25 p 178, Richards and Harris (2001).

## Chapter 7

# C'mon, Au$$ie

*'By the same people who gave you the Sharpeville massacre.' – Cartoon,* Sydney Morning Herald

Ali Bacher did not tend towards half-measures. In leading South Africa he had demanded a competitive resolve to match their formidable talent. When managing director of Transvaal Cricket Council his iron will was mirrored in the all-conquering 'Mean Machine'. And as recruiter-in-chief for the rebel tours he had not rested on his laurels despite the success of the 1982–83 West Indian series.

A few months after Lawrence Rowe's side left the republic for the first time, Bacher visited the United Kingdom for the 1983 World Cup. Clive Lloyd had been firm favourite to lift the trophy for a third time, particularly once the West Indies had reached the final at Lord's against India, a cricket nation previously characterised by Test pragmatism and one-day international illiteracy.[1] 'Show me a person who gave Kapil Dev's team any chance of winning the 1983 World Cup,' wrote the veteran Indian journalist Ayaz Memon, '[and] I will show you a liar and an opportunist.'[2] But a young, self-confident team did just that to precipitate a shift in world cricket's balance of power.

Relations between India and South Africa had been virtually non-existent and the attraction of a rebel Indian team was highly questionable. But after their victory at Lord's, Joe Pamensky approached the Hyderabad Blues with a view to arranging a South African tour. Sunil Gavaskar later said: 'The proposition was put to us after we won the World Cup, but to the great credit of the players they turned it down without another thought. It was just out of the question.'[3]

The political and economic structure of the Indian game meant that attracting any serious cricketers to South Africa would be nigh on impossible. The Indian players could expect to suffer the same extreme stigmatisation at home as had the West Indian rebels. And unlike many West Indians, they would not be able to fall back on professional contracts in England – they were largely employed full-time in India so would be exchanging their entire lives for a cricket tour. The same applied to the Pakistan team, and the idea of enticing players from either nation was dropped as quickly as it had arisen.

This uniform disinterest was in stark contrast to Australian players. If New Zealand were South Africa's fiercest rivals in rugby union then the closest equivalent in cricket was Australia. The cancelled 1971–72 tour had caused the Springboks far more distress than the 1970 visit to England, and not only because it had sentenced South African cricket to oblivion. The 4-0 whitewash of Bill Lawry's team had passed into South African sporting folklore and the prospect of renewing rivalries offered a natural yardstick to white Springbok fans in particular. Their attractiveness to SACU was obvious – and their availability likewise.

Ever since World Series Cricket, the stability of the Australian dressing room had been precarious as divisions between Packer men Greg Chappell, Dennis Lillee and Rod Marsh, and 'establishment loyalist' captain Kim Hughes contributed towards often inexplicable defeats, notably in the 1981 Ashes. Australia won back the urn for the first time since WSC in 1982–83 – and that in no small part because England had been weakened by the 1982 rebel tour. 'They were a pretty ragged lot those Poms without Boycott and Co.,' wrote Lillee. 'Easy meat for us but we tended to forget that as we celebrated after the series.'[4]

Despite that success, Hughes' side had remained weak and amid the factionalism were eliminated without distinction at the 1983 World Cup. It was then that Bacher began making serious offers. A year previously he had contacted Tony Greig to ask for advice on putting together a rebel tour but Kerry Packer, now the dominant figure in Australian cricket, was certain to oppose an idea that would damage the national side and therefore his own business interests. Greig suggested instead contacting the former Australian Test opener Bruce Francis, who had toured South Africa with the Derrick Robins XI and who remained a vocal supporter of bridge-building. An economics graduate, Francis took pride in his education and moved beyond the usual 'cricketer's position' to argue actively for sporting engagement. He relished the intellectual rough and tumble of the heated apartheid debate and would write a polemical book on the rebel tour furore in Australia.[5]

In particular, Francis argued forcefully that the sporting boycott had served its purpose with the advent of 'normal' cricket. The ruling whites would not 'surrender power', he declared, and apartheid would end only through the incremental change exemplified in cricket. Large-scale punishments such as economic sanctions, in contrast, would heighten the likelihood of 'bloody revolution'. Francis was adept at highlighting hypocrisies and inconsistencies in his own government's stance on South Africa and considered 'anyone remotely acquainted with the enormity of the South African problem' would attach little significance to the rebel tours and their value to the National Party government. However, the African National Congress and anti-apartheid movement in the republic, groups with some such acquaintance, continued to support the boycott and Francis' regard for his own analytical skills was not always shared by those who worked with him. 'He believed he was an authority on politics, whether they be Australian or South African,' Bacher said later, 'but as far as South Africa was concerned he was certainly no authority.'[6]

Bacher first met batsmen Graham Yallop, briefly Australian captain during the WSC exodus, and Kepler Wessels, the South African-born left-hander who had made his Australia debut in the 1982–83 Ashes. After the World Cup elimination, a further four players met with Bacher but the story was leaked to a newspaper and, with a second costly West Indian tour already imminent, plans were shelved.[7] In early 1984 the WSC kingpins Chappell, Lillee and Marsh retired, weakening Australia without an apparent improvement in spirit. A few months later the fast bowler Rodney Hogg threw a punch at captain Hughes on the field in the Port of Spain Test and respect for the still amateur, still distant Australian Cricket Board remained negligible.

Loyalty to the Board would be no stronger than eight years previously. In 1979 Sir Donald Bradman had advised the ACB to review the legal loopholes in their player contracts lest a Packer repeat occur. This advice had never been acted upon, and the ACB were to pay the price again. Chris Harte wrote in *A History of Australian Cricket*: 'The Board was shown up in April and May 1985 for what it had really become: totally toothless and even unable to provide its players with binding contracts. The irony of the situation was that, of the fourteen Board delegates at the time, three were actively involved in business in South Africa (one of whom was selling cricket equipment to the Western Province Cricket Union in Cape Town) whilst over the next two seasons four would watch part of the unofficial Test series.'[8]

Francis was highly motivated to arrange a tour that would bring financial and, in his view, political rewards and in September 1984 he began approaching disgruntled players. By the time Australia entered a five-Test home series with the West Indies the following month, only captain Hughes, Allan Border and Geoff Lawson in the 12-man squad had not signed to visit South Africa the following year. The West Indies, by now an irresistible force, won the first three Tests off the reel and Hughes stood down mid-series with a tearful resignation speech.

Australian cricket was entering its lowest ebb of the modern era, appointing Border to captain a squad in transition within which Hughes had been promised a place[9]. When the 17-man party for the 1985 Ashes was announced in March, Hughes' name was not there but eight players who had secretly signed for the rebel tour were. When a few weeks later two newspapers broke the story that 13 players had signed to visit South Africa at the end of the year[10], the eight players in both the Ashes and rebel parties were forced to make a choice between official and unofficial paymasters. SACU had their most formidable opponent yet in Packer, who promptly flexed his own financial muscle and five players were tempted back into the official fold[11]. The three players who had not jumped back over the fence were wicketkeeper Steve Rixon and fast bowlers Rod McCurdy and Terry Alderman. Needing replacements, the ACB then named John Maguire and Carl Rackemann as the substitute pacemen – only to learn they too had exchanged their international prospects for a SACU contract.

For critics of the Australian authorities, this was confirmation that honorary administrators experienced the real world from a safe distance. Warwick Hadfield wrote in *The Australian* that the players considered themselves 'not rebels but refugees from what they perceive as the parlous state of Australian cricket.'[12] No-one felt more resentful than Hughes, born on Australia Day and a vocal patriot. During the Packer affair, the fact that not one player leaked the news to the authorities had been taken as a show of universal contempt. As far as the rebel tours were concerned, only one man had broken ranks: after an approach by Francis in November 1982, the 'establishment loyalist' Hughes immediately informed the ACB. Now, having since been kept out of the loop by rebel planners who considered him a non-starter, he was offered the captaincy of the rebel Australian XI. Feeling abandoned by those who had promised him an Ashes place, he accepted in frustration and self-justification, telling a live television conference, 'I am going to South Africa with an open and, I hope, an intelligent mind. I believe I have the ability to judge right and wrong. I also believe I will be able to comment and suggest ways in which the situation can be improved.'[13]

Few among the rest of the party felt the need for such arguments. Although Hughes' conference had been met with anti-apartheid protests, the prevailing public and political mood in Australia was closer to England than the West Indies. The bridge-building vs. isolation debate was both hotly contested and easily ignored, and, facing the familiar cricketer's problem of balancing a professional career with the need to earn money elsewhere, A$100,000 per tour after tax was too good to turn down.[14] In the final 16-man squad, 15 were clear about their financial motive. As in England, it was difficult to find professional cricketers who had even addressed the moral question. Batsman David Hookes and fast bowler Jeff Thomson did not travel because their demands were excessive even by SACU standards; even Allan Border, who was not invited and was subsequently critical in his autobiography, later admitted, 'I'd have thought very hard about it … and the higher the offer, the longer I'd have thought.'[15]

The rebels received total condemnation from Prime Minister Bob Hawke, who told a press conference: 'I would have hoped that both Hughes and Yallop would have had a broader vision and understanding of their responsibilities as Australians and cricketers. We are uniquely placed as a cricketing nation, a sporting nation, to be able to do something to deny them a legitimacy which they seek through the instrument of international competition in sport.' And the media was similarly unflinching, as an editorial in *The Sunday Times* mocked, 'Presumably South Africa may even launch its own version of the Ashes. Steve Biko's, perhaps.'[16]

In assembling their party the South Africans felt they had 'out-Packered Packer' while the man himself was content that for the most part the rebel tour was ridding a stagnant Australian set-up of dead wood. In truth, neither could be entirely satisfied. Only with a late offer to Hughes had SACU given their Australian batting an outstanding individual alongside the talented trio of John Dyson, Steve Smith and Yallop. Hughes was an apt successor to Lawrence Rowe: an exceptional talent who, if lacking the consistency required for greatness, was nevertheless a figure of stature. In Steve Rixon, SACU had captured an outstanding wicketkeeper marginalised by the brilliant Marsh but, even allowing for the idiosyncrasies of selectors, the fact that only three of their final line-up had been first choices to tour England was inescapable.

Border, meanwhile, was missing four leading fast bowlers while including five men who had signed up with the rebels before Packer's intervention. The quintet were not popular with the rebels, as Rackemann said: 'I'm bitterly disappointed in those who have pulled out.

It should have been all or nothing. By bailing out they have made it harder for the other guys.'[17] And Border was equally unimpressed to be taking them back. Their initial disloyalty had been rewarded by Packer and they were now back in the fold.

This unrest was just one problem facing the new captain and he endured a torrid first series in England, winning only four of 24 matches to deepen Australian cricket's malaise. The trail of chaos left by South African cricket remained as impressive as ever.

When the Australian rebels arrived in South Africa in October 1985, the republic was an increasingly turbulent and unstable country compared to that which had hosted the earliest tours. The progress trumpeted by the Botha government in an international propaganda campaign was being undercut by brutal lawlessness back in the republic. The enduring political exclusion of blacks in the tricameral parliament was bolstered by a 'total onslaught' policy against 'resistance movements', including the ANC, and a violent cycle of repression and reaction prevailed.

The government was unpopular even among whites as unemployment rose, economic woes hardened and international antagonism grew. Racial tensions were at an all-time high. Frederik Van Zyl Slabbert would resign in 1986 after seven years as leader of the opposition and later said: 'Parliament as an institution was increasingly rendered powerless through two conflicting, polarising tendencies: the extra parliamentary struggle for the freedom of the ANC and the Total Strategy of an increasingly military autocracy under the leadership of PW Botha.'[18]

The Australian rebels would be guarded by a small army of security personnel but with typical alacrity Ali Bacher harnessed the backdrop as he set about his promotional pitch: 'There is a recession and small businesses are going under. There are problems in the townships. The Australians' cricket tour is the only bright ray of hope in 1985 and 1986. There is cricket euphoria. People feel that Don Bradman and his 1948 team are arriving ... They are a credit to Australia ... Their determination, motivation and spirit ... you've got to see it to believe it.'

And as the English had been forgotten upon the West Indian arrival, so SACU now suffered amnesia about Lawrence Rowe's side. Bacher said: 'Our players were a little bit agitated about the money being paid to visiting teams, but they are much more amenable now. Our players have never been fully motivated for these types of tours. They often have gone through the motions, but not this time round. This is the closest thing we have had to proper international cricket since the Australian Test team was here in 1970 and our chaps want to show the world we are still a top cricketing nation. It should be a hell of a contest.'[19]

Certainly the promised Australian commitment was in evidence upon their arrival. At the inaugural dinner at the Carlton Hotel in Johannesburg, Kim Hughes promised: 'You will see what we are all about. We are true-blue Australians ... We aren't the official team but we will be giving it the same effort as any athletic side that has left Australian shores.'

This intent was embraced by local media, who hailed a team with the professionalism and pedigree to present a sustained challenge to the Springboks. The same week the television programme *Network* trumpeted the qualities of their visitors compared to Allan Border's official side, dismissing the Australian government and cricket board as out of touch with public opinion. The South African press rarely needed encouragement to heap praise on visiting rebel cricketers but were handed a front-page gift when Hughes presented home counterpart Clive Rice with his green Australian Test blazer.

The mutual appreciation did not end there as one senior player, voicing the tourists' general contempt for the ACB, hailed the management of South African cricket: 'We have been totally impressed with the professionalism of Ali Bacher and Joe Pamensky. They treat cricket as a professional occupation and we appreciate their understanding. If these two ran cricket in Australia, you would not have the factionalism which is pulling the game apart back home.'[20]

The wisdom of praising unity in South African governance was rarely rock solid, and almost immediately Hassan Howa's SACB announced that any of their members attending Australian tour matches would be banned from the organisation for life.

For the first time since isolation an 'international' team visiting South Africa had agreed a schedule comparable to their official counterparts. The tour started for real against Orange Free State in Bloemfontein on 22nd November 1985, the same day the official side had begun their second Test against New Zealand in Sydney. But by this time the Australian XI had already played four unofficial one-day warm-up matches with 20 days' further cricket scheduled before the first 'Test' against South Africa starting 26th December. This itinerary would take them to many a SACU outpost, exposing the tourists not only to local cricket supporters but also to local committee men.

Each match was punctuated by an official function of one type or another, events generally filled with interminable speeches and meet-and-greets yet fulsomely attended by the tourists under a three-line whip from management.

Greg Shipperd recalls: 'There were way too many social activities on our schedule and we had to pare it back because we couldn't expect to get to all these functions and then play our best cricket. But we were accommodated beautifully, looked after very well and it was a pleasant time; notwithstanding the high level of security that was around the team.'

Unfortunately for the cricket, the organisers' eye for hospitality detail was not matched on the field. The Australians understandably focused on conditioning rather than results in the early tour matches, losing and drawing three apiece in their first eight before victories over strong Western Province and Natal sides in mid-December as the 'Tests' approached. But their preparations were repeatedly undermined by quite astonishingly incompetent contributions from the scorers and umpires.

After day one of the opening tour match against OFS at the Ramblers Club, journalists spent almost two hours at the close with the official scorebooks trying to reach a coherent set of figures for the Australians' innings.[21] For the second game with Northern Transvaal, one scorer had the home team totalling 209, the other 212; they eventually settled on 211.

If erratic scoring might be hushed up then there was no such hope for the umpiring, the low standard of which had blighted the rebel tours since Geoffrey Boycott's on-field confrontations in 1982. Officiating in the Australians' first two matches at Bloemfontein and Pretoria was charitably described as inconsistent and by the third outing it could no longer be ignored. Despite a comfortable five-wicket win over a South African President's XI at Berea Park, the tourists were aggrieved by the dismissals of three front-line batsmen. Steve Smith, Mike Haysman and Mick Taylor felt triggered by suggestible umpires who reacted quickly to the enthusiasm of the home side rather than the merits of the appeal. Hughes arranged discussions with SACU to clear up the issue.

This simmering unrest came to a head in the sixth tour match, a day/night affair against Eastern Province at St George's Park on 11 December. Despite one or two questionable dismissals the Australians had made 222-7 from their 50 overs. In response the home side had started slowly but a late flurry of boundaries brought them back into it: 11 runs were needed from the final over and then a six from Smith's final delivery. The batsman on strike, Kenny Watson, stepped back for a big swing only to see the ball pass between his pads and the stumps, and umpire Sandy Matthews blithely signalled a wide. When the furious Australian players recovered the power of speech they explained the laws of the game to Matthews, who conceded 'you're right', removed the bails and walked from the pitch without another word or signal.

Twenty minutes later it was announced that Matthews had retracted his call and awarded the Australian XI a five-run victory. Hughes, whose straight-talking to journalists had already earned a supposed press ban from tour manager Bruce Francis, immediately told reporters: 'I intend to take up the whole matter of umpiring once again with the South African Cricket Union. With these sorts of mistakes Matthews should not be umpiring senior cricket. Both captains met the umpires before the game and now we are looking bad for querying his decision.'

It was probably just as well that Hughes remained oblivious to a further controversy among organisers: one scorer had the tourists' score at 217, which would have made the game a tie, and another at 220. The interjections of a radio scorer ensured that the 222-7 stood.[22]

After three weeks, the busy schedule had taken its toll on tourist bodies as well as tempers. Graham Yallop tore cartilage in his ribcage in the second match and would not be fully fit for the rest of the tour; before the internationals got under way Terry Alderman suffered a back injury that severely limited his participation throughout, while a regular stream of minor knocks hampered the tourists' search for rhythm. At Natal, in the final tour match before the 'internationals' started, Steve Smith and Rod McCurdy collected hamstring injuries that would rule them out of the first 'Test'.

Of more concern to many observers was the tour's underlying basic arithmetic. Educated cost estimates for two Australian tours suggested a total outlay of A$8.5million but the total sponsorship of the first tour's 'international' programme – National Panasonic ('Tests') and South African Yellow Pages ('ODIs') – was announced as amounting to less than A$1,000,000. With the West Indian excitement now lacking, ticket revenues were hardly likely to cover the shortfall. A week before the first 'Test' at Durban there was a break-in at Kingsmead with A$10,000 cash being stolen but 20,000 untraceable tickets left untouched.[23] The burglars evidently knew the market as sales remained very low throughout the build-up: SACU had taken less than five per cent of their estimated revenue in advance sales, including those for the first 'Test'. The SACB and anti-apartheid movement had long asked where the money for these tours was coming from, and in view of these figures only two possibilities remained. Either the tours were receiving unpublicised funding from elsewhere, or the Ramblers Club scorers were moonlighting in SACU's finance department.

The most compelling reason to relish an 'international' between South Africa and a visiting representative XI had arguably not changed since the inaugural one-day win over South African Breweries some four years earlier. Graeme Pollock, now 41 years old, had reversed a private decision to retire after the West Indian tours once he heard of the imminent Australian visit. There was still no doubting the veteran's potency – he had just become the fifth South African to reach 20,000 runs despite rarely playing outside the republic since 1970[24] – but his inclusion did point to a concern for the Springboks: a batting line-up virtually unchanged since being derided as 'golden oldies' three years earlier.

The great left-hander had first encountered Kim Hughes' Australians in a day/night match for Transvaal on 4 December. The 'Mean Machine' was now in full swing, halfway through a run of five Currie Cup titles in six seasons, and had inflicted a 58-run defeat at Wanderers, the heaviest of the tour to date by a comfortable margin. Inevitably, Pollock had made a muscular contribution – an unbeaten 59 from 46 balls – and the only question mark around the veteran was his increasing reliance on boundaries. Was this on account of a slowing pace between the wickets, a weak hamstring, or a corporate 'rands for runs' sponsorship that rewarded him for each four and six?

The South African selection panel, which earned vocal and pointed approval from the Australians for comprising four former Test players in Peter van der Merwe, Jackie McGlew, John Waite and now retired Mike Procter, had named an experienced line-up. Only 23-year-old right-arm seamer Hugh Page, another Transvaal player, had not earned Springbok colours in a previous rebel tour. Already deprived of Steve Smith, Rod McCurdy and Terry Alderman for the first 'Test', the Australians lost Graham Yallop shortly before play was to begin and Mick Taylor stepped into his middle-order shoes. With Peter Faulkner the only member of the party available and not playing, the tourists fielded a team of contrasting experience, 166 Test caps between them but 138 of these shared among John Dyson, Kim Hughes and Rodney Hogg. Four Australians – Greg Shipperd,

Mike Haysman, Mick Taylor and Trevor Hohns – were considered in South Africa at least to be earning first Test caps, but no amount of SACU spin would make them baggy green.

The crowd at Durban was noticeably poor after a boycott by the SACB, and particularly the local Indian community, hit the gate takings. Attendance apart, the most notable thing about day one, an even-handed contest that left the Springboks on 179-4, was the finish 15 minutes after tea due to bad light; it was lost time that a four-day 'Test' could hardly afford. And on day two, during which Pollock registered a 62nd first-class century in a first-innings total of 393, Australia were cut short on 72-2 with more than an hour's play still scheduled.

At the halfway stage, the match appeared destined for a draw but on the third morning a regular procession of Australian wickets had SACU worried the game might finish early meaning revenue would be lost. Mick Taylor, an uncapped 30-year-old Victorian included only after others had dropped out in April, was the last recognised batsman at 185-6, still 58 short of avoiding the follow-on. But he and Tom Hogan put on 79 in scarcely an hour before Taylor fell for 109, the match killed stone dead. Hogan ended on 53 from 68 balls as the close came at 334-8 shortly after 4 p.m.

The third-day Saturday crowd of 4,800 was a huge disappointment, down 20 per cent even on the two previous days, but perhaps understandable given the fare on offer. Making a convincing case for viewing the matches as Tests was hard enough without them being reduced to four two-session days.

Under pressure to produce some entertainment, the Springboks briefly lost their heads on the final morning. The Australians had been all out for 359 after 38 minutes and Hughes turned to Hogg and Rackemann, five wickets apiece in the first innings, to renew acquaintances with the Kingsmead surface. First blood was drawn by Hogg, removing Cook and Kirsten in single figures; shortly afterwards Rackemann claimed Pollock, Ken McEwan and Rice so that at lunch South Africa were 37-5 with only Henry Fotheringham, who had sustained bruised ligaments in his hand in the first innings, left among the recognised batsmen. Facing a first-innings deficit of just 34, the Australians suddenly had South Africa on the rack, but to widespread bewilderment Hughes recalled Hogan and Maguire after the lunch break, allowing Fotheringham and Jennings to guide the hosts to safety. Hogg, who had professed his readiness to bowl all day, was recalled with the scoreboard reading 174-5 and though Fotheringham deserved credit for his courage the home side had been let off the hook in no uncertain fashion. Once the opener had reached his century, a gutsy effort good enough to beat Pollock and Taylor to the batting prize, Rice declared and Australia eked out a pointless 32-2 before the match was drawn.

For the Springboks it was another welcome experience, as Jimmy Cook explains: 'Some of the guys had played against Australia but I certainly hadn't, and it was just good to play guys from different countries and say, "I played Sri Lanka, I played England, I played the West Indies, I played Australia", so it was just a new challenge to say, "Gee, let's see how we can do against these guys." It was a shame that they were only four-day Tests.'

'Test' sponsor Panasonic's influence was evident after the game as the presentation ceremony was delayed for 45 minutes to coincide with the national news, Hogg and Rackemann sharing the bowling prize but doubtless wondering what might have been. There was predictably no prize for Hughes after his bewildering final-day tactics but he was consoled with a nomination from back home: the public had voted him onto the shortlist for

Australian of the Year, highlighting the public support for the tourists.

Keeping the sponsors happy was more important than ever after a total attendance over four days of 18,856, a world away from the 30,000 previously cited by Natal Cricket Association as the break-even point. The NCA bemoaned a boycott by Indian communities and the SACB as pivotal: the attendance from these groups alone over four days had been estimated at 20,000 but had hardly broken four figures.

SACU were faced with a conundrum The cricket had initially looked shaky – Bacher had hailed Taylor as a saviour who had SACU 'laughing all the way to the bank' when he rescued the tourists from a possible follow-on – but ultimately had been prevented from realising its potential. The spectacle had been spoiled by only five and a half hours' play per day on average over four days. There was a clear argument, then, for extending the 'Tests' to five-day affairs but, after four loss-making days in Kingsmead, this would incur an even greater financial liability if public interest did not urgently rise. There was also a worry that the Australians were already operating at something near full throttle, which might make any future fifth day obsolete. Not for the first time, SACU decided to gamble: 24 hours after fearing that the first 'Test' would not last four days, Bacher announced that the third 'Test' at Johannesburg would now go the full international distance.

Two days later, the teams met at Newlands on 1 January, 1986. As in Durban the strong home batting line-up justified Clive Rice's confidence at the toss, despite losing Henry Fotheringham to a fine catch by Steve Rixon off the bowling of Carl Rackemann. Jimmy Cook and Peter Kirsten put on 132 either side of lunch before the opener became fit-again Rod McCurdy's first scalp of the series on 91. And his departure prompted the arrival of Graeme Pollock, who made 76 in partnership with Kirsten (72) and Rice (21). It was a demanding day for both sides as South Africa's batsmen negotiated a slow pitch requiring patience, and Australia's bowlers ran hard for limited rewards. The home side were on top in closing on 293-5 and the next morning their tail wagged. Garth Le Roux, Stephen Jefferies and Hugh Page contribed 100 runs between them to carry the home side to 430 all out by the middle of day two.

In the four-day format this immediately placed South Africa in an inviolable position and, with the weakness in Australian batting, set up a straightforward siege for the remainder of the match. Stephen Jefferies bowled both Greg Shipperd and the struggling Mike Haysman off inside edges but the greater experience of John Dyson and Kim Hughes, evident in a methodical stand of 105, ended in the final over of the day when Peter Kirsten captured the wicket of the captain.

The third morning in Cape Town posed multiple embarrassments for the tourists. The previous evening their hotel had been vandalised with the legend 'The Au$$ies play for blood money' and on their return to Newlands the stadium announcer was enjoying himself reporting news from the third Test at the SCG: 'The other Australia team – the B team – have taken four wickets in Sydney against India, who have scored 600 runs.'[25]

This news may have pleased the South African public, who continued to fret over the comparative strength of the official and unofficial Australian XIs, but was an outright insult to the visiting players who considered themselves both patriots and colleagues of Allan Border. One visiting player was prevented from entering the announcer's box to bring a forceful end to the pantomime, but the message obviously got through as there was no repeat.

On the field, they continued to struggle for confidence. They had Dyson (95) to thank for building a respectable response and the muscular Tom Hogan (28) for avoiding the follow-on, Le Roux completing his four-wicket rout of the tail only after the tourists had passed 300. In reply Cook and Fotheringham put on 86 for the first wicket before the latter fell to Rackemann in the bowler's 13th consecutive over, the 25-year-old now indisputably Hughes' most dangerous bowler. He and McCurdy were able to pin the hosts back to 138-3 at the close but South Africa went into the final day in a position of dominance, 264 ahead with seven wickets in hand.

They suffered a setback when Cook fell to Rackemann having added only five runs to his overnight 65. The Springboks promoted the hard-hitting Le Roux to buy some quick runs and were rewarded with 15 from 11 balls before he holed out to Haysman at long off, Rackemann's sixteenth victim in two 'Tests'.

McKenzie then joined his captain Rice and turned the tables on the bowler, hitting two towering sixes down the ground to help the score to 202-5. Rice declared, setting Australia 329 in five and a half hours. When Shipperd and the influential Dyson were removed with only 54 on the board, Hughes and his partner Haysman took no chances in their afternoon progress. With 20 overs to go, the Australians required a further 131 to win with Hughes and Yallop at the wicket on a good pitch in fine light. They batted for a draw, the captain ending unbeaten on 97 and heading to the pavilion without apparent thought at the first opportunity. Ivo Tennant wrote in the *The Times*: 'Not only was it a sad end to an otherwise interesting match, but we were also given an indication of how the Australians view this series. Hughes, having ensured the match would be drawn, turned tail and headed to the pavilion with five of the 20 overs left ... The anomaly was that Hughes had 97 runs to his name. There has been talk here of whether these are Test matches proper. Hughes, by his action, gave his verdict. He would never have rejected a Test century.'[26]

Public interest had fallen off sharply after the West Indian tour: the official match attendance totted up to 31,563 as against a projected 48,000 and break-even 40,000. The first day had attracted 12,000, aided by the New Year bank holiday, but dropped as it became quickly apparent that another draw was in the offing. A five-day rubber, at the result venue the Wanderers, was the last hope to salvage a moribund 'Test' series.

Despite the low-key start, spirits at SACU remained high. A new rebel tour always shook things up and with a five-day 'Test' followed by six 'one-day internationals', the format that most excited the public, there were reasons to be cheerful. As such it was almost inevitable that the golden rule of the rebel tours would reassert itself: just when on-field matters had begun to attract serious consideration, off-field distractions returned to the fore. The South African newspaper *Business Day* reported an interview with Ali Bacher in which the SACU chief had claimed: 'Gate money, advertising, sponsorships and a deal over television rights are our main source of revenue, and we're looking to a R3million profit when it's all over.'

This was news to those who had seen only one change to the early tour arithmetic – gate receipts persistently below pre-tour expectations – and was quickly retracted as SACU insisted the reporter had obviously misunderstood. The mystery over revenue streams deepened when SACU continued to announce inconsistent and highly bullish estimates on ticket sales for the final 'Test' at Johannesburg. It promised to be a spectacle, or at least Bacher promised it: 'We expect to get 70,000 in total for what should be five days of great cricket. We will match the 72,000 who turned up for the corresponding match two years ago against the West Indies. This fixture has caught the public's imagination in a big way.'[27]

Another concern for Bacher was that the tourists' injury problems had become an epidemic with only six fully fit players left in the squad. In addition to the accumulated bruises and strains, Peter Faulkner and Tom Hogan had flu while Carl Rackemann was suffering from a bronchial infection. Concern for Kim Hughes' star bowler was such that SACU immediately called in a leading specialist to nurse the seamer back to health. A combination of antibiotics and South African pleading worked as he took the field in a team with three changes from the previous 'Test': out-of-form Haysman was replaced by Steve Smith; Faulkner came in for Hogan; and the finally fit Terry Alderman took over from Rod McCurdy, who had strained a hamstring. The home side sprang a surprise with one change: Stephen Jefferies dropping out of the XI and Corrie van Zyl collecting his first Springbok cap.

Hughes won the toss under cloud cover and put the opposition in at the high-altitude home of South African fast bowling. Hogg and Alderman gave ample evidence that the decision had been the right one, troubling Jimmy Cook and Henry Fotheringham from the first ball with movement through the air. Cook (5) was yorked by Hogg, who promptly suffered a recurrence of his hamstring strain to deepen Hughes' problems though there was no immediate concern with Rackemann coming into the attack. After Alderman had collected a first 'international' wicket of the tour by trapping Fotheringham lbw, his new partner delivered a devastating day of quick bowling, claiming six wickets across four spells, working over the South African batsmen, noticeably so Rice whom he had caught for a torrid nine. Only the aggressive leg-side play of McKenzie (72) topped the 19 apiece scored by Fotheringham and Pollock as the home side closed on 184-8, but they could hardly be written off against a team with only two bowlers left on the pitch. Hogg was barely able to walk while Alderman had left the field with a hip injury. Following a twisted knee for Yallop in the field, the Australians had three substitute fielders in the evening session, and only Faulkner to support Rackemann with the ball.

The large, inelegant and previously much-maligned Queensland farmer hardly needed assistance. He took the final two wickets in the first hour the next morning, each caught at the wicket by Steve Rixon to bring the 'keeper's tally to six and the bowler's to eight in a meagre-looking 211 all out. The Australians' reply was stilted by the early loss of John Dyson but after lunch they reaped 110 runs without loss in a partnership of contrasts: the exuberant Smith enjoyed his tea on 116 not out after thrashing the out-of-form Kourie while Greg Shipperd batted as if wary of disturbing the scorers. At 159-1 the tourists were in a position of supreme strength but the second ball after tea Pollock dived full from second slip to remove Smith and give van Zyl a first Springbok wicket. The debutant pinned Hughes leg-before with his next delivery and though Taylor survived the hat-trick ball the course of the 'Test' had changed. Shipperd took intransigence to new heights – he took 11 overs to move from 37 to 38 – but could find no worthy partner as first Taylor (21) and Yallop, for 20 from the final ball of the day, sent the batting side in for the night on 214-5.

Belatedly, the series came to life. When Shipperd succumbed to his 311th ball the following morning for 44, the Australian tail was again caught short with Faulkner's contribution of 25 the only innings of consequence. Rackemann (8) at least provided the Tasmanian with support, batting for an hour under heavy fire as Rice wrought revenge for his day one humiliation. To the few fair-minded neutrals present this was an unworthy sight to a limited batsman but the South African captain was typically lacking in contrition afterwards, telling reporters: 'Any batsman is a good target whether he is experienced or otherwise. I gave Carl two useful deliveries and I was certainly not concerned when he fell to the ground. In fact, I was counting him out.' He had the backing of his home crowd, who were being treated to a finely balanced and competitive game and Kim Hughes, who said: 'It's not a bloody Sunday afternoon picnic. We bowl bouncers at their tailenders.'[28]

Jimmy Cook recalls: 'They were very competitive, their bowlers. They had Alderman, Hogg and Rackemann, and they were aggressive. But they were so bad with the bat that we used to give them a hell of a time. When they came in we used to have a full go at them: "Aah, you've got such a big bloody mouth when you're bowling, look at you now – you're bloody scared and you're running away." They were absolutely petrified of Ricey.'

Garth Le Roux adds: 'Cricket in that era was played like that by South Africans and Australians – and even the English guys. Sylvester Clarke wasn't a talker; he was just aggressive by what he did, whereas the Aussie guys were talkers. If they say something to you, you say something back. We played our domestic cricket like that as well. There weren't any cameras lip-reading you in those days. It was aggressive and it was verbal. Ricey was an aggressive type of cricketer, and we used to say things to people. It stayed on the park and then we had a beer afterwards. No problems.'

The tourists would carry a 56-run lead into the second innings but that represented at best a missed opportunity and perhaps an insufficient effort: Hogg had limped out to the middle with a runner at number 11, was bowled first ball by Rice and would not be fit to bowl in the Springbok reply. Despite his limited resources, Hughes saw off both openers before the arrears had been erased, Rackemann and Alderman removing Fotheringham and Cook respectively. When Faulkner's innocuous medium pace claimed its first scalp, Peter Kirsten for ten, to leave the score on 80-3, the tourists were back on top. But Pollock had rediscovered his early series form in hitting 51 at almost a run a ball. Michael Haysman later said, 'I have just never fielded before to a batsman who hits the ball so well and so accurately. It was, in many ways, an honour to be out there.'[29]

Rackemann in the end brought an end to the innings, but only by breaking the left-hander's finger to see him retire hurt. The on-field drama was compounded at tea when Rackemann fell to the dressing room floor, hyperventilating, due to fatigue after bowling almost non-stop throughout the session at altitude. With only Alderman, not fully fit, and Faulkner, not fully competitive, to bowl Rice and McKenzie navigated the evening session untroubled for almost 100 runs and an end-of-day total of 192-3. The Springboks were back in charge.

A Sunday rest day was the least the tourists deserved as they sought to fight their way back into the match from such a disadvantageous position but on Monday morning, when all eyes ought to have been trained on the climax to an absorbing 'Test', the golden rule struck again.

'An Act of Contempt' and 'Taxpayers hit for six!' trumpeted the *Business Day* newspaper in answering many questions and confirming many more suspicions on the fourth morning of the third 'Test'.[30] The South African Government, it was reported, were granting 90 per cent tax rebates to the tour's major sponsors in a measure that had not passed Parliament but was instead described as 'an executive decision taken at Cabinet level.' The high commercial exposure enjoyed by Panasonic and Yellow Pages had come not, as advertised, in return for bankrolling the tour; SACU had made representations to reinstate an old tax break scheme due to the 'unique problems faced by sporting bodies'.

It was a damning if not altogether surprising revelation. 'We couldn't get involved in a direct way,' one government source had told *Business Day*, 'because the credibility of the tour would suffer and companies would face the risk of boycott. Direct government funding would have been the kiss of death for the tour.'

However, this secrecy bore little relation to commercial caution. The legitimacy of the tours, dating back to the English rebels' angry dismissal of any political relevance, had been rooted in their commercial status. Tourists had been 'just playing cricket' and exercising their freedom to trade; they had explicitly claimed to be keeping politics out of sport – and with all the benefits this brings. For their part SACU had been unambiguous when asked about the source of funding: South African business, since there was no place for politics in cricket, the republic's progressive sporting beacon.

The irrefutable proof that SACU and their sponsors had instead funded the tours with covert National Party support invited savage criticism. Like most Australian newspapers, the *Sydney Morning Herald* carried the story on its front page the following day under the headline 'Pretoria paying rebels' wages' – and accompanied by a cartoon of two Australian cricketers marching out to bat as the stadium announcer says, 'Brought to you by the same people who gave you the Sharpeville massacre.'[31]

Gone was the pretence of sport separated from politics, of SACU working independently towards multi-racial sport. SACU had previously rejected direct government funding for the second West Indian tour but instead availed themselves of a tax break that amounted to the same thing – all tours, in fact, had been funded the same way in one form or another.[32] The 'moral obligation' trumpeted by Yellow Pages in sponsoring the series also looked rather forlorn at ten per cent of the advertised price.

Asif Iqbal had written scathingly of the English rebel tour in 1982: 'It is the height of hypocrisy to condemn apartheid [with whatever degree of sincerity], but to have no qualms about fraternising with those who perpetrate it.'[33] That analysis had been debatable – although they had enjoyed the luxury South African experience, the rebels had not fraternised with the National Party; Ali Bacher, SACU and South African cricketers were not perpetrating apartheid, indeed they considered themselves to be actively opposing it. Now the hypocrisy was more clear-cut.

To the staunchest defenders of the tour, even this revelation did not warrant condemnation. Bruce Francis later wrote that it was impossible 'to cite a single instance of the South African Government having made political, pro-apartheid propaganda from the tour.'[34] For the anti-apartheid movement and SACB, the association was propaganda: the tours did not need to promote South Africa explicitly; by their very existence they provided a veneer of normality to the regime.

Even sceptics of that position would have to agree that when such a regime is paying for something, it is sensible to question its motive – and even more so when done in secret. For the historian Andre Odendaal, that motive was clear enough: 'The rebel tours were really a foreign policy coup for an embattled regime in the 1980s. And the fact that they were paid for with taxpayers' money shows really how closely tied up they were to the project of trying to buy time for apartheid for it to go in a new direction.'[35]

While international reaction was largely 'told you so' scornful, the revelation caused great anger in the republic. Hidden use of public funds was a genuine scandal, a blatant example of bypassing democratic process – such as it was in South Africa – for political capital. The government was in secret funding favoured international projects at twice the rebate offered to local sporting events. *Business Day* castigated 'a prime example of the arrogance of the National Party' that showed 'contempt towards taxpayers ... contempt towards Parliament [with] concessions handed out on the whim of a politician based on his interpretation of the national interest ... It is all evidence of a government that no longer governs for the people, but for its own ends.' Progressive Federal Party spokesman Brian Goodall condemned the action as an indication of 'the contempt with which the National Party treats Parliament.' And Costa Divaris, a quoted tax expert, described himself as 'flabbergasted' at their political gall.

The scandal was compounded when SACU president Geoff Dakin sought to calm the storm in a sympathetic interview with John Tingle on the Sydney radio station 2GB. Under benign questioning he refuted the claim that SACU was having trouble finding financial sponsorship: 'Well that's nonsense because the total budget for the tours is over R9.5 million, of which, at a maximum, the sponsors are putting up R4 million. We are still left to find R5.5 million from other areas such as the gates, television rights, advertising and so on.'

In seeking to destroy claims that the government was fully funding the tour he had admitted first that the government was paying for almost half of it and secondly that much of the other half remained uncosted: R5.5 million to find with a R1.7 million television deal and no gate receipts to shout about left a minimal shortfall of R3 million over both tours. The tours to 'save South

African cricket' were bought and paid for by apartheid.[36] These were simply not questions that the white media was willing or able to face. From the beginning of the tours, they had ignored the financial incentives that had brought the cricketers to the republic and instead focused on their bravery in thumbing a nose to political humbug. Again their gaze returned unerringly to the Johannesburg 'Test', which promised a final two days of remarkable cricket theatre.

The fourth morning was very much a low-key set-up to the climax. Rackemann returned to the field after a Sunday of rest and fluids, but Hughes still had only a three-man attack to juggle. The tourists picked up five wickets before lunch as the Rackemann/Rixon partnership claimed their eighth and ninth victims in Rice (50) and Le Roux (18), Alderman trapped the now hapless Kourie leg-before for a duck and Page (2), and Jennings was run out after a mix-up with the still motoring McKenzie (87 not out out of 273-8). The pendulum had swung back to the Australians: they had their opponents effectively 217-8 when the heavens opened, flooding the Wanderers outfield and ending the fourth day's play after one session for the 4,500 who had turned up.

The fifth and final day of the third 'Test' would prove perhaps the most unpredictable of any played across a decade of rebel tours. When Rixon caught van Zyl off Alderman in the second over of the day he equalled the record number of dismissals in official and unofficial Test matches but McKenzie, still 13 short of a first Springbok century, stood his ground: Pollock was re-emerging with a heavily bound right hand. McKenzie understandably let rip, pivoting to hit repeatedly through his favoured leg side to move quickly to 110 but even this was arguably eclipsed by his new partner. In only 13 balls Pollock added another 14 to his total, including two boundaries played with only one hand off Alderman. He would finish unbeaten on 65 as Rackemann collected his 28th wicket of the three-'Test' series when Alderman caught McKenzie at slip; an outstanding display of fast bowling that would later earn him the man-of-the-series and South African Cricketer of the Year awards.

And so the stage was perfectly set: 250 needed to win the match and the series, and plenty of time with play starting an hour and a quarter before lunch. After 36 minutes the home pacemen made their breakthrough, van Zyl drawing an edge behind from first-innings centurion Smith. Then, with half an hour still to go until lunch, came a most spectacular collapse. Le Roux clean bowled Shipperd with the fourth ball of his sixth over and Hughes, on a 'King pair' inside-edged the next delivery behind to Jennings. When the hat-trick ball, a vicious off-cutter, rapped Taylor on the pads, the raised umpire's finger went up as if powered by the intensity of 'bullring' appeals; the batsman could only return to the pavilion for television replays that confirmed a delivery heading down the leg-side.

Re-emerging after lunch at 34-4, Rice gave himself the second over and clean bowled vice-captain Yallop with his first ball. After finishing with two wickets in successive balls at the end of the first innings this represented a hat-trick for the skipper too. From 36-5, it was all over in under an hour. Rice and Page shared the final five wickets as Dyson looked on in horror from the other end; his unbeaten 18 was the lowest score by any player carrying his bat in South African first-class cricket as a total 61 all out gave the Springboks a 188-run victory.

A shell-shocked Hughes lamented: 'All of our hard work since mid-November was lost in two hours.'

The South African media were enraptured, celebrating an historic 'Test' victory underpinned with statistical landmarks and the first success over 'Australia' in 17 years. SACU had predicted an attendance of 72,000. Fewer than half that number turned up.

The first Australian tour would finish with a 'one-day international' series that contrasted markedly from the 'Tests'. For one thing, the tourists started winning matches and claimed a 2-0 lead in a Johannesburg day/nighter and at Durban. And better still they did so in front of healthy crowds: all six internationals played to near-capacity turnouts that aggregated more than 100,000. The febrile atmosphere and coloured clothing – the Springboks in dark green, Australians a Packer-aping canary yellow – all helped to lift the one-day spectacles and SACU were rewarded with a genuinely competitive series.

Inspired by Clive Rice, who put his poor 'Test' form behind him to dominate, the Springboks levelled 2-2 after wins in Port Elizabeth and Cape Town ahead of a return to Wanderers. After the disappointment of defeat at Newlands, Kim Hughes had launched an extraordinary attack on his vice-captain for lacking the commitment to play through injury and Graham Yallop was therefore recalled in the frostiest of atmospheres for the Johannesburg showdown. When the game did get under way the disaffection with umpiring crossed the line into mutiny.

Previous complaints about the standard of officiating had remained essentially polite: mistakes were put down to inexperience and failure to deal with pressure rather than any active impropriety. That changed in the fifth 'ODI' when Springbok debutant Anton Ferreira took three wickets with no-balls; an analysis by TV commentators identified an extraordinary 31 no-balls in a ten-over spell of which only two were called. These were not punished with an extra delivery, meaning that

Ferreira bowled 58 balls, of which 27 were legitimate, in his ten-over spell.

Faced with a third consecutive defeat that put a series victory out of reach, Hughes vented his anger in the post-match press conference: 'Am I playing primary school cricket or international cricket? Surely to goodness they can count to six.'[37]

Somehow this amateur hour seemed to toll the bell for the Australians' competitive instincts. For a tour match at Griqualand West the injury-decimated tourists called up 44-year-old former Test bowler Garth McKenzie in a heavy defeat and the final 'international', another loss for Hughes' side, was blighted by another row over umpiring – one scorer counted it as the 50th decision to go against the Australians on the tour.

A tour inside the South African bubble had by now a long history of entrenching a siege mentality. Even allowing for the message he was sending to the ACB, Kim Hughes was in particularly bullish form at his final press conference of the tour: 'It's been the happiest cricket tour I've ever been on. The politics of my life have now been taken out of my cricket. This has been as normal a tour as I have been on. There were no disturbances, unlike my other tours. Usually, in the West Indies, India and Pakistan, we can expect at least one riot. But here in South Africa it has been quite peaceful. I am more convinced now that we made the right decision than I was when we first came.'[38]

It was quite extraordinary to claim that politics had been taken out of cricket a few weeks after learning that the South African government had been footing the bill. More than that, though, the Australian captain's views echoed the 'three wise monkeys' approach of the English rebels. Where many among the West Indians had understood that their visit had an impact, and viewed that impact as positive, only Bruce Francis among the Australian party was interested even in the arguments in favour of the tour. Having spent more than three months in a country engulfed by civil disorder, Hughes was comfortable with the peacefulness he and his colleagues had enjoyed.

The tourists' disinterest was summed up during a brief break between the first and second 'Tests', when they were given a choice between visiting Sun City and Soweto. After previous brief trips to the townships for painfully stage-managed press conferences, the casino option won by a landslide.

For SACU, the tour had been a qualified success. Chris Harte, the only Australian journalist to cover both tours in their entirety, assessed the cricket in positive fashion: 'A victory by Kim Hughes' team would have let the official Australian side's Test against India pale into insignificance. As both matches were being played concurrently, it was interesting to note the unexpectedly high exposure given to the Durban match. The game was drawn after four days of play, interrupted by rain and bad light. Australians wanted to know more of what had gone on. Suddenly our sports editors doubled our newspaper space, wanted features on all and sundry, and became interested in how the allegedly mighty Springboks had been held by the second string Hughes mob ... Anyone who had witnessed Test cricket being debased, as it surely has been in recent years, by the glut of boring, dull and nauseating India, Pakistan and Sri Lanka draws, would have classed this as a genuine Test of the highest caliber.'[39]

This was a generous analysis. Certainly the Australians had borne no comparison to the West Indian tourists, and they were a team some way beneath international standard. The similarities were obvious – fine fast bowling, sub-standard batting – but Hughes' side had lacked the extraordinary penetration and tail-end defiance that had equipped Lawrence Rowe's teams for victories. In addition their captain had struggled to impose himself as a tactician and batsman – and when he had the chance of a century, he passed on it.

Garth Le Roux recalls, 'They struggled. Like every team that comes here you need your top order to be heavy scorers to be a combative force. Although they had some very good seam bowlers, for any team to do well it obviously needs to bowl teams out but it also needs to score. You need one or two guys scoring heavily, and I don't think Hughes ever got going and he was meant to be their best batsman.'

Greg Shipperd adds, 'It was an outstanding South African team – experienced, very well balanced and when they had gaps the replacements were hungry and showed great potential. Some of us were playing our first games at that level in foreign conditions and there was quite a bit of rotation to give people opportunities. Probably we needed another season or two at that level and greater continuity in the team.'

The Australians had enjoyed greater opportunity to prepare than any previous visiting rebels and Shipperd believes that his side gave their best competitive effort. But other observers criticised the application from certain squad members, and the team as a whole for failing to put an ageing Springbok team under serious pressure. Instead of improved preparation, the lengthy schedule had given rise to cliques and unrest in the camp as the leadership of both Hughes and Francis had met with opposition.

Despite ebullient assessments equating unofficial visitors with official national teams, the claims to Test status were a pretence – and the facade was underscored by the tax revelations. The lower calibre of the matches had obviously translated into lower attendances for the

'Tests', though this was also a reflection of changing tastes in South African cricket. One-day matches were now the preferred format, and that six-match series had been a riotous sell-out. The tension between old and new South African cricket was clear in the sponsorship and clothing, and the win-at-all costs approach of a newly aggressive Springbok team under Clive Rice. It was noticeable, too, in the growing gulf between still-amateur umpires and professional players. South African cricket was ready to change but the world was not ready to let it.

1 In the two previous World Cups India had managed only one win – and that against the minnows of East Africa. Despite an ODI win in the Caribbean shortly before the World Cup India began the 1983 tournament as 66-1 shots – in what was, at most, a six-horse race.
2 Ayaz Memon, Cricinfo, 24 June 2008. htto://content.cricino.com/magazine/content/story/355915.html.
3 p 139, Bose (1994). The reluctance of Indian cricketers to engage in unofficial cricket had previously been shown by their total absence from World Series Cricket.
4 p 170, Lillee (1984). Bob Willis, who became England captain after the 1982 rebel tour, adds, 'We had a pretty ropey team. Fifteen players were unavailable; that was the bottom line. We played above ourselves to beat India 1-0 and Pakistan 2-0 at home, and got to the World Cup semi-final which was a good performance with the players we had. But on the two overseas tours we were totally outplayed.'
5 Francis (1989). The Australian moral position was particularly awkward due to their domestic treatment of the Aborigines: in crude terms Australia (who had never fielded an acknowledged Aborigine in Test cricket) were closer than other cricket nations to South Africa in racial integration, although clearly the parallel was partial at best.
6 p 196, Hartman (2004).
7 The six were Yallop, Wessels, Rodney Hogg, David Hookes, Jeff Thomson and Graeme Wood. Only Yallop and Hogg would travel on the first tour.
8 p 652, Harte with Whimpress (2003).

9 The Hughes family had begun looking at rental properties in southern England for the duration of the tour, so confident were they of Kim's inclusion.
10 Front, *Adelaide Advertiser*, 13 April 1985. The 13 were: Terry Alderman, Murray Bennett, John Dyson, Rodney Hogg, John Maguire, Rod McCurdy, Wayne Phillips, Carl Rackemann, Steve Rixon, Dirk Welham, Kepler Wessels, Graeme Wood and Graham Yallop. The full story of the Australian rebel tour recruitment is detailed in Harte & Hadfield (1985).
11 Phillips, Welham and Wood were courted for a return by Packer; Bennett reverted with them. Kepler Wessels also withdrew because, as a South African who had changed allegiance to Australia and recently received a top-tier ACB contract, his position was particularly sensitive.
12 *The Australian*, 19 November 1985.
13 p 265, Ryan (2009).
14 Pay for all players was constant after the West Indian mutiny amidst pay differentials. The average Sheffield Shield wage at the time was c. A$12,000.
15 pp 262–3, Ryan (2009). According to Ryan, fast bowler Mike Whitney was the only Australian to turn down SACU on moral grounds.
16 p 271, Ryan (2009).
17 p 68, Harte and Hadfield (1985).
18 p 202, Hartman (2004).
19 pp 22–3, Harte (1988).
20 p 41, Harte (1988).
21 p 31, Harte (1988).
22 p 55, Harte (1988).
23 p 17, *The Australian*, 20 December 1985.
24 Pollock joined Procter, McEwan, Rice and Richards, and at a significantly higher average than all but the last.
25 p 78, Harte (1988).
26 p 28, *The Times*, 6 January 1986.
27 p 87, Harte (1988).
28 p 25, *The Age*, 20 January 1986.
29 p 90, Harte (1988).
30 Front, *Business Day*, 20 January 1986.
31 Front, *Sydney Morning Herald*, 21 January 1986.
32 pp 184–5, Hartman (2004) details the unilateral investment offer from foreign minister Pik Botha. The Income Tax Act formalising the arrangements was brought in after the *Business Day* scandal but the previous informal arrangement had

funded the English, Sri Lankan and West Indian rebel tours too. pp 133–4, Bose (1994) and p 147, Booth (1998).

33 p 250, Rae (2001).

34 p 278, Francis (1989). Francis was writing of criticism by former Australia captain Ian Chappell, criticism made before the *Business Day* scoop. However, he was writing after the revelations and, oddly, still described the idea of Government funding as a 'canard'.

35 *Out of the Wilderness: Part II*, British Sky Broadcasting, first broadcast 19 July 2008.

36 p 97, Harte (1988).

37 p 116, Harte (1988).

38 p 125, Harte (1988).

39 p 25, *Sunday Times* (SA), 26 January 1986.

## Chapter 8

# End of the Road

*'These days the players are only interested in getting what they can out of cricket.'* – Ossie Schoof

By the end of the first Australian rebel tour the controversy surrounding such ventures had dimmed. After five tours there was no novelty or outrage and the source of the funding was now a matter of public record. With the republic entering and re-entering states of emergency and dire economic conditions hitting the poorest hardest, it was clear that the republic was heading towards an end game in which cricketers would not be playing a front-line role.

The Australian players had been banned for two years from domestic cricket and three years from internationals, which back-dated to 1985 with a second tour in the offing effectively meant a one-year ban from the official side on their return. The one exception was the Western Australia Cricket Association, which sought an indefinite ban for its rebels, including Kim Hughes, and during the winter the former Australia captain launched a legal challenge against his one-time employers.

In a court case costing hundreds of thousands of Australian dollars to either side, the judge upheld the domestic and international suspensions while over-turning the prospect of an indefinite ban – and awarding Hughes A$250 compensation. Leaping on any justification however minor, the South African press trumpeted the verdict as a notable victory.

On their return home in February 1986, the rebels were invited widely to speak at clubs and events to discuss their experiences as an intrigued public wanted to know exactly what had gone on behind the initial media and government furore. But by the time of their return to South Africa eight months later, the cricket public's attention had been drawn solely to the impending Ashes series with Mike Gatting's England. As ever, South Africa cast a shadow of sorts as the number of unavailable Australians had increased to 17. Kepler Wessels, or 'South African-born Kepler Wessels', as he was perennially known after eight years in Australia, had joined the party. At the end of the 1985–86 season he had captained losing Sheffield Shield finalists Queensland at Sydney, throwing his boots at the feet of the attendant Australian Cricket Board chairman at the close.

Wessels had recently seen his ACB contract downgraded from the highest to lowest rung of seniority and, like Hughes, was uncompromising in his view on where the blame for Australian cricket's malaise lay: amateur administrators without an international cap between them. After a four-year Test career he had earned 24 caps, scoring four centuries for an average of 42.95 at a time when the Australian side was engaged in a permanent struggle for respectability. Yet he had never achieved acceptance, feeling singular criticism for his background in both domestic and international cricket. It was time to go home.

If acceptance was the goal then there would be no quick fix. Wessels and Graham Yallop had been the first Australian internationals to speak with Ali Bacher back in 1983. Although Wessels had not, as was later implied, actively recruited any of his team-mates he had been involved in talks with SACU within months of his Test debut and had been an obvious source of counsel for those weighing an offer. He had subsequently pulled out of the first trip, along with the four men re-signed by Kerry Packer, and played in the 1985 Ashes instead. It was a decision that caused great anger among 16 rebels bearing the brunt of public and political criticism and, a year on from keeping his name out of the controversy, most balked at the prospect of his belated admittance.

Nor was he South African cricket's favourite sporting son. The decision to leave the republic to further his own career was understood but not appreciated, and re-acceptance into the Springboks would not come easily. Certainly not if he had returned in 1985 on a A$100,000 rebel contract while playing Currie Cup cricket. 'The South African players would have gone ballistic when they heard what he was earning,' said Ali Bacher. 'If he had come on both tours, he would have had to play provincial cricket in between and earn even more money.'[1]

A year on Wessels was returning to the republic for good and, despite his unique popularity on either side, Bacher was keen to use his services. His debut Test century against England in 1982 had been front-page news in South Africa ahead of the series with Arosa Sri Lanka and it was clear that, in either Australian or Springbok colours, he would put money on the gate: here was one of South Africa's own who had played and succeeded in genuine international cricket.

Wessels was technically signed to the ACB until 1988 and SACU had to pay off their Australian counterparts to ensure his availability. Once they had done so, it was not clear which side he ought to play for. The Springboks had a settled, Transvaal-dominated top six and any replacement of Henry Fotheringham or Kevin McKenzie with a so-called 'deserter' would not be popular. For the

Australians, however, he was the man who had taken a lead in the rebel tour organisation only to revert to the safe haven of official Test cricket when the public scandal broke. In the end Bacher decided that Hughes' side needed him more after the disappointing first-tour showing by some batsmen, notably the talented Yallop.

'I've felt an Australian for the past eight years and won 24 Test caps for them,' said Wessels. 'It would be wrong for me to jump ships now. As I've competed with and against all the touring Australian players many times over the past few years, I know them much better than I know the Springboks. I'll feel very much at home with them. Anyway, I'm just happy to be involved and I'm very eager to contribute to the success of the tour.'

His new captain also put on a brave face, telling reporters, 'We're delighted to have Kepler on our side and it's going to be 17 men pulling towards one goal. The decision to accept him was unanimous.'

That was not quite true. Bacher had canvassed opinion among the Australian squad on Wessels' inclusion, whereupon 14 objected and two abstained. SACU pushed the deal through anyway: Wessels would play one final season under an Australian banner. An unnamed fast bowler told Chris Harte of *The Australian*, 'So that's how they vote in South Africa.'[2]

Faced with bans in Australia, competitive matches had been elusive for the tourists in their eight months outside the republic. Terry Alderman played county cricket, Peter Faulkner English league cricket and Carl Rackemann for Natal, but no-one else had played at all. They were helped in this regard by a lengthy schedule and by the time Kepler Wessels joined the tourists on 1 December everyone around the tour had been busy. The Australians had played two first-class and four one-day matches, winning half, and SACU had announced the full international schedule: following the success of last season's 'one-day internationals', a reflection of a growing appetite for the shorter game in the republic, there would be two one-day series: four day/night matches and a further four one-day games sandwiching four five-day 'Tests'. Yellow Pages and Panasonic confirmed their willingness to continue sponsoring the tours for almost R2 million apiece but professed ignorance of their tax status. With over R1.5 million each to save, it was a plea worthy of some scepticism.

The early weeks of the tour mirrored those a year previously: low-key visits to some of South African cricket's less famous outposts, a gentle chance to tune up for the serious work, and a spate of suspect umpiring calls that once again had Kim Hughes' nose twitching. Despite a busy schedule the Australians were noticeably more relaxed than on their previous visit, no doubt because they were no longer in unknown territory, but there were mutterings among the assembled press that familiarity was breeding contempt. Practices were few and far between, and tensions between Bruce Francis, Kim Hughes and the rank and file now quite well known.

Wessels was not expected to be a unifying figure, even after he had marked his arrival with a century first time out against Border. Immediately after that match, the Australians had no choice but to be ready as the day/night series had arrived; a four-match series under floodlights beginning at the new Centurion Park with fireworks planned during play. It was another attempt, of sorts, to have South African cricket mirror that in the outside world.

Hughes called correctly at the first of a dozen tosses with Clive Rice and elected to bat on a pitch about which no-one was certain. Steve Smith's mercurial back-foot hitting provided a run-a-ball 59 so that, despite opening partner John Dyson's cheap dismissal the tourists were in a strong position when their captain joined Wessels at the wicket shortly after 3.15 p.m. Within 20 minutes Hughes availed himself of the right to ask for the floodlights to be turned on – but no-one could find the only set of keys to the electrical cupboard. Espying an opportunity, Rice reintroduced his fastest bowler Corrie van Zyl, who delivered four overs for seven runs and bowled Hughes through the gate in the process. The captain traipsed off in half-darkness and total distress, and the Australians were five down by the time the floodlight operator had been recalled to duty from a car park *braai*.

After a rain delay Faulkner hit out to set a respectable 239 to win from 44 overs. The game was swinging the home side's way, 104-2 at the halfway point, when Graeme Pollock arrived at the crease shortly after 8 p.m. The fireworks began ten minutes after this, creating a cacophony of noise and smoke that brought the game to a halt with fieldsmen sat on the floor waiting for the fall-out to clear. When it had done so, Pollock rediscovered his rhythm more quickly than the bowlers, striking a quick-fire 62 with support from Ken McEwan and Rice as the home side eased to a six-wicket victory in just over 40 overs.[3]

It was not only traditionalist onlookers who were appalled by the Centurion Park spectacle. Hughes had pledged that his side would refuse to continue if there were a repeat of the floodlight and firework fiascos in the second match at Wanderers, and was true to his word. Batting first again under Johannesburg cloud cover, Smith and Dyson called for the floodlights to be turned on almost immediately and ended up sat on the pitch-side; the rain clouds were quicker off the mark than the stadium management, the heavens opened and the batsmen went to sit down inside. Although the Australians completed a full innings, South Africa batted for only four balls before more rain brought a cancellation – long enough, though, to lose Henry Fotheringham for the season with a calf tear.

Despite the problematic start, a third sell-out greeted the teams in Cape Town where the Australians now had to win in order to keep their series hopes alive. Hughes honoured the tradition of any captain given the choice at Newlands after winning the toss and elected to bat. The innings began at 2.20 p.m. and in under an hour the Australians were 15-7, Smith top-scorer back in the pavilion with four. On the plus side, there would be no floodlight problems. Garth Le Roux, who bowled his ten-over allocation off the reel for 6-21, recalls, 'It was just one of those days where the ball swung nicely. It wasn't particularly fast or aggressive but the ball just swung and they kept nicking it. It was quite bizarre. We bowled them out before the lights came on. People were still coming in and the game was over.'

A rearguard effort by Mick Taylor, aided by Rodney Hogg and Rod McCurdy, eventually eked the innings out beyond two hours but the target was still only 85, which the South Africans knocked off in an effortless 15 overs for the loss of only two wickets. Faced with 15,000 paying customers who had been promised international cricket and a firework show, but had seen neither, Ali Bacher and Bruce Francis were in a panic. Jimmy Cook wrote: 'As far as the players were concerned that was that and we were changing into our plain clothes. But then Ali Bacher rushed into our dressing room and said we had to play another game. We declined, reasoning that we had done our job. Then the sponsors came along and offered us more money if we would play a scratch 25-over-a-side game. Reluctantly, we did, and we won this too.'[4]

Those who had voiced concern over the Australian preparation saw themselves vindicated, while more generally the day/night series had been a commercial shock to a cricketing culture that continued to resist professionalism. Polychromatic uniforms, orange stumps, floodlights, temperamental fireworks, sponsorship parades at the fall of every wicket and the Springboks agreeing to entertain a capacity Newlands crowd only when R10,000 was put on the table: these were the ingredients of a new era. Australia won the final rubber of the series at Kingsmead in another sell-out, but not before Smith had reacted to an lbw decision by umpire Ossie Schoof with wild gesticulation and a few well-chosen words. It was another breach of the amateur cricketing code and it was to the benefit of all parties that the experimental series had reached its end – to be succeeded promptly by the reassuring sight of four five-day 'Test' matches, even if both sides would be bearing logos in a fashion that the ICC could not contemplate.

The first 'Test' began at Wanderers on Christmas Eve, a venue at which the Springboks had proved vulnerable against the West Indians and might have lost the first Australian series without that dismal final-day collapse. The strength of the tourists' pace attack for the occasion was evidenced by their luxury in omitting Terry Alderman. Instead they named Carl Rackemann, whose modest start to the second tour had been offset by his nomination as a South African cricketer of the year in the 1985–86 *South African Cricket Annual*. The Springboks lost Corrie van Zyl to a foot injury. Stephen Jefferies was therefore reunited with his Western Province partner Garth Le Roux in a team missing the injured Graeme Pollock. When the veteran was replaced by Brian McMillan the Springboks had a five-man pace attack plus Alan Kourie's left-arm slow and the occasional off-spin of Peter Kirsten to use at the bowler-friendly bullring.

The Wanderers pitch, never encouraging for batsmen or those hoping for a full, five-day contest, was predictably unkind once Hughes had won the toss and put the home side in. Rod McCurdy and Rackemann each extracted pace and bounce to keep Springbok wickets falling and, in the absence of Pollock, significant resistance never materialised.

The Australians had the South Africans on 66-4 during lunch and 154-7 at tea with Clive Rice the only man to pass 30. After a Christmas Day break on 221-9, the final wicket pairing, Le Roux and Jefferies, brought together at 210 the previous evening, extended their partnership to 44. It was a fine rescue mission, but looked insufficient until the Australian batsmen took their own turn on the green top. Jefferies made an immediate impact to remove John Dyson and, armed with a seven-man attack, Rice rotated his bowlers mercilessly to maintain the pressure. The captain, Hugh Page and Brian McMillan all applied themselves with vigour on their home ground to ensure a steady stream of returning batsmen and when rain brought an end to the day shortly after tea it was a blessing for the shell-shocked tourists who were 125-7.

On the third morning Rice sensed an opportunity to press home the advantage and in true 'Mean Machine' fashion renewed the previous season's bouncer barrage on Rackemann. It was a tactic that drew disapproving muttering from certain quarters but undeniable rewards as the tourists were bundled out for 142; having confidently expected a first-innings lead the Australians were 112 in arrears. When McCurdy removed Cook almost immediately after the restart it was apparent that the pitch needed no help from the umpires, but the afternoon session was marred by a dismal pair of decisions. John Maguire had already claimed two middle-order victims when he appealed quite impertinently for an lbw decision against opener Brian Whitfield. The batsman's disdain for the question was matched only by his shock at the answer, Ted Wood raising a finger.

At 103-5 the match was back in the balance, even more so when the enormous McMillan was given out as a lifter flicked the top of his pad. Once Maguire had also cleaned up the disgruntled-looking Kourie he had taken five wickets in a session and given his side an outside chance. Kevin McKenzie was 40 not out after tea when he too was hit on the pads by Maguire and umpire Wood obligingly commuted sentence. Once Rackemann had claimed three wickets in eight balls to end the innings, the Australians had been set an imposing but attainable 294 to win with two full days to play. It was a matter of opinion whether their greatest challenge was a multi-faceted Springbok attack, a deteriorating pitch or trigger-happy officiating.

The Australian attempt began brightly on day four when Steve Smith took advantage of a drop in the third over but Page was proving an exciting heir to Le Roux, bowling fast and straight without the due rewards. Meanwhile McMillan distinguished himself as a go-to bowler: thrown the ball when batsmen were set, he claimed the prized scalps of Smith (36) and Wessels (49) with the Australians still short of the halfway mark at 143-4. Nevertheless the tourists considered themselves well in the game when the umpires returned to centre stage.

Hughes was still at the crease and was joined by Mick Taylor, who began with two confident boundaries before Rice reintroduced himself to the attack. The Springbok captain delivered a leg-cutter across the right-handed Taylor, who calmly withdrew his bat and the fieldsmen, as both sides had grown into the habit of doing, began an appeal before quickly subsiding into silence. The ball had missed the bat by six inches to three feet depending on who you listened to, yet the bullring crowd was on its feet, and batsman and bowler competed for greater surprise at umpire Dudley Schoof's index finger. Hughes was now out of specialist partners, and lost Faulkner before tea and Steve Rixon shortly afterwards. Still he batted on, bringing his team to 200-7 – with a day still to play there was no rush for the final 94 – when South Africa took the second new ball. Page dug one in short, Hughes shouldered arms at the last second and the ball flicked the captain's pad before bouncing in front of first slip Kourie and being gathered by the diving Dave Richardson. Again the habitual half-appeal for a caught-behind had gone up and died; again umpire Schoof raised the finger.

Hughes was making his unsteady way to the pavilion when Rice, having conferred with Richardson and Kourie, made the unusual decision to call him back. Almost immediately Hughes nicked the ball behind to Richardson, wasn't given out and stood his ground. Despite the Springboks making their opinion on this turn of events quite clear, the captain was unmoved. He persevered doughtily but was betrayed by his side's lack of tail, losing five partners for a total contribution of 35.

Hughes finished with an unbeaten half-century and batted with typical élan to the very end; he was still dancing down the wicket to hit paceman Page through cover for four with the match all but lost. Almost immediately afterwards Rackemann was out for 12 to give South Africa a 49-run win and 1-0 lead in the series but the quality and excitement of the contest, spiced perhaps by the Taylor controversy, had descended into farce with the Hughes decisions. Rice, who was given the man of the match award after top-scoring with 61 and claiming seven wickets, summed up the situation neatly in commenting afterwards, 'It was a bit of a shambles out there. The umpire's decision is final … but we changed one of them.'

Hughes was unashamedly furious with umpires Wood and Schoof, worrying that their indecision was leading players to take liberties and creating friction between the two sides: 'It was tough Test cricket but there were too many mistakes. Batsmen were given out lbw when they weren't out and they were given out when their bats never came near the ball. We don't know whether we are Martha or Arthur as far as the umpiring is concerned. Umpiring like this just shouldn't be tolerated. There was a lot at stake and you can understand why people get uptight. All of a sudden everybody starts appealing for everything.'[5]

A first 'Test' finish inside four days afforded the players the luxury of an extended break before the second 'Test' at Newlands: all of 72 hours. As 12 months previously, the Australians would begin 1987 at the picturesque Cape Town ground, the only South African venue where batting first was nothing short of an obligation for the captain who won the toss. Graeme Pollock had long enjoyed his visits to Newlands and returned to strengthen a winning South African side who had twice beaten the West Indians as well as drawing comfortably with the English and Australians at the venue since rebel tours had begun.

The South Africans' intent to bat themselves into strong positions, as teams leading 1-0 are always keen to do, was emphasized when Pollock replaced Stephen Jefferies; with Brian McMillan at seven and Alan Kourie two places lower there was no shortage of batting in the home side. It was therefore suicide for Kim Hughes the make the decision that followed his winning the toss: bowling first at Newlands, an inexplicable call that, coupled with concerns over the togetherness and determination of his side, gave the impression of a team on the drift. Two defeats in one evening during the day/night series had perhaps clouded his judgement, though no-one had sought to blame the pitch three weeks earlier.

Over two days the South Africans blithely tortured the visitors, making 437-5 from 141 overs. Peter Kirsten top-scored with 177 that included only one half-chance, to Kepler Wessels in the gully when 38, but the centre of attention remained Pollock. On his last 'international' innings at the iconic stadium, the batsman made only one from his first 13 balls and then 50 from his next 60, hammering ten fours and a six. When he fell to Maguire, who had shown admirable resilience in trying to tie down the left-hander, the disappointment among a sparse crowd was tangible.

In contrast to the Wanderers, it was soon plain that a re-run of the 1939 'timeless Test' might have been viable.[6] South Africa refused to declare despite their dominance and time lost to light, and were finally 493 all out on the third morning. They went into the field hoping to force a follow-on, met instead with the calm face of John Dyson who eased to 103 overnight and dominated day four with Mike Haysman, the pair putting on 225 for the fifth wicket before Haysman hit the ball to Brian Whitfield at backward point and Dyson, skittish on 198, called for a single that wasn't there.[7] His partner did not move an inch and the chance to be the first Australian to make a double century at Newlands was gone. A result out of the question, Hughes decided to bat on and his side were 467-8 overnight with a day to play but nothing to play for.

On the final day Haysman became the third man to pass 150 in the match before falling with 153 out of 496. The statisticians became yet more involved when Kirsten hit an unbeaten 105 in South Africa's reply of 257-3, becoming the first man to hit centuries in both innings of a rebel 'Test' and passing 1,000 runs in Springbok colours. Rice's apparent determination to defend his 1-0 lead said much for his commitment to the series as authentic Test cricket, a real results business, but everyone was hoping for greater entertainment in the second half of the series. Instead, off-field matters engulfed the tour once more.

In the space of a few days after the second 'Test' at Newlands, two decisions illustrated South African cricket's isolation, rebel tours or not. Before leaving Cape Town, Rice was again moved to criticise the officials, claiming that after the trigger-happy performance in Johannesburg the umpires had refused to make any decisions at all, contributing to a dead game: 'We are now playing cricket that is very much more professional than it used to be with far greater stakes available in terms of finance. But, while the players have become far better paid, the South African umpires are still basically amateurs who stand for the love of the game. They are not trained to stand the pressures that come out in a game.'[8]

The following day Ossie Schoof and Denzil Bezuidenhout, who had stood in Cape Town, announced that Rice's comments were 'the last straw' and that they would be retiring with immediate effect. Leading administrators, including Ali Bacher and Eddie Barlow, had spoken out in defence of the umpires, saying that admonishments from Rice and Kim Hughes were not in the interests of the game. But seeping commercialisation had hardened a long-standing gulf between players and officials. As the Currie Cup had remained amateur and enclosed from the world game, so South African umpiring had stagnated. Player professionalisation in general, and the money and prestige attached to rebel matches in particular, had exacerbated the gulf dramatically such that the officials were not capable of matching the standard of play, nor retaining full control of those striving for competitive and financial glory. Dissent to umpires in the official game was hardly unheard of but it was never so appeased or rewarded as in the rebel tour 'Tests'.

'This has been building up for many seasons,' said Schoof. 'I would probably have got out at the end of the season but I have decided to make a decision now. At the age of 53 I have started to ask myself what I am doing putting up with it. When I first started umpiring at the age of 20 the players were only too happy to have someone stand in their matches. They played the match for fun but that is no longer the case. You do not come across the Cheethams, McGlews and Dowlings anymore. These days the players are only interested in getting what they can out of cricket and I no longer want to be part of that.'[9]

A few days later, something altogether more complicated and extraordinary occurred. After ten years of 'normal' cricket, the South African selectors anointed a 'coloured' Springbok. Transvaal left-armer Alan Kourie had struggled throughout the second Australian series, apparently suffering a recurrence of long-standing weight problems and struggling to make an impact. That the left-armer would be dropped was to be expected. What had not been foreseen by any pundit was the identity of his replacement: Omar Henry of Boland.

Outstanding slow bowlers remained a rarity in the Currie Cup and Henry had ranked among the best for some time after a fine career with Western Province and Scotland. Yet he was now almost 35 and in his third season in the B section. Chairman of selectors Peter van der Merwe knew what was coming and emphatically stated that it was selection on merit: 'In his most recent first-class outing, Omar scored a hundred and took seven wickets. He's a genuine spinner and good batsman.'

Kourie did not agree and was quoted in *Business Day* vehemently denouncing the selection of a B section player at his expense, insisting that he could not understand the decision. It was an unwise move given the political baggage, not to mention his own poor form, and pundits rounded on the former Springbok mainstay. Within a week he had been fined and issued an abject apology, van der Merwe observing coolly: 'I'm not prepared to give details of why the selection panel dropped Kourie, save to say that in our opinion he did measure up to what was expected of him. In fact, some players can be grateful we don't say why they have been dropped.'

Only in South Africa could the replacement of one steady slow bowler with another become a hotly contested issue of political morality. For Henry personally, it was a triumph as he told reporters: 'I did not expect it. It has come as a big surprise. I feel it is just reward for the many years of hard work I've put into the game and I only hope I'll be worthy of the national selectors' faith in me and not let the Springboks down.'[10]

It would take a hard-hearted opponent to deny these words and aspirations. Until the age of 25 it had been illegal for Henry to play with whites, let alone in the sacred Springbok colours, and by any measure the journey travelled from deprivation to recognition represented a profound personal achievement. The difficulty was that this was not just personal, as Henry wrote: 'That moment of glory wasn't just for me, it was for the non-white community of South Africa ... It may sound a bit melodramatic, but I did believe that I was blazing a trail which others, in time, could follow.'[11]

Non-white community leaders had no intention of following Henry. He had been called a 'Nazi' and a 'traitor' for leaving Hassan Howa's SACBOC (the precursor to SACB) for SACU, even though Howa himself had instigated the decision by expelling Henry for watching the match of a rival board.[12] The pro-boycott angst was understandable enough: if the rebel tours were part of a wider strategy to buy more time for apartheid then the presence of a coloured player in the same international team, at a time when he could not go on the same beach as his team-mates, was a propaganda coup.[13] It was widely agreed that there were three or four non-white players in the SACB with a stronger claim to Springbok colours, but they were staying loyal to their wider cause. As such, the opposition to Henry only intensified with his elevation to the national side and in certain quarters became extreme: he received death threats and had armed guards stationed at his family home.

The Henry controversy highlighted the absurdity of apartheid and the limitations of Hassan Howa's unflinching response; if it was a propaganda coup then Howa himself had gifted it to his enemies with the expulsion ten years earlier. Norman Arendse, who was opposed to any concessions to SACU whatsoever and a vehement Henry detractor, recalls the conflicting emotions: 'The odd thing was always that with a guy of colour – like Sylvester Clarke who ended up playing for the Transvaal 'Mean Machine' – you always took great pleasure out of seeing that he took four or five wickets. Even a guy like Omar Henry, who was ostracised and called a 'sell-out' and so on. You would always take great pleasure from seeing in the paper that he took five or six wickets or scored a hundred or a fifty.'

While the South African press fretted over on-field comparisons between the official and rebel Australian teams, the two were competing keenly for greater off-field disarray. The official team had lost the fourth Ashes Test inside three days, the first such defeat in 85 years, and an inquest into the death of the Australian game was well under way. Analyses suggesting that this was due in any way to the absence of Kim Hughes' Australians were leapt upon and reproduced with glee in the republic.

In Australia, opinion on the rebels was softening as the national team faced its lowest point. They had been widely tipped to prevail against an England team that had lost home series to New Zealand and India. Instead, they were outplayed and the rebels' stock began to rise by virtue of not taking part. Hughes remained insistent that he would be good enough at 33 to merit a Test recall: 'I'm playing as well as I've ever played in my whole life.'[14]

Meanwhile 12 rebels had long felt incoherent leadership to be derailing their efforts in South Africa – one writer had gone so far as to say that Omar Henry's inclusion demonstrated that the Springboks felt they had won the series. Following internal discussions senior players Steve Rixon and John Dyson stood down from the selection panel, leaving Kim Hughes, with whom the majority disagreed in the first place, in sole charge.

Two 'Tests' to play and 1-0 down, Australia won the toss at Kingsmead, which was enveloped by mid-January humidity. Hughes elected to bat first on a pitch already showing cracks in the blistering heat and after the early loss of Dyson and Kepler Wessels, for a duck to an abysmal caught-behind decision, the Springboks tired. The flamboyant Steve Smith batted through the day, partnering Hughes (25) and Graham Yallop (36) before falling for 137 out of 220-6. Henry was able to cement his place in history with the wickets of Yallop and Smith and when the Australians were bowled out for 264, Garth Le Roux claiming 4-33 in just 14 overs of shock bowling, the fieldsmen were treated for dehydration in the dressing room.

The humidity at Durban was becoming the enemy of entertainment as on day two the South African top seven all reached double figures with only one half-century, from Brian Whitfield, to show for it. Concentration-sapping conditions were widely felt to be culpable though spinner Trevor Hohns deserved at least some of the credit: he had taken all five wickets, out of a total of 225 when bad light called an early end to proceedings.

Ken McEwan reached a century and 24,000 first-class runs in his career on the third morning but it was three-figure temperatures that preoccupied observers with medical experts cropping up across the media to demand that the 'Test' be suspended in the name of player safety. The Australians would have had few complaints had the advice been heeded: McEwan and Dave Richardson had built a first-innings lead of 86 and Clive Rice rotated himself, Brian McMillan, Hugh Page and Le Roux to maintain short, sharp bursts of aggressive pace from one end while Henry tied up the other. At the close of day three, again earlier than scheduled due to light, the rebels were 35-3 having lost their best three batsmen in Smith, Wessels and Hughes.

Divided behind closed doors and struggling on the field, the Australians might have been expected to fold. Hughes felt that his side had to bat throughout the fourth day to save the game, perhaps in hope rather than expectation given the batting line-up.

Instead they did so with some room to spare, guaranteeing themselves at least a draw to keep the series alive. Hohns was out in Le Roux's first spell as the long-serving paceman kept up his reputation for short, wicket-taking spells, bringing together Dyson and Mike Haysman at 50-4.

The pair batted for very nearly five hours, adding 203 runs, neither needing to take undue risks against a pace attack struggling in the heat with an old ball. At the other end they were forced to treat Henry with far greater respect as the cracks added turn to his variations in flight, but the debutant sent down 22 wicketless overs for just 31 runs. Shortly after his century Dyson became the second and last wicket of the day just before the close, a waft outside off-stump at Rice finding the edge. Haysman spent overnight on 110 not out with praise ringing in his ears.

Hughes was predictably delighted in declaring: 'In all my matches for various Australian teams I don't think I've ever been involved in such a stirring fightback.' The South African newspapers were not so kind. Rice's perceived negative tactics in Cape Town were even more criticised, notably the field placings that had made life too easy for Dyson and Haysman at 50-4. Ray Williams wrote in the *Sunday Times*, 'If ever a side learnt the lesson that a match is never over until it's lost, it was the Boks in this Test. A guarded Rice admitted that one can become "over-confident" – a concession which must rank as the understatement of the year.'[15]

There was a fifth day still to play but with the Springboks' obvious happiness with a draw and only man of the match Hohns able to exploit a crumbling wicket, a result was rarely on the cards. The Springboks never made an attempt at the 254 winning target in their four hours, wobbling slightly before closing on 143-7. It was enough for Hughes to bait his opposite number ahead of the final match in Port Elizabeth: 'You guys have got to accept that your batsmen don't play spin very well.' But Rice was derisive of suggestions the Boks were under growing pressure: 'Nonsense. Kim can chirrup all he likes. We may have given away a few wickets but we were never in danger of losing.' That appeared to be the way the Springbok captain liked it.

Going into the final 'Test', there was R12,000 for winning the series and R18,000 for winning the match up for grabs – but did the players deserve it? Lamenting that in 1970 South Africa were not only the best in the world but the most exciting, Michael Owen-Smith wrote in the *Cape Argus*: 'The Springboks have given the distinct impression in the last two Tests, particularly at Kingsmead, that they have been happy to sit on the series lead they established at Wanderers and wait for the Australians to make mistakes.'[16] With the prize money weighted as it was, the incentive to be more attacking at St George's Park was clear. They would also have greater ammunition to do so: Graeme Pollock, on his home ground at 42, was making his absolutely final appearance in Springbok colours.

It was a good toss to lose at Port Elizabeth where both sides intended to bowl; Kim Hughes called incorrectly and the Australians had to bat. Despite a thrusting debut from Allan Donald, who claimed two wickets in a four-over spell, the tourists had very much the better of the first day with Greg Shipperd and Steve Smith sharing 123, the best opening stand of the series, with Hughes adding 42 to reach 230-4 at the close. The second day belonged to the groundsman, who it transpired had prepared a better batting track even than that in Cape Town; to Omar Henry, who as in Durban was the pick of a Springbok attack nullified by the conditions; and to Kepler Wessels, who made a methodical century across all three sessions. Upon passing three figures the reaction was second only to that received by Pollock, who could attract a standing ovation for following a breath in with one out. Hughes declared on 455-9 to give Rodney Hogg and Terry Alderman an hour to put the Springboks under pressure but they could manage only one wicket, that of Brian Whitfield.

It all meant that the stage was set for a grand farewell. Jimmy Cook and Peter Kirsten kept the capacity crowd waiting for over an hour before the former captain was out lbw to Hogg for 34. Eleven thousand spectators rose to their feet to greet their greatest ever batsman, and perhaps the world's best since Donald Bradman, and were immediately given a nasty shock. Hogg still saw the match as within the Australians' grasp and sent through a ball at full tilt that found the outside edge before falling short of Steve Rixon and racing away to the rope. But this was Pollock's only fright. Four hours of clinical shot-making brought 22 more boundaries. As ever the left-hander was a slow starter, taking two hours to reach his half-century from 102 balls. The acceleration then began, a second 50 came in 73 balls and then a final 44 at quicker than a run a ball, singles ignored as boundary followed boundary. On 144 the 42-year-old's concentration failed him. He was clean bowled by Hogg and watched nationwide on television as he returned to the pavilion.

'It might have been Pollock at the age of 22 rather than 42,' wrote Michael Owen-Smith. 'The only obvious change is the much-discussed change of stance. But most of Pollock will never change: the superhuman gifts of eyesight and timing, that majestic cover drive, the delicate cuts and sweeps, the ferocious pulls to mid-wicket … they were all there in the Pollock of yesterday as much as the Pollock of yesteryear.'[17]

If the left-hander was the same batsman then he was no longer the same person of 20 years ago. Throughout the 1980s there had been a growing awareness and acceptance among Springboks of the rationale for the sporting boycott. With a platform to reflect on his career Pollock moved beyond talk of Trent Bridge 1965 or Kingsmead 1970 to say: 'I can see the justice of our cricket isolation now, though it was hard at the time.' Minister for Finance Barend du Plessis was wise enough not to berate a national hero at the peak of his popularity, responding curtly: 'He should be remembered as a great cricketer, and should not be involved in debates on constitutional developments.'[18]

The veteran had brought the stadium alive, but killed the series. On day four the South Africans travelled all the way to 533 and though the Australians made 85-2 in response, Hughes would begin the final day seven runs ahead with eight wickets in hand, needing both a serious target and ten South African wickets to save the series. It was simply impossible and so the St George's Park crowd were instead treated to a day of batting from Wessels, who made his second century in the match.

It was a suitably dull conclusion to a hugely disappointing second series. A year on from his endorsement of the 'Tests' as standing comparison with much international fare, Australian journalist Chris Harte reflected, 'Without Graeme Pollock and Garth Le Roux for the South Africans, and Steve Smith for the visitors, the four 'Test' series would have lacked virtually any entertainment value.'

Much of the blame fell on Rice, who even received criticism from his own selectors, but the pitches had not allowed a fair competition between bat and ball. Fully motivated or not, the Australian bowlers were a highly respectable unit while the home side also had a potent team attack on paper. Among them all only Le Roux, who was 32 by the season's end, had made a significant impact although the Springboks' new spinner would remember the experience for the rest of his life.

The Australian tours appeared to represent a natural end point for the rebel experiment. The English, Sri Lankan and West Indian series had all boasted novelty elements for an isolated game without ever achieving serious equivalence with Test cricket. Now, having fulfilled the desire for five-day matches it was apparent that a true re-creation was impossible. The questionable commitment and togetherness of the Australian players had brought to a head an obvious but little discussed problem: without roots in representation and community, the essence of Test cricket was necessarily absent.

Vince van der Bijl, veteran of three rebel series, explains it thus: 'County and provincial cricket is cricket at a pretty good standard but we always felt that we were not being truly tested. On a rebel tour we were playing against a small group of individuals without any backing of province or country and so there isn't this *gees*, there wasn't the drive, there isn't this ... you know, willingness to die for your country. You can't put the rebel tours contextually anywhere near Test cricket. So when I look at those results ... I'm happy to have taken some wickets, and I loved the experience – don't get me wrong on that. And I loved the privilege of playing against guys I'd read about. But statistics wise, it didn't mean that much. Like the Derrick Robins tours – great experience for us, but it didn't mean as much as playing for Natal or Transvaal.'

The question of a rebel team's comparative strength with the official team, or that of weaker Test nations, was a particular obsession in South African media but shown to be moot. Even with a full tour schedule for practice and preparation, a rebel team could not be fairly regarded as an equivalent to official national sides. The argument that with consistent selection some of the Australians might have had 50 caps was debatable on the players' various merits but in any case unsustainable. Elite sport is an unforgiving arena in which credentials cannot be forged. They simply did not have 50 caps and that was the end of it. In addition, the Australian team had, like their predecessors, borne essential imbalances. John Dyson, Steve Smith, Mick Taylor, Mike Haysman, Steve Rixon and Carl Rackemann had produced outstanding individual performances over the two tours but as a team they rarely threatened to win a 'Test' and were overwhelmed in the 'one-day internationals'. The Australians were notably low on lower-order batting and fielding skills, and whereas the English and Sri Lankans offered excuses in lack of preparation, and the West Indians wanted to prove themselves, the Australians did neither. Low pressure to perform translated into mediocre displays.

If anything the lesson to SACU had been 'be careful what you wish for'. Five-day cricket, replete with grinding draws and long passages of unremarkable play, had represented neither commercial nor competitive value. The day/night series, organisational circus aside, had provided a more interesting spectacle, and the four-match one-day series to finish the tour had been sold out as the Springboks won again, 3-1. But even their viability was in doubt: kit manufacturers Adidas had announced their withdrawal from future events because 'a large section of the population is offended by the rebel tours' while the black-dominated National Soccer League cut ties with Panasonic over their 'Test' sponsorship.

The Australians would be free to return to international cricket a year later but only three were recalled. Terry Alderman was able to repeat quite closely his pre-1985 career: 19 Test caps added to the first 22, and a stellar performance in the 1989 Ashes that eclipsed his record-breaking effort eight years previously. Rackemann and Trevor Hohns also visited England, claiming a further seven Test caps apiece before retirement. There was no return for Hughes, who like Lawrence Rowe and Graham Gooch became synonymous with South Africa. He had managed to find himself on the minority side of both the WSC and South African debates, and though not alone was a high-profile figure in both cases. He remained defiant, labelling his team 'ambassadors for humanity', but the sad demise continued with poor form during a couple of seasons with Natal before retirement. Hughes had not been helped by a lack of media support on the trip, and it was clear he could still use guidance when he said 20 years later: 'It was the first time I'd played cricket where we had a room to ourselves. All of a sudden, we had an administration that wanted the wives there. There was hardly a thing we wanted that we didn't get.'[19]

That analysis speaks for itself but Hughes also made a plausible argument in favour of the tours. Namely, that they 'kept cricket in South Africa alive.' It is noticeable across the first six series that the South African team had changed very little. By 1986–87 the selectors were still relying on a top six dominated by Jimmy Cook, 33; Peter Kirsten, 31; Graeme Pollock, 42; Ken McEwan, 34; Kevin McKenzie, 38; and Clive Rice, 37. Even allowing for the undeniable qualities of these players, and the freakish Pollock in particular, the absence of a generation raised on the 1970s scene was marked. Probably only Kirsten and Brian McMillan would make unanswerable cases as players of international class before the emergence of a new generation, raised on the 1980s rebel tours, including Hansie Cronje and Allan Donald.

The wider political situation in South Africa had become dire. The republic had been in and out of states of emergency throughout the two Australian tours, the government confiscating the presses of newspapers which voiced dissent.[20]

South Africa had become more or less ungovernable and it was during the Australian tours that Ali Bacher decided to tackle actively the racial divide in cricket in South Africa. He and his colleague Hoosain Ayob picked up an idea born in conversations with Alvin Kallicharran in 1982: mini-cricket, a simplified junior version of the game requiring minimal equipment or facilities. Bacher and Ayob started visiting the townships every Saturday, quickly introducing thousands of children to the game with the help of local coaches and corporate sponsorship.

It was unquestionably the best thing that SACU had done for non-white cricket but it was missing the essential ingredient of all unity attempts: full co-operation from black leaders. The development programme had been set up in the townships uninvited, and was viewed by resentful black leaders, for whom non-cooperation remained essential, to be patronising. This impression was somewhat confirmed by Bacher's admission that after a few weeks in the townships he began to realise for the first time the cricket potential among black youth. The development programme was well-intentioned and constructive, but it betrayed the fact that SACU had only now begun to understand the context they were facing. The fervour with which the township development programme was then flaunted abroad invited further suspicion and allegations of window-dressing, however unjust.

Another attempt at unity was also destined to fail. Hassan Howa invited Bacher to the SACB Under-19 national tournament at Mitchell's Plain to discuss access to the township development sponsorship funds: while SACU lacked the friends abroad, his SACB lacked money to develop their cricketers. For the first time he considered a co-operative relationship with SACU as they embarked upon a programme specifically targeted at non-whites. But opposition within the Western Province CB, opposition that Howa had founded and fostered, was too great. Rather than try co-operation the WPCB voted out their iconic leader, architect of a decade's immovable opposition, rather than join him in bringing down the barricades. After a decade seeking international approval and recognition SACU were faced with their own impotence. Without political assistance, the quest for re-admittance had reached the end of the road.

1 Pp 196–7, Hartman (2004).
2 P 147, Harte (1988).
3 pp 179-81, Harte (1988).
4 p 50, Cook with Cleary (1993).
5 p 22, *Cape Argus*, 29 December 1986.
6 3–14 March 1939 at Durban. South Africa (530 & 481) drew with England (316 & 654-5). The game was curtailed after ten days' play because England, who needed only 42 more to win, had a boat to catch.
7 Overnight Dyson had particular cause to curse the umpires as television replays showed that a boundary hit off Alan Kourie, signalled as a four, had in fact cleared the rope for six.

8 Page 24, *The Argus*, 7 January 1987.
9 p 26, *Sunday Tribune*, 11 January 1987.
10 p 16, *Daily News*, 13th January 1987.
11 p 141, Henry (1994).
12 pp 40–52, Henry (1994).
13 Henry later wrote, 'In point of fact I did go on the beach with [my team-mates at Durban], fully prepared to take the consequences' (p 143, Henry 1994). It would have been a brave young police officer who broke up the national cricket team at a time of acute racial tension on a petty apartheid charge. However, it was by no means impossible. In January 1987 Rev. Allan Hendrickse, leader of the Labour Party that dominated the coloured branch of Botha's tricameral Parliament, swam on a whites-only beach as a statement of defiance of enduring social segregation and was criticised on television by the Prime Minister for his transgression. Shortly afterwards Rev. EJ Manikkam, Indian Member of Parliament for the Solidarity Party, was asked to leave a whites-only restaurant.
14 p 40, *The Age*, 17 January 1987.
15 p 36, *Sunday Times* (SA), 25 January 1987.
16 p 28, *Cape Argus*, 29 January 1987.
17 p 14, *Cape Argus*, 2 February 1987.
18 p 261, Harte (1988).
19 *The Age*, 21 November 1985.
20 Adverts placed by the United Democratic Front, the National Education Crisis Committee and the South African Council of Churches calling for the unbanning of the ANC in newspapers on 7 and 8 January 1987 (*Daily News* in Durban, *Cape Argus* in Cape Town) led to government officials confiscating documents and printing plates, increasing restrictions on debate of banned organisations and a police investigation into their publication.

## Chapter 9

# Does Everyone Know Where They Stand?

*'The wrong place at the very wrong time.' –*
*Ian Wooldridge*

Cricket's global village was a restive place after six South African tours in five years. The bans on English participation in 1982 had already elapsed and those on the Australians had only a year to run, pitching former rebels against countries who felt they should not play international cricket again. This opposition was still led by national governments and it had become problematic for professionals with South African connections to enter India, Pakistan and certain Caribbean islands.

In June 1987 the West Indies and Sri Lanka proposed an ICC motion which would have banned indefinitely all those with South African ties. It was impracticable, legally unsustainable and quickly dropped, but there was an urgent need for a consistent ruling as relations between the 'white' and 'non-white' nations had become increasingly unstable.[1]

England in particular attracted criticism as the United Nations repeatedly ranked the UK most often in breach of the sporting boycott. Graham Gooch had become synonymous with boycott-breaking after his captaincy of the first rebels and had grown increasingly insular during his exile, resolving to return to Essex and 'let his bat do the talking'. The bat proved most persuasive, and it was no surprise when he was handed an international recall at the first opportunity to face Australia in 1985.

It proved a memorable summer for England, an emphatic victory over a team managing their own South African defection, and Gooch re-established himself as an international batsman of formidable presence with 487 runs including a first Ashes century. The equally unrepentant John Emburey also played in all six Tests while fellow South African Breweries veterans Peter Willey, Les Taylor and Arnie Sidebottom appeared in one apiece.

Storm clouds gathered with a West Indies tour scheduled for the following winter. In the initial 1982 furore all SAB rebels had been banned indefinitely from visiting most Caribbean nations and national governments reserved the right to revive the measure. Deputy Prime Minister of Antigua Lester Bird threatened to refuse Gooch entry to the island without an apology for his rebel tour participation. But the batsman had absolutely no intention of apologising and it was only after drawn-out political manoeuvres, including input from the Foreign and Commonwealth Office, that he issued an attempt at placating West Indian anger: 'Let me say that I strongly oppose apartheid. My visit to South Africa was certainly not motivated by any intention to support apartheid and naturally nothing I have said has been intended to be contemptuous of anti-apartheid opinion in the West Indies, or anywhere else in the world.'

Delivered without conviction or enthusiasm, it fell short of Antiguan demands on all counts and so it was to great surprise that Bird confirmed Gooch would be allowed into the country. Wary of the reception he would receive and tired of political interference, the batsman was reluctant to travel but did so at the urging of captain David Gower and the TCCB. He was met by placard-waving demonstrators and a statement from Bird's office that read, 'Mr Gooch's statement contains three elements which I had suggested were necessary to ensure his welcome to the Caribbean. He has stated that he would not return to South Africa, that he does not support apartheid and he has regretted the circumstances that took him there in the first place.'[2] One out of three ain't good, and Gooch was dismayed. The series, in which England were 'blackwashed' 5-0 by eye-watering margins of defeat, did little to improve his mood. He had served his time, however unjust he felt the sentence, and despaired of the ongoing political manipulation.

Gower was replaced as captain by Mike Gatting the following summer and England promptly retained the Ashes against a still hapless Australia in 1986–87. But despite reaching the 1987 World Cup final, Gatting's was a tumultuous reign. His first full year ended with the most ill-tempered Test series since Bodyline when an ugly on-field row with umpire Shakoor Rana soured relations between Pakistan and England.[3] Like Bodyline and Gooch vs. Bird, UK Government intervention was required to defuse diplomatic tension. By the summer of 1988, when the West Indies would be the visitors, Gatting had published a book detailing his side of the Pakistan controversy and the TCCB were resolved to changing captains. They were not without ammunition – the 2-1 Ashes win had provided Gatting's only victories in 22 Tests as captain – but lacked the clarity of thought and purpose to act.

Instead a bizarre and unedifying episode set the tone for extended chaos at the top of the English game. After a drawn first Test at Trent Bridge, a tabloid newspaper sting 'caught' Gatting taking a waitress to his hotel room, although the England captain denied any improper behaviour. He was sacked nonetheless, chairman of selectors Peter May[4] explaining, 'We don't think he made love to the barmaid, but he shouldn't have invited her to his room.'[5] Gatting, patently punished for the Rana affair, was left betrayed and resentful, and soon made himself unavailable to the national team for a year.

For an organisation that had made clear its opposition to drinking with women in the evening, the TCCB's moral leadership was a sight to behold. They appointed John Emburey as captain for the second and third Tests, which were lost heavily at Lord's and Old Trafford, and then changed nine of their squad between Manchester and the fourth match in Leeds. Emburey was among those jettisoned and replaced as captain by Chris Cowdrey, a Kent all-rounder who had played five Tests in India in 1984–85. Cowdrey was such an unfamiliar face that the gateman refused him entry to the players' car park at Headingley. He was rather better known to Peter May, being his godson.

Cowdrey affirmed appraisals that he was an intelligent captain short of Test class with bat and ball, and he could do nothing to prevent a third resounding defeat. He then suffered a foot injury playing for Kent so for the finale at The Oval the selectors required a fourth captain in five Tests. There was only one remaining option: Graham Gooch. Few had considered Gooch to be captaincy material but he accepted the responsibility for the defeat to the West Indies and was reappointed ahead of Cowdrey for an end-of-season Test against Sri Lanka.

Gooch's appointment was hotly contested amid questions over his character and commitment, and abysmally handled by the TCCB. Cowdrey was not informed in person that he had not been retained and when he complained publicly he was fined. At the same time the selectors dropped Matthew Maynard and Rob

Bailey, who had both made their debuts only against the fearsome Windies at The Oval, and handed out four new Test caps for a match where a victory, England's first in 19 Tests, was more or less inevitable.

Such fickleness generated enormous dressing room discord while Gooch's strong South African connections made him a provocative choice internationally. England were now due to tour India when their new captain had plans to winter with Western Province, where he could spend more time with his family.[6] Gooch had passed on the previous winter's Ashes on the same basis, staying in Essex, and he was beginning to consider, at 35, the end of his international career. But when the selectors reached a belated decision and in September asked him to captain his country he accepted. The England side needed a period of stability after a chaotic 12 months. And then the tour was immediately cancelled.

The Indian government was enraged by Graham Gooch's appointment, announcing that no player 'having or likely to have sporting contact with South Africa' would be granted a visa.[7] Since the captain was one of eight players in the squad on a UN blacklist, that meant abandonment, and the political tensions among the ICC resurfaced. Critics of the 'black' position questioned why Indian concerns had been muted a year earlier when Gooch and John Emburey were in England's World Cup squad on the Asian subcontinent.

Sympathisers believed that the silence was not to protect their substantial tournament income but a begrudging exception to accommodate the global game – and on the strict proviso that an international agreement on South Africa be reached. The West Indies and Sri Lanka backed India's position, and a replacement triangular series between New Zealand, Pakistan and England also proved unviable.

There were suspicions that the TCCB had been unduly provocative in appointing a captain who would otherwise have been in Cape Town. 'It was a situation made, if not designed, to aggravate the Indian government,' wrote *Wisden* editor Graeme Wright. These suspicions were apparently confirmed when Peter May told *The Cricketer* that he was interested only in picking the best possible team: 'We don't pick teams for political reasons. In any case Graham Gooch had been perfectly acceptable to India at the World Cup...'[8] At the very least the 'best possible team' defence did not tally with their recent treatment of Mike Gatting.

The South African question required a new answer, a unified international response before world cricket began to fracture again. All sides appreciated the urgency and in January 1989 they unanimously agreed a motion that inserted political aspects in the ICC constitution for the first time. Essentially any participation – playing, coaching or administration – in South African cricket would make players liable for a ban of three, four or five years depending on age and the nature of contact. A list of such players would be kept by the ICC, collectively agreed. At the same time the slate was wiped clean for those who had visited South Africa in the past.

It was a clear compromise measure. To close the door on South African cricket 'for the last time' the 'non-white' nations had agreed to shorter bans and an amnesty on previous contact. In exchange the TCCB, weakened at home and abroad by a wretched 12 months, accepted explicitly for the first time that other nations could dictate which players they might and might not select. In return for their sacrifices, with which hard-line elements in all countries could find problems, the reward was a standard to which all players could be held. As one TCCB official said, 'At least everyone knows where he stands. The players have a straightforward choice.'[9]

Crucially, the new-found clarity was no deterrent. The uncertainty of the professionals over international futures, compared to the guaranteed pay day of a South African visit, had been a key motivation since the earliest rebel tours. Moreover, SACU had been big losers in the ICC ruling: coaches could no longer visit South Africa without withdrawing from international cricket and so Ali Bacher's township coaching programme was suffering. The SACU chief visited London in April 1989 to champion the development programme's achievements at the *Wisden* dinner. He received a standing ovation despite dropping an unmistakable hint on his other plans: 'The development programme is extremely costly and the funds come only from the South African Cricket Union and the business community. As any cricket-playing country knows, most central funds come from tours; and if we are to keep the momentum going for our development and motivational programmes, we are going to have tours again soon. If South Africa is not to be granted tours through the front door it will be forced to use the back door.'

Despite Bacher's reservations about further rebel tours, SACU's members needed another financial injection. And having exhausted the West Indian and Australian markets, there was only one place left to turn. India and Pakistan remained impossible; a third string from New Zealand or Sri Lanka would mean a return to Cuckooland.[10] And so months before the dinner Bacher had begun recruiting a second English rebel squad, first making contact with John Emburey, who would have the unique distinction of travelling on both English tours, and David Graveney, who became player-manager. Emburey began approaching players for a trip to the republic at the start of the 1989 season, his place in the England team allowing easy access to a dressing room in impressive disarray and still lacking a captain.

England began the Ashes series with a new chairman of selectors, Ted Dexter, who had made his opinion of Gooch quite clear in an earlier newspaper column: 'If you've ever been hit in the face with a wet fish you'll know how I've been feeling this week ever since England's latest Test leader voiced his opinions on the business of captaincy.'

Gooch was not even interviewed for the job he theoretically held. Dexter wanted to reinstate Mike Gatting and told him as much in private in March. But the decision was vetoed on 'non-cricket grounds' by another selector, Ossie Wheatley. Gatting was humiliated again and the TCCB reverted instead to David Gower.

The result was a shambles. After 1988 it had been assumed that English cricket could not sink any lower, but such an assumption is never less than dangerous. Whereas the summer of four captains had been characterised by comical ineptitude, 1989 brought disrepute in a comprehensive series defeat bereft of pride, commitment and belief. Gower's men began the Ashes series as favourites but were thoroughly outplayed, relinquishing the urn in the fourth Test at Old Trafford where Australia, led by the returning Terry Alderman, went 3-0 up. The home team had used a scarcely believable 21 players in those four Tests and, unbeknownst to the captain, nine of them had signed to tour South Africa. The Manchester Test was lost in spectacular fashion on the last day of July and the newspapers demanded Gower's head. The following morning they were distracted, as baying hordes are wont to be. A second English rebel squad had been leaked to the press.

The revolving doors of captaincy and team selection had created a large group each nursing grievances, precisely the environment in which SACU contract offers thrived. One of five county captains, Chris Cowdrey was a predictable signatory after his treatment from the

TCCB the previous summer; batsman Chris Broad and all-rounder Phil De Freitas nurtured their own senses of injustice at treatment from the hierarchy. Ageing and injury-prone players with few international prospects were easier still to identify and SACU added a further eight men with no discernible long-term future at Test level. The surprise names were Matthew Maynard and Paul Jarvis, both of whom had been expected to play a central role for England, and the identity of the captain who had signed only at the last moment: Mike Gatting. Few had been more committed to England's cause through the turbulent 1980s but the establishment's betrayals had corroded his loyalty.

For opponents and supporters alike, the studied ignorance of many tourists remained unfathomable. De Freitas and Roland Butcher, at 36 one of those with no career to endanger, were black yet had not anticipated any specific problems as a consequence; they were pressurised, lampooned and immediately withdrew to be replaced by Alan Wells and Greg Thomas. And like Gooch before him, in accepting the captaincy Gatting instantly made himself a poster boy for South African collaboration. Improbably, Gatting was even more naive on the political ramifications of the trip; he admitted that he knew nothing of apartheid and was just coming to learn the fundamentals of segregation. Alongside the more articulate Graveney, the only uncapped member of a 16-man party, the now familiar arguments were heard again, and in particular that multi-racial cricket was thriving: SACU claimed 40,000 black children were now in the township development scheme.[11]

Graveney provided the confident spokesman that previous tours had so badly lacked, but active argument also invited better targeted responses. Frank Keating wrote in the *Guardian*, 'What about the 29,960,000 non-members? ... Gatting's £200,000 seems reasonably generous in light of the fact that for every R1,000 spent on white sport, just R1 is spent on black sport.'[12]

News of a tour was seized on by the Anti-Apartheid Movement, who put together their biggest sports campaign since 1970 with protests at more than 50 first-class matches. Front pages were given over once again to 'Traitors!' (*Daily Mirror*), 'Blood Money Cricket Storm' (*Daily Mail*) and 'Rebel threat to British Sport' (*The Times*), with only one exception ('Wrinkly rocker stole my Page 3 girl' – *The Sun*).[13] The *Daily Mirror* declared, 'The 16 England cricketers who are to tour South Africa have betrayed their country. They have sold themselves for money which is stained with suffering. The cost to the regime is negligible. The price others will play is incalculable ... Judas would've been proud of them all.'[14] And Bacher became the focus of particular ire as South African temptation's human face: the 'Pirate King' destroying the international game with his sack of krugerrands.

In typically uncomplicated fashion Gatting pledged to meet any protesters in South Africa, insisting, 'I'm no traitor. I do not see myself as a traitor because I am going off to earn a living by playing cricket in South Africa. I think I've been a loyal person. I've given a lot of my life to cricket. It's time for me to put my family first.'[15] There were few Kit Wright fans in the party. Jarvis cited his £66,500 mortgage and 'large overdraft', and Graveney responded that his decision had been made 'bearing in mind my responsibilities for my family': 'I am not going to propagate anything for South Africa. I will be there as a cricketer to help SACU break down apartheid.'[16]

Since 1982 a minority of the cricketers visiting South Africa had laid claim to a knowledge of apartheid and, in some cases, a modest influence towards its demise; by late 1989 few politicians in the country understood the prevailing climate. Since the mid-1980s there had been a fearfully thin line between ongoing unrest and all-out civil war. But the view within progressive white political circles was that apartheid would endure at least until the end of the century as the National Party held grimly to power. It was on this basis that Ali Bacher had resolved to pursue the second English rebel tour, discounting his doubts over their disruption overseas in the belief that they were essential to the future of South African cricket.

That analysis, made in the latter half of 1988, was bankrupt within a year. In January 1989 President PW Botha had a stroke and the acrimonious battle to succeed him was won by FW De Klerk, a lifelong apartheid adherent who surprised everybody with a programme of reforms. Prominent among these was lifting the prohibition on political protests in September 1989, which would make the visiting cricketers a target for demonstrations.

Meanwhile the African National Congress, many of whose leaders were in exile, had begun making serious efforts to harness sporting and cultural events with an eye on the 'endgame': reconciliation and unification. They had formed a new democratic sporting wing, the National Sports Congress, which resolved to promote and support conciliatory sporting projects while opposing those they considered exclusive. Rebel cricket tours assuredly fell into the latter category and when the NSC and SACU met for the first time in October 1989, Bacher was told that the rebel tour ought to be cancelled and that his township coaching programme, however well-intentioned, was a paternalistic intrusion. The NSC asked SACU to call off the tour, predicting that 'blood will flow' in the demonstrations if it went ahead.

Faced with battle-hardened veterans of a profound political struggle, those running cricket were in over their heads; the lack of visible animosity to previous tours had consoled not only visiting players but resident administrators too, and only now was the reality of their world becoming obvious. But the tour had been instigated in the first place purely for financial reasons and those remained. SACU was dominated by provincial heads who still needed the income and the next day they voted against cancellation. Immediately the NSC began preparing opposition for the new year.

By the time the tourists arrived in South Africa in mid-January 1990, a potentially explosive mix awaited them. The NSC had arranged marches and consumer boycotts, but would not apply to an illegitimate government for the legally required permission to protest. The demonstrations would be monitored by a police force that not only had no experience of managing mass protests but no previous obligation to treat black South Africans as equals; the fact that they had not applied for permission would give licence for further brutality. As the *Guardian*'s Johannesburg correspondent John Perlman wrote, 'What Bacher, the South African Cricket Union, Mike Gatting and his men are about to find out is that the sports boycott of South Africa no longer operates from London or the United Nations.'[17]

Timing is everything. After a growing irrelevance towards the end of the Australian tours, cricket was back on the front line in the battle against apartheid. Contrary to their convictions in organising and announcing the tour, neither SACU nor the rebels knew where they stood.

An introduction was provided immediately upon arrival at Jan Smuts Airport, where a demonstration against the tour was violently disbanded. An editorial in township newspaper *The Sowetan* warned of the dangers to come: 'We have no sympathy for Mike Gatting and his men. The treatment of blacks at the airport when police fired tear-smoke at protestors should have convinced them that they are not welcome. Instead Gatting said the tour would go ahead as scheduled and it was up to the South African Cricket Union to ensure that everything went according to plan. They would only reconsider if it became dangerous for their personal lives.

'Well, it has become dangerous, and for the lives of our people. As happened at the airport on Friday the police will be taking strong action against protestors. We know our police much better than Gatting and his greedy band of mercenaries.'[18]

It was just the beginning. The first tour match scheduled for East London, a town known for a high level of political activism, was moved to Kimberely to escape the ANC. But news of the switch was leaked 48 hours beforehand and a mass demonstration arranged. The government offered to suppress it but SACU's Geoff Dakin declined; instead a short distance from the ground there was a disquieting stand-off between police and a thousand protesters as the town was given over to anti-tour sentiment. As promised, the NSC had not applied for a permit so as to expose the fallacy of demonstration without democratic freedom. When police threatened to break up the illegal gathering, Ali Bacher was called to the scene. He insisted that he had no objection to peaceful protest, and was met with a snarling response from the police captain: 'Listen, you do your job, and I'll do mine!'

As officers then began moving among the crowd with batons, Bacher appreciated the imminent threat of appalling violence. He took it upon himself to arrange the permit on the demonstrators' behalf, using the phone in a nearby house. He later recalled: 'The owner of the house, a very nice man, turned out to be an uncle of the Howell twins who played cricket for Border. There we were, all hell breaking loose outside, Kimberley up in flames, me under siege, and all this man wanted to talk about was Hugh Tayfield and what I thought of him as a bowler.'[19]

The acquisition of the permit was a masterstroke, avoiding violent reprisals in Kimberley and raising Bacher's standing among the protestors. But the tour was clearly established as a focal point for black dissent and Gatting's hopeless incomprehension was reiterated in his response: 'As far as I'm concerned there were a few people singing and dancing and that's it.'[20]

Remarkably, the tour match had proceeded with a comfortable English win against weak opposition. The caravan then proceeded to Bloemfontein, where the English players were made further aware of local feeling. Journalist Richard Evans wrote in his diary of the tour: 'If you want the black waiter to bring you a pot of tea it is necessary to convince him you are not a member of the English cricket team. The team are in an alcove around the corner, near the self-service buffet, cordoned off from the main, multi-racial dining room. The irony is not easy to miss. Apartheid at breakfast.'[21]

Gatting met this union activism at one restaurant by going into the kitchen and cooking steaks himself, a gesture that was viewed alternately as defiant good humour and patronising disrespect. During the match at Bloemfontein, a draw with South African Universities notable for a stylish century from their captain Hansie Cronje, the tourists were outwitted again. Outside the ground black protests had been broken up using tear gas and rubber bullets, and white extremists were said to be co-ordinating a response on the town's outskirts.

Gatting and David Graveney agreed to meet with anti-tour leaders who wanted to present a petition during the tea break on the final day. Reporters and photographers were lined up, and as the paper was handed over, the shirt of one petitioner, John Sogoneco, was dramatically removed to reveal buckshot wounds from a police action some days previously. It was a set-up, and one Gatting was ill-equipped to combat. He asked if the wounds had been collected at the cricket and, when informed they had not, he responded, 'Then it is nothing to do with us. We can't be held responsible for anything that happens away from the ground.'

Gatting had a point, of course, but it was an expression of insensitivity that sat neatly next to the newspaper pictures the following day.

The tourists left Bloemfontein immediately that evening, heading to Pietermaritzburg for their third and final date before back-to-back 'Test' matches. That was 1 February 1990. The next morning FW De Klerk went further than his previous reforms had hinted and few had imagined possible. After years of secret talks between ANC and Afrikaaner representatives, the President used a televised speech at the opening of parliament in Cape Town to lift restrictions on the ANC, the smaller Pan African Congress and the South African Communist Party; Nelson Mandela would be released from prison in the near future at an unspecified date.

Ian Wooldridge wrote in the *Daily Mail*, 'Mike Gatting finds himself in the wrong place at the very wrong time.'[22]

At Pietermaritzbug, Mike Gatting showed a different face to the hapless and bewildered figure engulfed by events that few could understand. At tea on day one the word came through that another petition was waiting to be presented outside the stadium. Leaving the confines of the turnstile barrier, Gatting, John Emburey, David Graveney and Ali Bacher were confronted with a massed crowd.

A representative of the protest committee told Gatting that he had to receive the petition on a podium 150 yards into the melee. Richard Evans wrote: 'The look on

Ali's face told all one needed to know about how safe he thought it would be for the English captain to walk out through a crowd of 5,000 people, all of whom were shouting his name, all of whom were hot, tired and angry. "Gatting go home! Gatting go home!" [...] In a very real sense Gatting was putting his life on the line and he must have known it. But he had said he would listen to anyone and receive any legitimate protest petition and he is not the sort of man who goes back on his word.'

The protest representative led the tour quartet as, rancour and tension in the air, the crowd was parted by marshals. Gatting accepted the petition and walked the 150 yards back, never once flinching or changing expression even as stones and drinks cans rained in from above. Evans added: 'Nor did he break stride when he finally made it back into the ground. Marching into the dressing room he picked up his hat and called out, "Come on, lads, time to go." And then he bowled the second over after tea.'

It was a remarkable moment that confirmed Gatting's credentials as a courageous and straightforward man who simply did not understand what he had got himself into. Adrian Kuiper recalls: 'It must have been horrendous for him. He was incredibly brave. None of the South Africans had to go and do that.'

The tour, now confronted with the depth of anger it had created, went on to Johannesburg for the first 'Test'. The extraordinary manner in which cricket had remained divorced from the outside world persisted. On the first day two and a half hours were lost to rain and the English XI made 113-3 on a dreadful pitch, prompting reporters to castigate the inexperienced South African bowlers Allan Donald and Richard Snell for not taking full advantage of a lively surface.

But all sides were by now under incalculable psychological pressure, as Donald later said: 'It wasn't real. We were representing our country, we had the green cap and it just meant nothing.'[23]

The match had been watched by hundreds of black spectators, bussed in by a previously unknown group called Freedom in Sport on the promise of work at the stadium, to ensure a multi-racial audience for television cameras. At the close police distributed sheets detailing their action against protestors; permits to protest had been refused and 2,000 demonstrators were dispersed with tear gas.

On the second morning the English XI did the series a big favour, losing seven wickets for 43 runs to an improved Donald and Snell, who each took a wicket in his first over and maintained the barrage in helpful conditions. Sixteen wickets fell in the day and only Kuiper, a blight of the first rebel tour eight years earlier, managed more than 23. Brought to the crease at 40-4 he flayed the English bowlers for 84 as the home team closed on 203-9. A crowd of around 10,000 saw the third day's play – and a result. The sorry English XI were all out for 122, setting just 76 to win, which was achieved for the loss of three wickets. Both Gatting and the Springbok captain Jimmy Cook lamented the pitch, one of the few variables still under SACU's control.

The second 'Test' no longer fell into that category and it was cancelled after an explosion near the intended venue in Cape Town. The NSC and Mass Democratic Movement were delighted, declaring: 'If Gatting can make his own food, then he ought to be quite capable of making his way back to London in an emergency situation.'[24]

Nelson Mandela was released the morning after the 'Test', sparking new waves of euphoria, violence and turmoil across the republic. The situation was now quite clearly very dangerous. Death threats continued against Ali Bacher as a high-profile 'friend of government'; leaders implored the rebels to go home. Instead, a compromise was reached. In exchange for a NSC promise that no further demonstrations would disrupt the tour, the schedule was curtailed from a second 'Test' and seven 'one-day internationals' to four one-day games.

These would be kept away from Cape Town and Port Elizabeth, where fears of increased violence prevailed, and they proceeded in the most incongruous fashion. Kepler Wessels would not be present after leaving the South African squad at Wanderers amid dressing room unrest over his Australia links. The Springboks nevertheless won the first two matches and clinched the series in farcical circumstances at Bloemfontein. First the hosts set 301 to win after Kuiper hit 117 from 66 deliveries and then the floodlights failed. England were all out for 94 with the appalling light plainly culpable but the rebels were no longer in a position to make complaints or demands. They won the fourth match as a consolation and, with threats to their lives still very real, hurried out of the country.

'No more inglorious, downright disgraced and discredited team of sportsmen wearing the badge of "England" can ever have returned through customs with such nothingness to declare,' wrote Frank Keating in the *Guardian*.[25] The *Daily Mirror* added, 'Mike Gatting and his jackals of cricket are coming home early with their bats between their legs. Having disgraced their country and their sport, it is only fitting that they should be abandoned by the South Africa to which they sold their reputations.'[26]

For the first time it was difficult to find anyone providing the alternate view.

The tour had been a fiasco. SACU had proclaimed two key objectives for the visit: development of grassroots cricket, and in particular the townships coaching programme, and the bolstering of elite competition at the top of the domestic game. But it had been a financial disaster, with only seven days of 'international' cricket rather than the scheduled 17. Trickle-down to Soweto would be non-existent and the circumstances had rendered on-field activity among the most forgettable in the game's history. David Graveney said that he expected the second tour to proceed in 1990–91, an extraordinary notion that marked more or less the final such declaration recognising an airtight seal between cricket and wider considerations.

Despite the spectacular embarrassment the tour had become, it had at least two vital instrumental impacts; Graveney's ambition 'to help break down apartheid' was fulfilled in spectacular if inadvertent fashion. First, it had provided a forum for black dissent and demonstration that gave SACU an unequivocal insight into what the majority in South Africa thought of the rebel tours. The first six tours had been protected entirely from the anger that their visits had caused; the legalisation of protest meant the seventh became a crucible of recriminations for centuries-old injustice. Here was the answer to the bridge-builders' question, 'Whose cause would be advanced by cricketers not touring?'

Sam Ramsamy, who had led the international sporting boycott movement with SANROC for decades, hailed 'a vindication of everything we have strived for … they never anticipated the magnitude of the protests from the blacks.'[27] Secondly, the tour proved a catalyst for negotiations between SACU and the SACB. Empowered by Nelson Mandela's release, and the mood of reconciliation the ANC then espoused, the two groups met in September 1990 and agreed to 'forge ahead with plans to bring about one controlling body for all cricketers in the country'. Three months later a timetable for unity had been set and agreed, and on 20th April 1991 the formation of the United Cricket Board of South Africa was confirmed.[28]

In July 1991, two and a half years after closing the door on South Africa 'for the last time', the ICC re-opened it. Only the West Indies among 26 full and associate members abstained from a vote in favour of UCBSA admission, and that because the WICBC had not had the chance to discuss the proposal with their individual national boards. To countries steeped in the trench warfare of the international apartheid struggle it was a counter-intuitive manoeuvre – South Africa remained three years away from full democratic elections – but they complied at the urging of the ANC, who wanted South Africa to regain membership of the international community as soon as possible.

Donald Woods wrote for *Wisden*: 'South African cricket began to be riven instead by the same disputes that characterise the game elsewhere, mostly over the eccentricities of the selectors. This argument reached its peak when Jimmy Cook and Clive Rice were left out of the World Cup squad.'[29] A 'nationwide petition' was raised in Johannesburg to explore 'legal aims' for the restoration of the Transvaal pair with the stated aim of acquiring two million signatures, an ambition that rapidly dissolved into silence. The contrast with the cricket petitions two years earlier was expressive.

South Africa returned to the international stage at the 1992 World Cup. Three of the four previous events had been won by nations they had never faced before and the outcome was remarkable. Kepler Wessels, who might have considered his international career over after walking out on the Springboks in Johannesburg two years earlier and who could never have imagined it when playing for Kim Hughes' Australians, led a young team without Cook and Rice but including Peter Kirsten, Adrian Kuiper, Omar Henry, Brian McMillan, Allan Donald and Hansie Cronje. They beat the West Indies and Australia by big margins, India and eventual winners Pakistan before being eliminated at the semi-final stage against England in Sydney under farcical 'rain rule' circumstances.

Kuiper recalls, 'When we got into the World Cup 1992 I wasn't ready for it, because we'd played a little bit of rebel cricket but we'd never played against the real cricketers of the world. And we got to the World Cup in 1992 and we hadn't played against Pakistan, India, West Indies. We didn't know who they were, what they were … I'd only read about them in magazines. "Crikey, these are the best cricketers in the world, who the hell are we?" It showed that rebel cricket had been artificial in a sense. First we had to prove ourselves.'

It was very nearly a spectacular homecoming but would hardly have signified redemption. As Woods added, there was a new generation of stars to find as representatives of the new South Africa.

The readiness to forgive South African links, as with the readiness to resist them, varied greatly by country as world cricket began its own reconciliation.

England recalled Mike Gatting and John Emburey with what some considered indecent haste when their suspensions were curtailed in 1992–93, although they were restricted to eleven and seven Tests respectively as retirement neared. Matthew Maynard and Alan Wells were a source of widespread regret: two batsmen who might have taken Gatting's place in the early 1990s were instead reduced to forgettable international careers.[30] Paul Jarvis and Neil Foster also earned recalls without ever becoming established at international level, and, of course, all were playing under the captaincy of Graham Gooch.

It would be wholly wrong to say that Gooch redeemed himself by his subsequent captaincy of the England team. He never sought forgiveness and his opponents had no intention of conferring it. It was, however, an ironic conclusion to the rebel period that Gooch, the most recognisable name linked with South African cricket from 1982 onwards, should be the man to whom the TCCB turned in seeking to rescue a second rebel catastrophe.[31] Having been derided as lacking both the personality and commitment to captain his country he proved a resilient and impressive leader at a time when, as Gooch himself memorably said, English talent gave him 'the makings of a goodish side.'[32]

In 1991 his arch critic Michael Manley felt England had 'a leader in Graham Gooch in whom the players had confidence and who had earned the respect of the cricket world by the tough and uncompromising professionalism with which he was steering English cricket back towards self-respect.'[33] By the end of the decade England's cricket team was exclusively in the hands of former South African visitors: Gooch, Gatting and David Graveney picked the England team, although only Graveney showed any great aptitude for the job. He held his selector's position for almost a decade and made an unheralded contribution to the run that culminated in the 2005 Ashes victory, England's most successful period for some decades.

Similarly in Australia, forgiveness was quickly forthcoming. It was said that their tours generated more front-page coverage than any sporting event, including World Series Cricket. But the Australian game quickly moved on. Three of the squad were back to win the Ashes in 1989, two years after leaving South Africa. They rejoined a squad that had begun to lay foundations for 15 years of global dominance – perhaps Packer had been right about the dead wood. A number of the Australians slipped quickly out of the first-class scene, but Peter Faulkner, Greg Shipperd and Tom Hogan became influential figures at state level while Trevor Hohns graduated to be chairman of the national selectors and Steve Rixon was a successful coach of New Zealand. Most interestingly, John Dyson was in 2007 appointed West Indies coach; it was still impossible to imagine one of the West Indian rebels rising to such a position.

The plight of returning West Indian cricketers has already been highlighted, but much less well known is that of the Sri Lankans. Excluded from all levels of cricket until well past their prime, careers were laid to waste. Theirs was the only squad from which no-one played international cricket again. Some were able to build new lives with their money but others, notably the young batsman Anura Ranasinghe, found themselves ostracised; he died an alcoholic at just 42. Forgiveness was forthcoming, though always hard won. Mahes Goonatilleke and Lalith Kaluperuma have worked as national selectors, and Bernard Perera was the manager of the Sri Lanka women's team. Many were not only lost to the game but to their societies at large.

The most remarkable renaissance of all, of course, was that of Ali Bacher. After a decade as the most recognisable and controversial face of South African cricket authority, 1990 had been a disaster for him personally. His twin operations to better South African cricket, international tours and township development coaching, had both been destroyed by the unleashing of powers beyond his control. Those projects had been launched in archetypal Bacher fashion: identifying a target, assessing the best possible means of achieving it, and setting off purposefully on that path.

His great disadvantage previously had not been a lack of skill or good intentions but a limited appreciation of the South African reality. Both the rebel tours and township programme had been arranged without a full knowledge of their context. In managing South African cricket's reunification with Steve Tshwete, the former ANC military commander, and a host of figures from across the South African spectrum, Bacher was finally equipped with that understanding. He ultimately fulfilled the ambition of leading a unified South African cricket board and, twenty years after beginning his rebel tour recruitment at the World Cup in London, he took the tournament to South Africa in 2003.

1 pp 51–55, Jack Bailey, 'ICC and South Africa', *Wisden*, 1990. Much of the debate remained unmoved. For the Bicentenary Test between MCC and a Rest of the World XI at Lord's in 1987, Graeme Pollock was not invited as per the rationale for his Packer exclusion 20 years previously; Clive Rice was allowed to play by virtue of his Nottinghamshire connections.
2 pp 117–8, Gooch and Keating (1995).
3 Pakistan v England, 2nd Test at Faisalabad, 7-12 December 1987. Acres of print have been dedicated to the episode. An amusing and informative summary is provided pp 192–5, Rae (2001).
4 PBH May, England. 66 Tests, 4537 runs at 46.77 (1951–61); chairman of selectors (1982–8).
5 Front, *The Sun*, 9 June 1988.
6 pp 102–3, Tennant (1993).
7 p 105, Tennant (1993).
8 p 47, Notes by the Editor, *Wisden* 1989.
9 pp 51–55, Jack Bailey, 'ICC and South Africa', *Wisden*, 1990.
10 A New Zealand team had been due to visit South Africa should the Australian trips have fallen through but it would have faced a particularly acute version of the credibility question: without two or three outstanding individuals, any unofficial New Zealand XI would have struggled to assert itself as international class.
11 Bacher himself had claimed 60,000 at the *Wisden* dinner a few months earlier.
12 p 19, *Guardian*, 19 January 1989. Gatting's fee was double that on offer to rank-and-file players, who agreed to £50,000 per tour. The promotional significance of a captain of stature was evident throughout the tours. See also pp 67–8, Booth (1998) for details of the grotesque disparity between investment in white and black sport: in 1983 Ken Andrew MP, of the Progressive Federal Party, calculated that spending was 2,400 times higher on white children than black. The government refuted the figures but took some three years to do so.
13 2 August 1989.

14 p 2, *Daily Mirror,* 2 August 1989. In an indication of the rolling door of outrage that cricket rebellions engendered, Tony Greig gave an interview to *The Sun*, 2 August 1989, declaring 'good riddance' to those who were not committed 100% to England. Others, however, remained unmoved; John Woodcock accompanied the tour for *The Times* and remained supportive of the venture, declaring, 'It's the hypocrisy I can't stand.' (p 75, Evans 1990).
15 p 36, *Daily Mirror,* 3 August 1989.
16 Front, *The Times*, 2 August 1989.
17 p 19, *Guardian*, 3 August 1989.
18 p 6, *The Sowetan*, 22 January 1990.
19 p 224, Hartman (2004).
20 p 210, Bose (1994).
21 p 6, Evans (1990).
22 p 46, *Daily Mail*, 14 February 1990.
23 *Out of the Wilderness: Part II*, British Sky Broadcasting, first broadcast 19 July 2008.
24 Front, *Cape Argus*, 13 February 1990.
25 p 15, *Guardian*, 14 February 1990.
26 p 70, Evans (1990).
27 p 48, *The Times*, 14 February 1990.
28 The full story of South African Cricket's reunification is detailed, inter alia, in Hartman (2004) and Bose (1994).
29 pp 19–22, *Wisden* 1993.
30 Maynard added three caps to his 1988 debut but managed only 87 runs in eight innings; he also failed to transfer his outstanding one-day form to the international arena, top-scoring with 41 in 14 outings. Wells received a belated first Test cap aged 33 and was out first ball to Curtly Ambrose (6th Test at The Oval, August 1995); his only one-day cap also came that summer.
31 The story of what happened afterwards is expertly covered in Gooch and Keating (1995) and Tennant (1993). Having considered retirement at 35 with 68 Test caps, 4,500 runs, eight centuries and an average of 38.15 he played a further 50 Tests, finishing with a world-record 8,900 runs including 20 centuries at 42.58.
32 The results during Gooch's reign were mixed, as the talent at his disposal necessitated, but he began shaping a team in his own image with young, mentally strong players. Michael Atherton, Alec Stewart and Nasser Hussain all benefited from the rebel exodus and Gooch's leadership.
33 p 393, Manley (2002).

# Afterword

Many people associated with the rebel tours were wary of contributing to this book. A typical response came, 'Why do you need to go dragging all that up again?' The honest answer was modest: curiosity in a remarkable episode of cricket history that dominated my first ten years watching the game without prompting much objective examination. I have tried to stay true to that curiosity, writing primarily a cricket history while all the time aware that a wider context is essential. This brief conclusion is offered in the name of completion rather than provocation.

Viewed from the lofty hilltops of hindsight, the rebel tours are an unfortunate spectacle. Anyone familiar with the noble game knows that nobility has been in short supply throughout its history but the tours bear a particular notoriety. The self-justifying parallel most commonly drawn was with World Series Cricket, but this was obviously destined to fail. In his 30th anniversary afterword to *The Cricket War,* Gideon Haigh's assessment of the myriad consequences echoes that of Zhou Enlai on the French Revolution: it is too early to tell.

In contrast, it became obvious even during the final rebel tour that they had been a damaging miscalculation. Ali Bacher quickly conceded that an earlier knowledge of the anger and resentment among black South Africans, which became so apparent leading the English rebels around a nation in revolt, might have dissuaded him from pursuing the rebel option. The tours did stimulate players within SACU, providing a benchmark for excellence and a new competitive challenge, and the stature of the leading SACU cricketers is hopefully done justice in this book. However, those benefits were offset by wider consequences, and there is little dispute among the Springboks themselves that sporting isolation was retrospectively justified.

An arch cynic might say that the organisers and players have had little choice but to repent. The African National Congress became the dominant force in South Africa from 1990, and so to dispute the significance of the boycott movement during apartheid is to swim against the current. To pursue this line of thought is to do a disservice both to the depth of opposition to the tours and to the reconciliation that followed them.

For those who would still pursue the counter-arguments, there is little in the way of comfort. The much-vaunted multi-racial cricket did indeed prove an exercise in government propaganda, as John Arlott and the anti-apartheid movement had warned. Levels of investment in black and white sport through the 1980s bore a dramatic disparity. The greatest positive influence on sporting integration in the republic came courtesy of the boycott between 1970 and 1976. And the traumatic 1989–90 tour provided a vivid illustration that far from mitigating the wretched apartheid status quo, South Africa's cricket establishment was yet to understand it.

The 'inconsistency' of sporting links with other unpalatable regimes such as the Soviet Union was always an empty vessel: 'if someone else is doing something then it must be acceptable for me to do so' is the logic of the playground. Moreover, South Africa *was* uniquely affected by a sporting isolation. Politics does not entail the use of one all-purpose strategy but those measures justified by their effectiveness and legitimacy.

The boycott had done as much as anything to force measurable change in the republic.

Most insightful is reconsideration of the argument that the rebel tours were a 'business proposition like any other'. It is possible to debate when and how economic engagement with a disgraced government is desirable, although the 'inconsistency' justification is insufficient here too – the fact that an international bank is doing something does not qualify this as a productive or wise course of action. Still, there might be times when economic engagement is indeed productive or wise but the tax concessions make the argument moot in this case.

The rebel tours were not a business proposition like any other. At the commercial level, the tours made no sense. The size and source of the payments received by the rebel cricketers are condemnatory. Viv Richards was fully vindicated in his assessment that the amount of money on offer 'showed things were not really right.'

This is not to say that the rebel tours were essential in propping up apartheid. Clearly, it is preposterous to suggest that the National Party would have dismantled apartheid for a game of cricket. In his exhaustive review of the Anti-Apartheid Movement Roger Fieldhouse writes: 'Ultimately, the campaign to discourage economic collaboration and investment in South Africa was probably the most significant and influential of all the campaigns.'[1] Whether or not sport was a religion in white South Africa, the finances probably mattered rather more.

Instead sport was a publicity tool for the boycott movement. Isolation raised the profile of apartheid reality in the hope that economic and political links, the essentials to sustain apartheid government, were adversely affected and that internal pressure on the government would grow. Such as they understood it, the rebel cricketers objected to being used by a protest movement. But the publicity enjoyed and endured by elite sportsmen is not easily escaped. In breaking the boycott they were instead used by the National Party.

Few rebel tourists would accept this conclusion – public expressions of reflection or doubt have been rare among those who visited South Africa. But it is difficult to construct any logical case for government payment, and in secret, due to the anger it would cause among most taxpayers, except the veneer of respectability that the tours provided. Inside South Africa their presentation as international matches contributed to a sense of normality while highlighting overseas support for the status quo. Outside South Africa they certainly received intense criticism but also provided a high-profile validation of international engagement with a regime that required such engagement to survive. The anger kept from the first six rebel tours, and then unleashed with interest on the seventh, was aimed not only at a cricket tour but at engagement generally. The idea that the tours had nothing to do with the apartheid struggle was erased once those directly involved in the struggle were given a serious voice.

None of this denies that the choice was anything but each player's. The rebels ought to have been free to go – but then they always were. The majority who opposed them were engaged in a campaign of persuasion and ultimately vindicated in their representations on sporting links. The tours were a source of support for the apartheid regime. The democratic rights the rebels were so happy to brandish were precisely those denied to the majority of South Africans who funded their tours.

1 p 87, Fieldhouse (2004).

# Schedules and Results

## South African Breweries XI, 1981–82

3–4 March: Tour match at Berea Park, Pretoria. SAB XI (152-7d & 32-2) drew with South African Under-25s (170-8d).

6 March: First 'ODI' at St George's Park, Port Elizabeth. SAB XI (240-5) lost to South Africa (244-3) by seven wickets.

8–10 March: Tour match at Newlands, Cape Town. Western Province (263-8d & 204-7d) drew with SAB XI (219 & 225-8).

12–15 March: First 'Test' at Wanderers, Johannesburg. South Africa (400-7d & 37-2) beat SAB XI (150 & 283) by eight wickets.

17 March: Second 'ODI' at Kingsmead, Durban. South Africa (231-6) beat SAB XI (152) by 79 runs.

19–22 March: Second 'Test' at Newlands, Cape Town. SAB XI (223 & 249-3d) drew with South Africa (235 & 38-0).

24 March: Third 'ODI' at Wanderers, Johannesburg. South Africa (243-5) beat SAB XI (111-7 from 23 overs) on faster scoring rate.

26–29 March: Third 'Test' at Kingsmead, Durban. South Africa (181-9d & 143-2) drew with SAB XI (311-8d).

**Squad:** Graham Gooch (captain), Dennis Amiss, Geoffrey Boycott, John Emburey, Mike Hendrick, Geoff Humpage, Alan Knott, Wayne Larkins, John Lever, Chris Old, Arnold Sidebottom, Les Taylor, Derek Underwood, Peter Willey, Bob Woolmer.

**Notes:**

'ODIs' 50 overs per innings. South Africa won the three-match series 3-0.
'Tests' four days. South Africa won the three-match series 1-0.

## Arosa Sri Lanka, 1982–83

26–28 October: Tour match at Berea Park, Pretoria. Arosa Sri Lanka (315-9d & 123) lost to Combined Transvaal XI (313-4d & 127-4) by six wickets.

30 October, 1 November: Tour match at Newlands, Cape Town. Arosa Sri Lanka (275 & 307) drew with Western Province (400-7d & 106-6).

3–4 November: Tour match at Oude Libertas, Stellenbosch. Arosa Sri Lanka (208 & 79) lost to Boland (141 & 149-5) by five wickets.

6 November: First 'ODI' at Wanderers, Johannesburg. South Africa (291-4) beat Arosa Sri Lanka (102) by 189 runs.

8 November: Second 'ODI' at Berea Park, Pretoria. South Africa (281-5) beat Arosa Sri Lanka (174-5) by 107 runs.

10–11 November: Tour match at Jan Smuts Ground, East London. Arosa Sri Lanka (275 & 188-6) drew with Eastern Cape Invitational XI (181-6d).

13–15 November: Tour match at St George's Park, Port Elizabeth. Arosa Sri Lanka (223 & 321-8d) drew with Eastern Province (287-5d & 162-8).

17 November: Third 'ODI' at Kingsmead, Durban. Arosa Sri Lanka (140) lost to South Africa (143-2) by eight wickets.

19, 20, 22, 23 November: First 'Test' at Wanderers, Johannesburg. Arosa Sri Lanka (213 & 141) lost to South Africa (378) by an innings and 24 runs.

25 November: 45-over day-night match at Jan Smuts Stadium, Pietermaritzburg. Arosa Sri Lanka (181) lost to Natal Invitational XI (183-2) by eight wickets.

27–29 November: Tour match at Kingsmead, Durban. Arosa Sri Lanka (129 & 104) lost to Natal (328) by an innings and 95 runs.

1 December: Fourth 'ODI' at St George's Park, Port Elizabeth. Arosa Sri Lanka (276-9) lost to South Africa (278-4) by six wickets.

4–6 December: Tour match at Wanderers, Johannesburg. Arosa Sri Lanka (122 & 200) lost to Transvaal (362-1d) by an innings and 40 runs

9, 10, 11, 13 December: Second 'Test' at Newlands, Cape Town. Arosa Sri Lanka (282 & 281) lost to South Africa (663-6d) by an innings and 100 runs.

Squad: Bandula Warnapura (captain), Flavian Aponso, Hemantha Devapriya, Lantra Fernando, Mahes Goonatilleke, Nirmal Hettiaratchi, Lalith Kaluperuma, Susantha Karunaratne, Bernard Perera, Anura Ranasinghe, Ajit de Silva, Bandula de Silva, Jeryl Woutersz, Tony Opatha (player-manager).

**Notes:**
'ODIs' 55 overs per innings. South Africa won the four-match series 4-0.
'Tests' four days. South Africa won the two-match series 2-0.
One informal warm-up match was played: 24 October: v Nicky Oppenheimer's XI at Sandton.

## West Indian XI, 1982–83

15 January: 50-over match at Newlands, Cape Town. West Indian XI (204-9) beat Western Province (183) by 21 runs.

17 January: 50-over match at January: Smuts Ground, East London. Border (100-8) lost to West Indian XI (101-3) by seven wickets.

19 January: 50-over match at St George's Park, Port Elizabeth. West Indian XI (243) beat Eastern Province (158) by 85 runs.

21, 22, 24, 25 January: First 'Test' at Newlands, Cape Town. South Africa (449 & 108-5) beat West Indian XI (246 & 309) by five wickets.

28, 29, 31 Jan,1 February: Second 'Test' at Wanderers, Johannesburg. West Indian XI (267 & 176) beat South Africa (233 & 181) by 29 runs.

3 February: 50-over match at Kingsmead, Durban. Natal (202-8) beat West Indian XI (118) by 84 runs.

5 February: First 'ODI' at St George's Park, Port Elizabeth. South Africa (250-7) beat West Indian XI (159) by 91 runs.

7 February: Second 'ODI' at Newlands, Cape Town. South Africa (194-8) beat West Indian XI (151) by 43 runs.

9 February: Third 'ODI' at Berea Park, Pretoria. South Africa (179-9) beat West Indian XI (167) by 12 runs.

11 February: Fourth 'ODI' at Wanderers, Johannesburg. South Africa (139) lost to

West Indian XI (141-3) by seven wickets.

12 February: Fifth 'ODI' at Wanderers, Johannesburg. South Africa (228-6) beat West Indian XI (171) by 57 runs.

13 February: Sixth 'ODI' at Kingsmead, Durban. West Indian XI (155) beat South Africa (71) by 84 runs.

Squad: Lawrence Rowe (captain), Richard Austin, Herbert Chang, Sylvester Clarke, Colin Croft, Alvin Greenidge, Bernard Julien, Alvin Kallicharran, Collis King, Everton Mattis, Ezra Moseley, David Murray, Derick Parry, Franklyn Stephenson, Emmerson Trotman, Ray Wynter, Albert Padmore (player-manager).

**Notes:**
'ODIs' 50 overs per innings. South Africa won the six-match series 4-2.
'Tests' four days. Two-match series drawn 1-1.

## West Indian XI, 1983–84

19, 21, 22 November: Tour match at Berea Park, Pretoria. Northern Transvaal (288-9d & 136-5d) drew with West Indian XI (153 & 183-5).

24 November: 50-over match at Oude Libertas, Stellenbosch. Boland (132-8) lost to West Indian XI (133-6) by four wickets.

25, 26, 28 November: Tour match at Newlands, Cape Town. West Indian XI (291 & 300) drew with Western Province (322-8d & 57-1).

30 November: 50-over match at the January: Smuts Ground, East London. West Indian XI (247-6) beat Border (119) by 128 runs.

2, 3, 4 December: Tour match at Kingsmead, Durban. West Indian XI (397 & 168-9d) drew with Natal (239 & 160-3).

7 December: First 'ODI' (day-night) at Wanderers, Johannesburg. South Africa (233-7) lost to West Indian XI (235-8) by two wickets.

10 December: 50-over match at Ramblers, Bloemfontein. West Indian XI (290-6) beat Orange Free State (232-6) by 58 runs.

12, 13, 14 December: Tour match at St George's Park, Port Elizabeth. Eastern Province (314 & 161) drew with West Indian XI (242-7d & 181-7).

17, 18, 19 December: Tour match at Wanderers, Johannesburg. West Indian XI (230 & 172) lost to Transvaal (310-9d & 94-6) by four wickets.

23, 24, 26, 27 December: First 'Test' at Kingsmead, Durban. West Indian XI (529-7d) drew with South Africa (333 & 59-0).

30, 31 December, 2, 3 January: Second 'Test' at Newlands, Cape Town. West Indian XI (252 & 268) lost to South Africa (404 & 117-0) by 10 wickets.

6 January: Second 'ODI' at St George's Park, Port Elizabeth. West Indian XI (260-8) lost to South Africa (261-6) by four wickets.

8 January: Third 'ODI' at Kingsmead, Durban. South Africa (220) lost to West Indian XI (194-4 from 40 overs) on faster scoring rate.

10 January: Fourth 'ODI' at Newlands, Cape Town. South Africa (149) lost to West Indian XI (150-2) by eight wickets.

13, 14, 16, 17 January: Third 'Test' at Wanderers, Johannesburg. South Africa (160 & 236) lost to West Indian XI (193 & 205-9) by one wicket.

21 January: Fifth 'ODI' at Wanderers, Johannesburg. South Africa (279-3) lost to

West Indian XI (208-7 from 34.2 overs) on a faster scoring rate.

23 January: Sixth 'ODI' at Berea Park, Pretoria. South Africa (227-7) beat West Indian XI (54) by 173 runs.

25 January: 50-over match at De Beers Country Club, Kimberley. West Indian XI (316-9) beat Griqualand West (193) by 123 runs.

27, 28, 30, 31 January: 4th 'Test' at St George's Park, Port Elizabeth. South Africa (277 & 127) lost to West Indian XI (199 & 206-4) by six wickets.

Squad: Lawrence Rowe (captain), Hartley Alleyne, Faoud Bacchus, Sylvester Clarke, Colin Croft, Alvin Greenidge, Bernard Julien, Alvin Kallicharan, Collis King, Monte Lynch, Everton Mattis, Ezra Moseley, David Murray, Derick Parry, Franklyn Stephenson, Emmerson Trotman, Albert Padmore (player-manager).

**Notes:**
'ODIs' 50 overs per innings. West Indian XI won the six-match series 4-2.
'Tests' four days. West Indian XI won the four-match series 2-1.

## Australian XI, 1985–86

22, 23, 25 November: Tour match at Ramblers Club, Bloemfontein. Australian XI (345-8d & 301-5d) drew with Orange Free State (319 & 76-1).

27 November: 50-over (day-night) match at Technikon Ground, Pretoria. Northern Transvaal (211-9) beat Australian XI (204) by seven runs.

29, 30 November, 2 December: Tour match at Berea Park, Pretoria. South Africa Board President's XI (150 & 126) lost to Australian XI (186 & 91-5) by five wickets.

4 December: 50-over (day-night) match at Wanderers, Johannesburg. Transvaal (269-3) beat Australian XI (211-6) by 58 runs.

6–8 December: Tour match at January: Smuts Ground, East London. Border (168) drew with Australian XI (236-8).

11 December: 50-over (day-night) match at St George's Park, Port Elizabeth. Australian XI (222-7) beat Eastern Province (217-9) by five runs.

13–15 December: Tour match at St George's Park, Port Elizabeth. Australian XI (382-9d & 101-1d) lost to Eastern Province (235 & 250-8) by two wickets.

17-19 December: Tour match at Oude Libertas, Stellenbosch. Boland (271 & 159-6) drew with Australian XI (456-9d).

21 December: 50-over match at Newlands, Cape Town. Australian XI (260-4) beat Western Province (212-9) by 48 runs.

23 December: 50-over (day-night) match at Kingsmead, Durban. Australian XI (234-6) beat Natal (206) by 28 runs.

26-29 December: 1st 'Test' at Kingsmead, Durban. South Africa (393 & 203-7d) drew with Australian XI (359 & 32-2).

1–4 January: 2nd 'Test' at Newlands, Cape Town. South Africa (430 & 202-5d) drew with Australian XI (304 & 224-4).

6-8 January: Tour match at St George's Park, Port Elizabeth. South African Universities (219 & 237-5d) drew with Australian XI (220-9d & 203-9).

10, 11, 13 January: Tour match at Berea Park, Pretoria. Australian XI (229 & 326-2d) beat Northern Transvaal (190 & 340) by 25 runs.

16, 17, 18, 20, 21 January: 3rd 'Test' at Wanderers, Johannesburg. South Africa

(211 & 305) beat Australian XI (267 & 61) by 188 runs.

24 January: 1st 'ODI' (day-night) at Wanderers, Johannesburg. Australian XI (197-5) beat South Africa (151) by 46 runs.

26 January: 2nd 'ODI' at Kingsmead, Durban. South Africa (221-6) lost to Australian XI (224-6) by four wickets.

28 January: 3rd 'ODI' at St George's Park, Port Elizabeth. South Africa (223-9) beat Australian XI (151) by 72 runs.

30 January: 4th 'ODI' at Newlands, Cape Town. South Africa (234-9) beat Australian XI (210) by 24 runs.

1 February: 5th 'ODI' at Wanderers, Johannesburg. Australian XI (185-7 from 49 overs) lost to South Africa (189-5) by five wickets.

3 February: 50-over match at De Beers Country Club, Kimberley. Australian XI (219-9) lost to Griqualand West (221-4) by six wickets.

5 February: 6th 'ODI' at Berea Park, Pretoria. Australian XI (272-6) lost to South Africa (273-4) by six wickets.

Squad: Kim Hughes (captain), Terry Alderman, John Dyson, Peter Faulkner, Mike Haysman, Tom Hogan, Rodney Hogg, Trevor Hohns, John Maguire, Rod McCurdy, Carl Rackemann, Steve Rixon, Greg Shipperd, Steve Smith, Mick Taylor, Graham Yallop.

**Notes:**
'ODIs' 50 overs per innings. South Africa won the six-match series 4-2.
1st and 2nd 'Tests' four days, 3rd 'Test' five days. South Africa won the three-match series 1-0.
Four informal warm-up matches were played: 9 November: v Northern Transvaal County Districts Invitation XI at Nelspruit, 10 November: v Northern Transvaal County Districts at Nelspruit, 16 November: v Orange Free State County Districts at Virginia, 18 November: v Transvaal County Districts at Orkney.

## Australian XI, 1986-87

17 November: 50-over match at Oude Libertas, Stellenbosch. Australian XI (180-8) beat Boland (178-9) by two runs.

18 November: 50-over match at Danie Craven Stadium, Stellenbosch. Australian XI (198-8) lost to Boland Invitation XI (202-7) by three wickets.

21, 22, 24 November: Tour match at University Ground, Bloemfontein. Australian XI (412d-9 & 100-1) drew with Orange Free State (367).

25 November: 50-over match at De Beers Country Club, Kimberley. Australian XI (248-5) beat Griqualand West (168) by 80 runs.

27–29 November: Tour match at Harmony Cricket Club, Virginia. Australian XI (347-6d & 128-5d) lost to President's XI (215-5d & 261-7) by three wickets.

30 November: 50-over match at Harmony Cricket Club, Virginia. President's XI (185) lost to Australian XI (149-9 from 39.5 overs) on faster scoring rate.

2, 3, 4 December: Tour match at January: Smuts Ground, East London. Border (358) drew with Australian XI (519-8).

6 December: 1st 'Day-Night International' at Centurion Park, Verwoerdburg. Australian XI (238-5 from 44 overs) lost to South Africa (239-4) by six wickets.

8 December: 2nd 'Day-Night International' at Wanderers, Johannesburg. Australian

XI (149 from 40 overs); South Africa (3-1). No result due to rain.

10 December: 3rd 'Day-Night International' at Newlands, Cape Town. Australian XI (85) lost to South Africa (86-2) by eight wickets.

10 December: 25-over match at Newlands, Cape Town. Australian XI (153-5) lost to South Africa (154-4) by six wickets.

12–14 December: Tour match at St George's Park, Port Elizabeth. Eastern Province (117 & 125) lost to Australian XI (326-7d) by an innings and 84 runs.

17 December: 4th 'Day-Night International' at Kingsmead, Durban. South Africa (183-9 from 48 overs) lost to Australian XI (153-4 from 39.1 overs) on faster scoring rate.

19–21 December: Tour match at Kingsmead, Durban. Australian XI (227-2d & 238-6d) lost to Natal (234-3d & 232-4) by six wickets.

24, 26, 27, 28 December: 1st 'Test' at Wanderers, Johannesburg. South Africa (254 & 182) beat Australian XI (142 & 245) by 49 runs.

1, 2, 3, 5, 6 January: 2nd 'Test' at Newlands, Cape Town. South Africa (493 & 257-3) drew with Australian XI (496).

9–11 January: Tour match at January: Smuts Ground, East London. South African Invitation XI (165 & 121) lost to Australian XI (332) by an innings and 46 runs.

13–15 January: Tour match at January: Smuts Stadium, Pietermaritzburg. South African Universities XI (240-9d & 128-2) drew with Australian XI (448).

17, 19, 20, 21, 22 January: 3rd 'Test' at Kingsmead Durban. Australian XI (264 & 339) drew with South Africa (350 & 143-7).

24, 26, 27 January: Tour match at Centurion Park, Verwoerdburg. Northern Transvaal (315-8d & 217-9d) drew with Australian XI (281-3d & 219-7).

30, 31 January, 1, 3, 4 February: 4th 'Test' at St George's Park, Port Elizabeth. Australian XI (455-9d & 333-4) drew with South Africa (533).

7 February: 1st 'ODI' at St George's Park, Port Elizabeth. South Africa (316-6) beat Australian XI (310) by six runs.

10 February: 2nd 'ODI' at Newlands, Cape Town. Australian XI (199-7 from 47.4 overs) lost to South Africa (188-2 from 40.3 overs) on faster scoring rate.

12 February: 3rd 'ODI' at Centurion Park, Verwoerdburg. South Africa (237-9) lost to Australian XI (238-5) by five wickets.

14 February: 4th 'ODI' at Wanderers, Johannesburg. Australian XI (175-9) lost to South Africa (176-6) by four wickets.

Squad: Kim Hughes (captain), Terry Alderman, John Dyson, Peter Faulkner, Mike Haysman, Tom Hogan, Rodney Hogg, Trevor Hohns, John Maguire, Rod McCurdy, Carl Rackemann, Steve Rixon, Greg Shipperd, Steve Smith, Mick Taylor, Kepler Wessels, Graham Yallop.

**Notes:**
'Day-Night Internationals' 50 overs per innings. South Africa won the four-match series 2-1.
'ODIs' 50 overs per innings. South Africa won the four-match series 3-1.
'Tests' five days. South Africa won the four-match series 1-0.
Two informal warm-up matches were played:14 November: v Southern Cape at Oudtshoorn, 15 November: v Southern Cape Invitation XI at Oudtshoorn.

## English XI, 1989–90

26–28 January: Tour match at De Beers Country Club, Kimberley. English XI (305 & 206-4d) beat Combined Bowl XI (152 & 105) by 254 runs.

30, 31 January, 1 February: Tour match at Springbok Park, Bloemfontein. South African Universities (328-6d & 160-9d) drew with English XI (212 & 75-4)

3, 4, 5 February: Tour match at January: Smuts Stadium, Pietermaritzburg. South African Invitation XI (305-2d & 315-2d) drew with English XI (292-5d & 198-5).

8, 9, 10 February: 1st 'Test' at Wanderers, Johannesburg. English XI (156 & 122) lost to South Africa (203 & 76-3) by seven wickets.

16 February: 2nd 'Test' at Newlands, Cape Town. Match cancelled.

16 February: 1st 'ODI' at Centurion Park, Verwoerdburg. English XI (217) lost to South Africa (218-5) by five wickets.

18 February: 2nd 'ODI' at Kingsmead, Durban. South Africa (219-5) beat English XI (205-7) by 14 runs.

20 February: 3rd 'ODI' at Springbok Park, Bloemfontein. South Africa (301-7) beat English XI (94) by 207 runs.

22 February: 4th 'ODI' at Wanderers, Johannesburg. English XI (296-8) beat South Africa (162) by 134 runs.

Squad: Mike Gatting (captain), Bill Athey, Kim Barnett, Chris Broad, Chris Cowdrey, Graham Dilley, Richard Ellison, John Emburey, Neil Foster, Bruce French, Paul Jarvis, Matthew Maynard, Tim Robinson, Greg Thomas, Alan Wells, David Graveney (player-manager).

**Notes:**
'ODIs' 55 overs per innings. South Africa won the four-match series 3-1.
'Test' five days. South Africa won the only 'Test'

## 'Test' Match Scorecards

## South African Breweries XI , 1981–82

**1st 'Test' South Africa v SAB XI**
Wanderers, Johannesburg
12,13,14,15 March 1982
Result: South Africa won by 8 wickets

South Africa won toss
Umpires: PR Hurwitz and BC Smith

| **South Africa 1st innings** | | | |
|---|---|---|---|
| BA Richards | c Amiss | b Underwood | 66 |
| SJ Cook | c Gooch | b Taylor | 114 |
| PN Kirsten | c Gooch | b Taylor | 88 |
| RG Pollock | not out | | 64 |
| CEB Rice | c Knott | b Taylor | 1 |
| *MJ Procter | c Knott | b Lever | 1 |
| AJ Kourie | lbw | b Old | 14 |
| †RV Jennings | c Knott | b Lever | 24 |
| GS Le Roux | not out | | 6 |
| Extras | (lb 17, w 4, nb 1) | | 22 |
| Total | (7 wkts dec., 116 overs) | | 400 |

DNB: ST Jefferies, VAP van der Bijl
FoW: 1-117, 2-278, 3-286, 4-290, 5-295, 6-331, 7-388

| | O | M | R | W |
|---|---|---|---|---|
| Taylor | 31 | 7 | 73 | 3 |
| Lever | 32 | 3 | 122 | 2 |
| Old | 28 | 10 | 76 | 1 |
| Underwood | 23 | 1 | 92 | 1 |
| Gooch | 2 | 0 | 15 | 0 |

**SAB XI 1st innings**

| | | | |
|---|---|---|---|
| *GA Gooch | b Le Roux | 30 | |
| G Boycott | c Cook | b van der Bijl | 5 |
| W Larkins | lbw | b van der Bijl | 2 |
| DL Amiss | not out | | 66 |
| RA Woolmer | c Jennings | b Kourie | 14 |
| P Willey | lbw | b Jefferies | 1 |
| DL Underwood | c Cook | b van der Bijl | 8 |
| †APE Knott | c Richards | b van der Bijl | 5 |
| CM Old | c Kourie | b van der Bijl | 1 |
| JK Lever | | b Kourie | 9 |
| LB Taylor | | b Jefferies | 0 |
| Extras | | (b 1, lb 5, w 2, nb 1) | 9 |
| Total | (all out, 63 overs) | | 150 |

FoW: 1-38, 2-38, 3-42, 4-73, 5-80, 6-90, 7-124, 8-130, 9-142

| | O | M | R | W |
|---|---|---|---|---|
| van der Bijl | 22 | 8 | 25 | 5 |
| Jefferies | 20 | 5 | 59 | 2 |
| Kourie | 11 | 2 | 19 | 2 |
| Le Roux | 10 | 2 | 38 | 1 |

**SAB XI 2nd innings**

| | | | |
|---|---|---|---|
| *GA Gooch | c Jennings | b van der Bijl | 109 |
| G Boycott | lbw | b van der Bijl | 36 |
| W Larkins | c Kourie | b van der Bijl | 20 |
| DL Amiss | c Procter | b Jefferies | 24 |
| RA Woolmer | lbw | b Le Roux | 21 |
| P Willey | lbw | b Le Roux | 24 |
| †APE Knott | lbw | b van der Bijl | 9 |
| CM Old | | b Le Roux | 11 |
| JK Lever | not out | | 10 |
| DL Underwood | lbw | b van der Bijl | 6 |
| LB Taylor | c Pollock | b Le Roux | 0 |
| Extras | | (b 4, lb 3, w 2, nb 4) | 13 |
| Total | (all out, 103.2 overs) | | 283 |

FoW: 1-119, 2-174, 3-179, 4-207, 5-229, 6-252, 7-258, 8-267, 9-278

| | O | M | R | W |
|---|---|---|---|---|
| van der Bijl | 31 | 9 | 79 | 5 |
| Jefferies | 27 | 4 | 88 | 1 |
| Kourie | 16 | 7 | 53 | 0 |
| Le Roux | 22.2 | 5 | 44 | 4 |
| Procter | 6 | 3 | 6 | 0 |

**South Africa 2nd innings**

| | | | |
|---|---|---|---|
| SJ Cook | | c & b Old | 2 |
| BA Richards | lbw | b Lever | 4 |
| PN Kirsten | not out | | 20 |
| RG Pollock | not out | | 9 |
| Extras | | (lb 2) | 2 |
| Total | (2 wkts, 11.4 overs) | | 37 |

DNB: CEB Rice, *MJ Procter, AJ Kourie, †RV Jennings, GS Le Roux, ST Jefferies, VAP van der Bijl
FoW: 1-8, 2-14

| | O | M | R | W |
|---|---|---|---|---|
| Lever | 5.4 | 1 | 27 | 1 |
| Old | 6 | 1 | 8 | 1 |

**2nd 'Test' South Africa v SAB XI**
Newlands, Cape Town
19,20,21,22 March 1982
Result: Match drawn

SAB XI won toss
Umpires: OR Schoof and BC Smith

**SAB XI 1st innings**

| | | | |
|---|---|---|---|
| *GA Gooch | hit wicket | b Kourie | 83 |
| G Boycott | c Kuiper | b Kourie | 16 |
| W Larkins | c Richards | b Kourie | 29 |
| DL Amiss | c Jennings | b Jefferies | 13 |
| RA Woolmer | c & | b Kourie | 2 |
| P Willey | c Kourie | b van der Bijl | 39 |
| †APE Knott | | b van der Bijl | 16 |
| CM Old | c Jennings | b Jefferies | 1 |
| JK Lever | | b Jefferies | 8 |
| DL Underwood | c Richards | b van der Bijl | 0 |
| LB Taylor | not out | | 10 |
| Extras | | (lb 2, w 2, nb 2) | 6 |
| Total | (all out, 102.4 overs) | | 223 |

FoW: 1-27, 2-104, 3-140, 4-144, 5-148, 6-189, 7-199, 8-205, 9-207

| | O | M | R | W |
|---|---|---|---|---|
| van der Bijl | 33 | 12 | 61 | 3 |
| Jefferies | 24.4 | 9 | 56 | 3 |
| Hobson | 13 | 3 | 48 | 0 |
| Kourie | 32 | 15 | 52 | 4 |

**South Africa 1st innings**

| | | | |
|---|---|---|---|
| SJ Cook | c Knott | b Lever | 18 |
| *BA Richards | lbw | b Taylor | 8 |
| PN Kirsten | lbw | b Lever | 114 |
| RG Pollock | c Knott | b Lever | 0 |
| CEB Rice | lbw | b Taylor | 12 |

| | | | |
|---|---|---|---|
| AP Kuiper | c Willey | b Underwood | 1 |
| AJ Kourie | c Knott | b Lever | 18 |
| †RV Jennings | c sub | b Lever | 32 |
| ST Jefferies | c Knott | b Lever | 3 |
| VAP van der Bijl | not out | | 4 |
| DL Hobson | | b Taylor | 2 |
| Extras | | (lb 6, w 1, nb 16) | 23 |
| Total | (all out, 108 overs) | | 235 |

FoW: 1-11, 2-43, 3-43, 4-85, 5-87, 6-144, 7-212, 8-218, 9-232

| | O | M | R | W |
|---|---|---|---|---|
| Taylor | 27 | 8 | 49 | 3 |
| Lever | 37 | 11 | 86 | 6 |
| Old | 18 | 6 | 33 | 0 |
| Underwood | 22 | 9 | 36 | 1 |
| Willey | 4 | 1 | 8 | 0 |

**SAB XI 2nd innings**

| | | | |
|---|---|---|---|
| *GA Gooch | c Kourie | b Hobson | 68 |
| G Boycott | c Jennings | b Jefferies | 1 |
| W Larkins | lbw | b Kirsten | 95 |
| DL Amiss | not out | | 73 |
| RA Woolmer | not out | | 1 |
| Extras | | (b 4, lb 7) | 11 |
| Total | (3 wkts dec., 93 overs) | | 249 |

DNB: P Willey, †APE Knott, CM Old, JK Lever, DL Underwood, LB Taylor
FoW: 1-8, 2-112, 3-231

| | O | M | R | W |
|---|---|---|---|---|
| van der Bijl | 21 | 6 | 53 | 0 |
| Jefferies | 14 | 5 | 39 | 1 |
| Hobson | 30 | 7 | 86 | 1 |
| Kourie | 16 | 4 | 38 | 0 |
| Kirsten | 4 | 2 | 7 | 1 |
| Kuiper | 8 | 2 | 15 | 0 |

**South Africa 2nd innings**

| | | | |
|---|---|---|---|
| †RV Jennings | not out | | 28 |
| AP Kuiper | not out | | 9 |
| Extras | | (lb 1) | 1 |
| Total | (0 wkts, 7 overs) | | 38 |

DNB: SJ Cook, *BA Richards, PN Kirsten, RG Pollock, CEB Rice, AJ Kourie, †RV Jennings, VAP van der Bijl, DL Hobson

| | O | M | R | W |
|---|---|---|---|---|
| Lever | 3 | 0 | 22 | 0 |
| Old | 4 | 0 | 15 | 0 |

**3rd 'Test' South Africa v SAB XI**
Kingsmead, Durban
26,27,28,29 March 1982
Result: Match drawn
SAB XI won toss
Umpires: DD Schoof and OR Schoof

**South Africa 1st innings**

| | | | |
|---|---|---|---|
| SJ Cook | c Gooch | b Lever | 11 |
| *BA Richards | c Knott | b Hendrick | 41 |
| PN Kirsten | c Gooch | b Hendrick | 11 |
| RG Pollock | | b Taylor | 15 |
| CEB Rice | c Gooch | b Hendrick | 9 |
| AP Kuiper | | b Taylor | 0 |
| AJ Kourie | not out | | 50 |
| †RV Jennings | c Knott | b Taylor | 22 |
| GS Le Roux | c Knott | b Taylor | 0 |
| VAP van der Bijl | c Knott | b Taylor | 0 |
| WK Watson | not out | | 4 |
| Extras | | (lb 11, w 7) | 18 |
| Total | (9 wkts dec., 70.3 overs) | | 181 |

FoW: 1-48, 2-61, 3-77, 4-92, 5-92, 6-111, 7-168, 8-170, 9-170

| | O | M | R | W |
|---|---|---|---|---|
| Taylor | 25.3 | 5 | 61 | 5 |
| Lever | 13 | 1 | 53 | 1 |
| Old | 11 | 3 | 21 | 0 |
| Hendrick | 21 | 9 | 28 | 3 |

**SAB XI 1st innings**

| | | | |
|---|---|---|---|
| *GA Gooch | c Kourie | b Le Roux | 48 |
| G Boycott | c Jennings | b van der Bijl | 31 |
| W Larkins | lbw | b van der Bijl | 39 |
| DL Amiss | c Cook | b van der Bijl | 50 |
| RA Woolmer | c Kourie | b Watson | 100 |
| P Willey | | b Watson | 15 |
| †APE Knott | c Kirsten | b van der Bijl | 6 |
| CM Old | c Rice | b van der Bijl | 10 |
| JK Lever | not out | | 4 |
| Extras | | (lb 7, w 1) | 8 |
| Total | (8 wkts dec., 111.2 overs) | | 311 |

DNB: M Hendrick, LB Taylor
FoW: 1-67, 2-95, 3-137, 4-217, 5-259, 6-270, 7-301, 8-311

| | O | M | R | W |
|---|---|---|---|---|
| van der Bijl | 40 | 14 | 97 | 5 |
| Watson | 25.1 | 4 | 79 | 2 |
| Le Roux | 24 | 5 | 71 | 1 |
| Kourie | 17 | 3 | 43 | 0 |
| Kuiper | 3 | 1 | 8 | 0 |
| Kirsten | 2 | 1 | 5 | 0 |

**South Africa 2nd innings**

| | | | |
|---|---|---|---|
| SJ Cook | not out | | 50 |
| *BA Richards | retired hurt | | 17 |
| PN Kirsten | c Knott | b Lever | 14 |
| RG Pollock | c Hendrick | b Larkins | 12 |
| CEB Rice | not out | | 39 |
| Extras | | (lb 4, nb 7) | 11 |
| Total | (2 wkts, 48 overs) | | 143 |

DNB: AP Kuiper, AJ Kourie, †RV Jennings, GS Le Roux, VAP van der Bijl, WK Watson
FoW: 1-61, 2-91

| | O | M | R | W |
|---|---|---|---|---|
| Taylor | 8 | 2 | 23 | 0 |
| Lever | 16 | 9 | 25 | 1 |
| Old | 6 | 2 | 18 | 0 |
| Hendrick | 12 | 3 | 37 | 0 |
| Larkins | 5 | 0 | 24 | 1 |
| Knott | 1 | 0 | 5 | 0 |

## Arosa Sri Lanka 1982–83

**1st 'Test' South Africa v Arosa Sri Lanka**
Wanderers, Johannesburg
19,20,22,23 November: ember 1982
Result: South Africa won by an innings and 24 runs

Arosa Sri Lanka won toss
Umpires: CJ Mitchley and OR Schoof

**Arosa Sri Lanka 1st innings**

| | | | |
|---|---|---|---|
| NDP Hettiaratchi | c Jennings | b Le Roux | 1 |
| PB de Silva | c Jennings | b Jefferies | 70 |
| *B Warnapura | lbw | b Jefferies | 15 |
| GJAF Aponso | lbw | b Le Roux | 12 |
| JNB Perera | c Jennings | b Kuiper | 2 |
| JF Woutersz | lbw | b Le Roux | 51 |
| PLJ Fernando | c Rice | b van der Bijl | 21 |
| LW Kaluperuma | c Rice | b Le Roux | 2 |
| †HM Goonatilleke | not out | | 15 |
| ARM Opatha | c Jennings | b Le Roux | 9 |
| GRA de Silva | c Jennings | b Le Roux | 0 |
| Extras | | (lb 5, w 9, nb 1) | 15 |
| Total | (all out, 72.3 overs) | | 213 |

FoW: 1-10, 2-34, 3-73, 4-76, 5-134, 6-176, 7-179, 8-193, 9-213

| | O | M | R | W |
|---|---|---|---|---|
| van der Bijl | 21 | 4 | 51 | 1 |
| Le Roux | 18.3 | 1 | 55 | 6 |
| Jefferies | 14 | 3 | 44 | 2 |
| Kourie | 15 | 2 | 42 | 0 |
| Kuiper | 4 | 0 | 6 | 1 |

**South Africa 1st innings**

| | | | |
|---|---|---|---|
| SJ Cook | | b Perera | 169 |
| BA Richards | | b Opatha | 1 |
| ST Jefferies | c Fernando | b Kaluperuma | 45 |
| *PN Kirsten | c Goonatilleke | b Opatha | 3 |
| RG Pollock | | c & b Kaluperuma | 79 |
| CEB Rice | | b Kaluperuma | 19 |
| AP Kuiper | c Opatha | b Kaluperuma | 11 |
| AJ Kourie | lbw | b Opatha | 11 |
| †RV Jennings | lbw | b Kaluperuma | 2 |
| GS Le Roux | c Kaluperuma | b Perera | 6 |
| VAP van der Bijl | not out | | 4 |
| Extras | | (b 6, lb 3, w 16, nb 3) | 28 |
| Total | (all out, 106.5 overs) | | 378 |

FoW: 1-4, 2-93, 3-96, 4-261, 5-291, 6-317, 7-348, 8-357, 9-373

| | O | M | R | W |
|---|---|---|---|---|
| Opatha | 29 | 4 | 111 | 3 |
| Fernando | 7 | 1 | 24 | 0 |
| Woutersz | 2 | 0 | 11 | 0 |
| Kaluperuma | 45 | 7 | 123 | 5 |
| GRA de Silva | 5 | 0 | 33 | 0 |
| Perera | 18.5 | 2 | 48 | 2 |

**Arosa Sri Lanka 2nd innings**

| | | | |
|---|---|---|---|
| NDP Hettiaratchi | lbw | b Le Roux | 1 |
| PB de Silva | | c & b Kourie | 3 |
| *B Warnapura | c Jennings | b Jefferies | 31 |
| GJAF Aponso | c Jefferies | b Kirsten | 44 |
| JNB Perera | c Pollock | b Jefferies | 0 |
| JF Woutersz | c Kuiper | b Kourie | 0 |
| LW Kaluperuma | c Richards | b Kourie | 39 |
| †HM Goonatilleke | | b Kourie | 2 |
| ARM Opatha | | c & b Kourie | 4 |
| GRA de Silva | not out | | 8 |
| PLJ Fernando | absent hurt | | - |
| Extras | | (b 4, lb 3, w 2) | 9 |
| Total | (all out, 62.1 overs) | | 141 |

FoW: 1-6, 2-46, 3-46, 4-49, 5-51, 6-103, 7-123, 8-131, 9-141

| | O | M | R | W |
|---|---|---|---|---|
| van der Bijl | 14 | 8 | 22 | 0 |
| Le Roux | 8 | 1 | 22 | 1 |
| Jefferies | 14 | 4 | 29 | 2 |
| Kourie | 22 | 6 | 54 | 5 |
| Kirsten | 4.1 | 2 | 5 | 1 |

**2nd 'Test' South Africa v Arosa Sri Lanka**

Newlands, Cape Town
9,10,11,13 December 1982
Result: South Africa won by an innings and 100 runs

South Africa won toss
Umpires: BC Smith and DD Schoof

**Arosa Sri Lanka 1st innings**

| | | | |
|---|---|---|---|
| NDP Hettiaratchi | c Jennings | b Le Roux | 4 |
| HH Devapriya | c Seeff | b Kuiper | 29 |
| *B Warnapura | c Pollock | b Kuiper | 21 |
| GJAF Aponso | c sub | b Kirsten | 81 |
| AN Ranasinghe | c Hobson | b Jefferies | 54 |
| JNB Perera | c Seeff | b Hobson | 13 |
| JF Woutersz | c Jennings | b Le Roux | 31 |
| †HM Goonatilleke | | b Jefferies | 19 |
| LW Kaluperuma | | b Jefferies | 9 |
| ARM Opatha | not out | | 5 |
| GRA de Silva | | b Le Roux | 0 |
| Extras | | (lb 6, w 4, nb 6) | 16 |
| Total | (all out, 90.5 overs) | | 282 |

FoW: 1-4, 2-47, 3-77, 4-150, 5-174, 6-229, 7-268, 8-268, 9-281

| | O | M | R | W |
|---|---|---|---|---|
| Le Roux | 18.5 | 5 | 69 | 3 |
| Jefferies | 18 | 5 | 43 | 3 |
| Kuiper | 13 | 3 | 37 | 2 |
| Kourie | 6 | 0 | 12 | 0 |
| Hobson | 25 | 2 | 77 | 1 |
| Kirsten | 10 | 1 | 28 | 1 |

**South Africa 1st innings**

| | | | |
|---|---|---|---|
| SJ Cook | | b Ranasinghe | 112 |
| L Seeff | c Woutersz | b Perera | 188 |
| *PN Kirsten | run out | | 27 |
| RG Pollock | c Goonatilleke | b Perera | 197 |
| CEB Rice | c Perera | b Opatha | 37 |
| AP Kuiper | st Goonatilleke | b Woutersz | 66 |
| †RV Jennings | not out | | 11 |
| Extras | | (b 2, lb 12, w 2, nb 9) | 25 |
| Total | (6 wkts dec., 159.3 overs) | | 663 |

DNB: GS Le Roux, ST Jefferies, AJ Kourie, DL Hobson
FoW: 1-250, 2-328, 3-344, 4-449, 5-623, 6-663

| | O | M | R | W |
|---|---|---|---|---|
| Opatha | 42 | 5 | 150 | 1 |
| Ranasinghe | 36 | 3 | 123 | 1 |
| de Silva | 7 | 0 | 41 | 0 |
| Kaluperuma | 16 | 0 | 110 | 0 |
| Perera | 42.3 | 3 | 154 | 2 |
| Woutersz | 16 | 0 | 60 | 1 |

**Arosa Sri Lanka 2nd innings**

| | | | |
|---|---|---|---|
| *B Warnapura | | b Jefferies | 14 |
| HH Devapriya | st Jennings | b Hobson | 53 |

| | | | |
|---|---|---|---|
| NDP Hettiaratchi | | b Hobson | 10 |
| GJAF Aponso | | b Kuiper | 7 |
| AN Ranasinghe | | b Kuiper | 9 |
| JNB Perera | c Rice | b Jefferies | 102 |
| JF Woutersz | c Jefferies | b Hobson | 32 |
| †HM Goonatilleke | c Pollock | b Le Roux | 10 |
| ARM Opatha | lbw | b Jefferies | 20 |
| LW Kaluperuma | not out | | 1 |
| GRA de Silva | st Jennings | b Kirsten | 0 |
| Extras | | (lb 15, w 4, nb 4) | 23 |
| Total | (all out, 81.2 overs) | | 281 |

FoW: 1-48, 2-83, 3-90, 4-102, 5-109, 6-186, 7-236, 8-271, 9-280

| | O | M | R | W |
|---|---|---|---|---|
| Le Roux | 12 | 3 | 39 | 1 |
| Jefferies | 19 | 6 | 76 | 3 |
| Kuiper | 12 | 3 | 33 | 2 |
| Hobson | 34 | 9 | 87 | 3 |
| Kirsten | 4.2 | 0 | 23 | 1 |

## West Indian XI, 1982–83

**1st 'Test' South Africa v West Indian XI**
Newlands, Cape Town
21,22,24,25 January 1983
Result: South Africa won by 5 wickets

South Africa won toss
Umpires: BC Smith and OR Schoof

**South Africa 1st innings**

| | | | |
|---|---|---|---|
| SJ Cook | c Murray | b Stephenson | 73 |
| BA Richards | c Rowe | b Moseley | 49 |
| *PN Kirsten | lbw | b Parry | 2 |
| RG Pollock | | b Moseley | 100 |
| CEB Rice | lbw | b Parry | 16 |
| KA McKenzie | lbw | b Parry | 4 |
| AJ Kourie | c Murray | b Moseley | 69 |
| †RV Jennings | | b Parry | 15 |
| GS Le Roux | | c & b Stephenson | 30 |
| VAP van der Bijl | c Stephenson | b Parry | 10 |
| ST Jefferies | not out | | 40 |
| Extras | | (b 18, lb 13, w 2, nb 8) | 41 |
| Total | (all out, 132.4 overs) | | 449 |

FoW: 1-85, 2-98, 3-201, 4-264, 5-270, 6-276, 7-351, 8-371, 9-382

| | O | M | R | W |
|---|---|---|---|---|
| Clarke | 34 | 9 | 88 | 0 |
| Moseley | 25 | 3 | 87 | 3 |
| Stephenson | 23.4 | 0 | 93 | 2 |
| Parry | 43 | 10 | 117 | 5 |
| Austin | 7 | 1 | 23 | 0 |

**West Indian XI 1st innings**

| | | | |
|---|---|---|---|
| RA Austin | c Jennings | b van der Bijl | 93 |
| AE Greenidge | | b Jefferies | 4 |
| EH Mattis | lbw | b Le Roux | 0 |
| AI Kallicharran | | b van der Bijl | 21 |
| *LG Rowe | c Kourie | b van der Bijl | 9 |
| CL King | c Jennings | b van der Bijl | 19 |
| †DA Murray | | b Kourie | 3 |
| DR Parry | | b Kourie | 18 |
| FD Stephenson | run out | | 56 |
| EA Moseley | st Jennings | b Kourie | 8 |
| ST Clarke | not out | | 5 |
| Extras | | (b 1, lb 7, nb 2) | 10 |
| Total | (all out, 75 overs) | | 246 |

FoW: 1-8, 2-9, 3-46, 4-66, 5-86, 6-89, 7-129, 8-212, 9-232

| | O | M | R | W |
|---|---|---|---|---|
| Le Roux | 17 | 4 | 56 | 1 |
| Jefferies | 9 | 4 | 28 | 1 |
| van der Bijl | 20 | 6 | 44 | 4 |
| Kourie | 28 | 6 | 101 | 3 |
| Kirsten | 1 | 0 | 7 | 0 |

**West Indian XI 2nd innings**

| | | | |
|---|---|---|---|
| RA Austin | | b Kourie | 23 |
| AE Greenidge | lbw | b Le Roux | 23 |
| EH Mattis | c Jennings | b Le Roux | 19 |
| AI Kallicharran | st Jennings | b Kourie | 89 |
| *LG Rowe | lbw | b Jefferies | 26 |
| CL King | | b Jefferies | 13 |
| †DA Murray | c Jennings | b Le Roux | 27 |
| DR Parry | lbw | b Jefferies | 29 |
| FD Stephenson | | b Jefferies | 16 |
| EA Moseley | c Kirsten | b van der Bijl | 25 |
| ST Clarke | not out | | 0 |
| Extras | (b 3, lb 9, w 3, nb 4) 19 | | |
| Total | (all out, 122.4 overs) | | 309 |

FoW: 1-43, 2-70, 3-73, 4-127, 5-177, 6-198, 7-253, 8-280, 9-308

| | O | M | R | W |
|---|---|---|---|---|
| Le Roux | 21 | 5 | 71 | 3 |
| Jefferies | 35.4 | 17 | 58 | 4 |
| van der Bijl | 22 | 4 | 46 | 1 |
| Kourie | 31 | 4 | 94 | 2 |
| Kirsten | 13 | 3 | 21 | 0 |

**South Africa 2nd innings**

| | | | |
|---|---|---|---|
| SJ Cook | c Rowe | b Moseley | 6 |
| BA Richards | c Parry | b Clarke | 7 |
| *PN Kirsten | | b Parry | 13 |
| RG Pollock | not out | | 43 |

| | | | |
|---|---|---|---|
| CEB Rice | lbw | b Clarke | 6 |
| KA McKenzie | lbw | b Parry | 0 |
| AJ Kourie | not out | | 12 |
| Extras | | (b 8, lb 5, w 5, nb 3) | 21 |
| Total | (5 wkts, 30 overs) | | 108 |

DNB: †RV Jennings, GS Le Roux, VAP van der Bijl, ST Jefferies
FoW: 1-14, 2-18, 3-65, 4-82, 5-85

| | O | M | R | W |
|---|---|---|---|---|
| Clarke | 15 | 4 | 22 | 2 |
| Moseley | 8 | 1 | 25 | 1 |
| Parry | 7 | 1 | 40 | 2 |

**2nd 'Test' South Africa v West Indian XI**
Wanderers, Johannesburg
28,29,31 January, 1 February 1983
Result: West Indian XI won by 29 runs

South Africa won toss
Umpires: DD Schoof and CJ Mitchley

**West Indian XI 1st innings**

| | | | |
|---|---|---|---|
| RA Austin | c Pollock | b van der Bijl | 4 |
| AE Greenidge | not out | | 42 |
| EH Mattis | lbw | b Le Roux | 3 |
| AI Kallicharran | | b Kourie | 37 |
| *LG Rowe | | b van der Bijl | 0 |
| CL King | lbw | b Kourie | 101 |
| †DA Murray | c Pollock | b van der Bijl | 8 |
| DR Parry | | b Kourie | 20 |
| FD Stephenson | c Pollock | b Kourie | 0 |
| ST Clarke | c Rice | b Kourie | 25 |
| RA Wynter | | b Kourie | 9 |
| Extras | | (lb 9, w 2, nb 7) | 18 |
| Total | (all out, 78 overs) | | 267 |

FoW: 1-13, 2-16, 3-39, 4-104, 5-164, 6-185, 7-185, 8-222, 9-233

| | O | M | R | W |
|---|---|---|---|---|
| Le Roux | 17 | 2 | 58 | 1 |
| Jefferies | 16 | 3 | 62 | 0 |
| van der Bijl | 16 | 3 | 74 | 3 |
| Kourie | 29 | 9 | 55 | 6 |

**South Africa 1st innings**

| | | | |
|---|---|---|---|
| SJ Cook | c Wynter | b Stephenson | 0 |
| BA Richards | c Kallicharran | b Clarke | 0 |
| †RV Jennings | c Parry | b Clarke | 0 |
| *PN Kirsten | | b Clarke | 56 |
| RG Pollock | | b Stephenson | 73 |
| CEB Rice | c Austin | b Parry | 38 |
| KA McKenzie | c Rowe | b Wynter | 27 |

| | | | |
|---|---|---|---|
| AJ Kourie | lbw | b Clarke | 17 |
| GS Le Roux | lbw | b Wynter | 0 |
| ST Jefferies | | b Clarke | 11 |
| VAP van der Bijl | not out | | 1 |
| Extras | | (lb 7, w 1, nb 2) | 10 |
| Total | (all out, 78.3 overs) | | 233 |

FoW: 1-1, 2-1, 3-8, 4-122, 5-151, 6-199, 7-203, 8-204, 9-230

| | O | M | R | W |
|---|---|---|---|---|
| Clarke | 23.3 | 4 | 66 | 5 |
| Wynter | 11 | 3 | 26 | 2 |
| Stephenson | 18 | 1 | 68 | 2 |
| King | 7 | 2 | 29 | 0 |
| Parry | 17 | 5 | 25 | 1 |
| Austin | 2 | 0 | 9 | 0 |

**West Indian XI 2nd innings**

| | | | |
|---|---|---|---|
| RA Austin | c McKenzie | b van der Bijl | 14 |
| AE Greenidge | c Jennings | b Le Roux | 48 |
| EH Mattis | | b Jefferies | 21 |
| AI Kallicharran | | b van der Bijl | 13 |
| *LG Rowe | | b Jefferies | 0 |
| CL King | lbw | b Kourie | 39 |
| †DA Murray | c Cook | b Jefferies | 4 |
| DR Parry | | b Kourie | 15 |
| FD Stephenson | c Pollock | b Le Roux | 4 |
| ST Clarke | c Kourie | b Le Roux | 0 |
| RA Wynter | not out | | 0 |
| Extras | | (b 4, lb 4, w 5, nb 5) | 18 |
| Total | (all out, 62.1 overs) | | 176 |

FoW: 1-33, 2-56, 3-56, 4-57, 5-65, 6-70, 7-70, 8-105, 9-176

| | O | M | R | W |
|---|---|---|---|---|
| Le Roux | 15.1 | 3 | 46 | 3 |
| Jefferies | 22 | 8 | 66 | 3 |
| van der Bijl | 16 | 7 | 24 | 2 |
| Kourie | 9 | 2 | 22 | 2 |

**South Africa 2nd innings**

| | | | |
|---|---|---|---|
| SJ Cook | c King | b Clarke | 27 |
| BA Richards | | b Parry | 59 |
| †RV Jennings | c Murray | b Clarke | 0 |
| *PN Kirsten | | b Clarke | 7 |
| RG Pollock | c King | b Clarke | 1 |
| CEB Rice | c Austin | b Clarke | 12 |
| KA McKenzie | not out | | 26 |
| AJ Kourie | c Murray | b Clarke | 5 |
| GS Le Roux | lbw | b King | 2 |
| ST Jefferies | run out | | 31 |
| VAP van der Bijl | | b Clarke | 2 |
| Extras | | (b 1, lb 4, w 1, nb 3) | 9 |
| Total | (all out, 71.2 overs) | | 181 |

FoW: 1-87, 2-97, 3-97, 4-100, 5-111, 6-117, 7-119, 8-124, 9-179

| | O | M | R | W |
|---|---|---|---|---|
| Clarke | 22.2 | 10 | 34 | 7 |
| Wynter | 9 | 0 | 33 | 0 |
| Stephenson | 18 | 3 | 47 | 0 |
| King | 1 | 0 | 3 | 1 |
| Parry | 20 | 3 | 51 | 1 |
| Austin | 1 | 0 | 4 | 0 |

## West Indian XI, 1983–84

**1st 'Test' South Africa v West Indian XI**
Kingsmead, Durban
23,24,26,27 December 1983
Result: Match drawn

West Indian XI won toss
Umpires: DD Schoof and DH Bezuidenhout

**West Indian XI 1st innings**

| | | | |
|---|---|---|---|
| SFAF Bacchus | retired hurt | | 19 |
| EN Trotman | c Pollock | b Le Roux | 21 |
| MA Lynch | c Hobson | b Kourie | 26 |
| AI Kallicharran | c Hobson | b Le Roux | 103 |
| CL King | c Jefferies | b Rice | 0 |
| *LG Rowe | lbw | b Jefferies | 157 |
| †DA Murray | c Kourie | b Le Roux | 32 |
| FD Stephenson | | b Hobson | 53 |
| DR Parry | not out | | 63 |
| EA Moseley | not out | | 33 |
| Extras | (b 5, lb 9, w 2, nb 6) 22 | | |
| Total | (7 wkts dec., 135 overs) | | 529 |

DNB: ST Clarke
FoW: 1-34, 2-86, 3-87, 4-241, 5-311, 6-392, 7-468

| | O | M | R | W |
|---|---|---|---|---|
| Le Roux | 27 | 2 | 88 | 3 |
| Jefferies | 31 | 3 | 132 | 1 |
| Kourie | 36 | 5 | 123 | 1 |
| Rice | 21 | 4 | 65 | 1 |
| Hobson | 19 | 1 | 95 | 1 |
| Kirsten | 1 | 0 | 4 | 0 |

**South Africa 1st innings**

| | | | |
|---|---|---|---|
| SJ Cook | c Murray | b Clarke | 69 |
| HR Fotheringham | lbw | b Moseley | 0 |
| *PN Kirsten | c Murray | b Moseley | 84 |
| RG Pollock | | b Parry | 62 |
| KS McEwan | c sub | b Moseley | 11 |
| CEB Rice | | c & b Parry | 7 |
| AJ Kourie | | b Clarke | 32 |

| | | | |
|---|---|---|---|
| †RV Jennings | | b Clarke | 18 |
| GS Le Roux | c Stephenson | b Clarke | 11 |
| ST Jefferies | | b Clarke | 0 |
| DL Hobson | | not out | 12 |
| Extras | | (b 4, lb 9, w 1, nb 13) | 27 |
| Total | (all out, 106.1 overs) | | 333 |

FoW: 1-2, 2-132, 3-219, 4-239, 5-249, 6-257, 7-302, 8-313, 9-313

| | O | M | R | W |
|---|---|---|---|---|
| Clarke | 32.1 | 11 | 105 | 5 |
| Moseley | 26 | 5 | 76 | 3 |
| Stephenson | 21 | 5 | 61 | 0 |
| Parry | 25 | 7 | 62 | 2 |
| King | 2 | 1 | 2 | 0 |

**South Africa 2nd innings**

| | | | |
|---|---|---|---|
| SJ Cook | not out | | 30 |
| HR Fotheringham | not out | | 22 |
| Extras | | (b 2, nb 5) | 7 |
| Total | (0 wkts, 24 overs) | | 59 |

DNB: *PN Kirsten, RG Pollock, KS McEwan, CEB Rice, AJ Kourie, †RV Jennings, GS Le Roux, ST Jefferies, DL Hobson

| | O | M | R | W |
|---|---|---|---|---|
| Clarke | 3 | 0 | 9 | 0 |
| Moseley | 4 | 2 | 8 | 0 |
| Stephenson | 6 | 1 | 16 | 0 |
| King | 6 | 2 | 13 | 0 |
| Kallicharran | 5 | 2 | 6 | 0 |

**2nd 'Test' South Africa v West Indian XI**
Newlands, Cape Town
30,31 December 1983, 2,3 January 1984
Result: South Africa won by 10 wickets

West Indian XI won toss
Umpires: CJ Mitchley and SG Moore

**West Indian XI 1st innings**

| | | | |
|---|---|---|---|
| EN Trotman | c Jennings | b Kourie | 28 |
| EH Mattis | lbw | b Jefferies | 6 |
| MA Lynch | c Jennings | b Kourie | 2 |
| AI Kallicharran | c Fotheringham | b Kourie | 8 |
| CL King | c Kourie | b Jefferies | 83 |
| *LG Rowe | | c & b Kourie | 0 |
| †DA Murray | lbw | b Rice | 39 |
| FD Stephenson | c Pollock | b Kourie | 7 |
| BD Julien | not out | | 33 |
| DR Parry | c & | b Le Roux | 30 |
| ST Clarke | lbw | b Jefferies | 0 |
| Extras | (b 4, lb 7, w 1, nb 4) | 16 | |
| Total | (all out, 87.4 overs) | | 252 |

FoW: 1-31, 2-38, 3-46, 4-49, 5-49, 6-156, 7-183, 8-183, 9-247

| | O | M | R | W |
|---|---|---|---|---|
| Le Roux | 17 | 6 | 34 | 1 |
| Jefferies | 20.4 | 6 | 63 | 3 |
| Kourie | 22 | 6 | 66 | 5 |
| Hobson | 20 | 5 | 49 | 0 |
| Rice | 8 | 1 | 24 | 1 |

**South Africa 1st innings**

| | | | |
|---|---|---|---|
| SJ Cook | c Murray | b Clarke | 45 |
| HR Fotheringham | c Julien | b Stephenson | 20 |
| *PN Kirsten | c Parry | b Julien | 88 |
| RG Pollock | c Murray | b Parry | 102 |
| KS McEwan | c Murray | b Clarke | 32 |
| CEB Rice | not out | | 71 |
| AJ Kourie | lbw | b Clarke | 1 |
| †RV Jennings | lbw | b Parry | 8 |
| GS Le Roux | c Mattis | b Clarke | 11 |
| ST Jefferies | c Julien | b Parry | 1 |
| DL Hobson | | c & b Clarke | 1 |
| Extras | | (lb 17, w 6, nb 1) | 24 |
| Total | (all out, 132.5 overs) | | 404 |

FoW: 1-61, 2-84, 3-267, 4-273, 5-315, 6-317, 7-364, 8-393, 9-398

| | O | M | R | W |
|---|---|---|---|---|
| Clarke | 37.5 | 13 | 92 | 5 |
| Julien | 24 | 5 | 71 | 1 |
| Stephenson | 27 | 5 | 95 | 1 |
| Parry | 36 | 8 | 79 | 3 |
| King | 5 | 1 | 21 | 0 |
| Kallicharran | 3 | 0 | 22 | 0 |

**West Indian XI 2nd innings**

| | | | |
|---|---|---|---|
| EN Trotman | c Jennings | b Jefferies | 1 |
| EH Mattis | c Rice | b Kourie | 26 |
| MA Lynch | run out | | 23 |
| AI Kallicharran | lbw | b Kourie | 17 |
| CL King | c Pollock | b Jefferies | 26 |
| *LG Rowe | c Cook | b Hobson | 31 |
| †DA Murray | c Fotheringham | b Kourie | 40 |
| FD Stephenson | lbw | b Le Roux | 7 |
| BD Julien | c Kirsten | b Le Roux | 18 |
| DR Parry | c Pollock | b Rice | 58 |
| ST Clarke | not out | | 3 |
| Extras | | (b 4, lb 7, w 6, nb 1) | 18 |
| Total | (all out, 96.3 overs) | | 268 |

FoW: 1-5, 2-53, 3-63, 4-86, 5-100, 6-178, 7-206, 8-232, 9-260

| | O | M | R | W |
|---|---|---|---|---|
| Le Roux | 17.3 | 5 | 50 | 2 |
| Jefferies | 16 | 6 | 62 | 2 |
| Kourie | 27 | 11 | 61 | 3 |

| | | | | |
|---|---|---|---|---|
| Hobson | 15 | 2 | 36 | 1 |
| Rice | 15 | 8 | 21 | 1 |
| Kirsten | 6 | 1 | 20 | 0 |

**South Africa 2nd innings**

| | | | |
|---|---|---|---|
| SJ Cook | not out | | 40 |
| HR Fotheringham | not out | | 71 |
| Extras | | (lb 5, w 1) | 6 |
| Total | (0 wkts, 21.2 overs) | | 117 |

DNB: *PN Kirsten, RG Pollock, KS McEwan, CEB Rice, AJ Kourie, †RV Jennings, GS Le Roux, ST Jefferies, DL Hobson

| | O | M | R | W |
|---|---|---|---|---|
| Clarke | 6 | 0 | 23 | 0 |
| Julien | 2 | 0 | 11 | 0 |
| Stephenson | 2 | 0 | 11 | 0 |
| Parry | 8 | 0 | 36 | 0 |
| King | 3 | 0 | 22 | 0 |
| Kallicharran | 0.2 | 0 | 8 | 0 |

**'3rd Test' South Africa v West Indian XI**

Wanderers, Johannesburg
13,14,16,17 January 1984
Result: West Indian XI won by 1 wicket

West Indian XI won toss
Umpires: SG Moore and DD Schoof

**South Africa 1st innings**

| | | | |
|---|---|---|---|
| SJ Cook | lbw | b Clarke | 7 |
| HR Fotheringham | | b Moseley | 8 |
| PN Kirsten | c Murray | b Alleyne | 67 |
| RG Pollock | c Moseley | b Alleyne | 41 |
| KS McEwan | c Murray | b Alleyne | 0 |
| *CEB Rice | c Trotman | b Stephenson | 4 |
| AP Kuiper | lbw | b Alleyne | 16 |
| AJ Kourie | not out | | 7 |
| †RV Jennings | c sub | b Moseley | 1 |
| WK Watson | lbw | b Moseley | 0 |
| RW Hanley | c Murray | b Moseley | 0 |
| Extras | | (lb 4, nb 5) | 9 |
| Total | (all out, 45.4 overs) | | 160 |

FoW: 1-16, 2-24, 3-91, 4-92, 5-102, 6-151, 7-154, 8-160, 9-160

| | O | M | R | W |
|---|---|---|---|---|
| Clarke | 13 | 6 | 17 | 1 |
| Moseley | 10.4 | 2 | 45 | 4 |
| Alleyne | 12 | 1 | 54 | 4 |
| Stephenson | 9 | 2 | 34 | 1 |
| King | 1 | 0 | 1 | 0 |

**West Indian XI 1st innings**

| | | | |
|---|---|---|---|
| EN Trotman | c Fotheringham | b Hanley | 3 |
| AE Greenidge | c Jennings | b Kuiper | 20 |
| EH Mattis | lbw | b Watson | 0 |
| MA Lynch | lbw | b Rice | 9 |
| CL King | c Jennings | b Watson | 54 |
| †DA Murray | c Pollock | b Kuiper | 43 |
| *AI Kallicharran | lbw | b Hanley | 18 |
| FD Stephenson | not out | | 30 |
| EA Moseley | c Pollock | b Kuiper | 0 |
| ST Clarke | lbw | b Kuiper | 9 |
| HL Alleyne | c sub | b Kuiper | 0 |
| Extras | | (lb 3, w 1, nb 3) | 7 |
| Total | (all out, 52.5 overs) | | 193 |

FoW: 1-6, 2-11, 3-23, 4-69, 5-106, 6-142, 7-154, 8-154, 9-189

| | O | M | R | W |
|---|---|---|---|---|
| Watson | 16 | 5 | 42 | 2 |
| Hanley | 13 | 4 | 26 | 2 |
| Rice | 6 | 1 | 46 | 1 |
| Kuiper | 11.5 | 0 | 50 | 5 |
| Kourie | 6 | 1 | 22 | 0 |

**South Africa 2nd innings**

| | | | |
|---|---|---|---|
| SJ Cook | c Greenidge | b Alleyne | 17 |
| HR Fotheringham | lbw | b Moseley | 4 |
| PN Kirsten | c King | b Moseley | 61 |
| RG Pollock | | b Stephenson | 46 |
| KS McEwan | c Stephenson | b Alleyne | 0 |
| *CEB Rice | c Murray | b Clarke | 47 |
| AP Kuiper | c Mattis | b Alleyne | 10 |
| AJ Kourie | | b Alleyne | 31 |
| †RV Jennings | lbw | b Alleyne | 0 |
| WK Watson | not out | | 6 |
| RW Hanley | c Stephenson | b Clarke | 0 |
| Extras | | (b 3, lb 5, w 4, nb 2) | 14 |
| Total | (all out, 56.3 overs) | | 236 |

FoW: 1-6, 2-44, 3-127, 4-149, 5-169, 6-169, 7-169, 8-216, 9-236

| | O | M | R | W |
|---|---|---|---|---|
| Clarke | 24.3 | 5 | 74 | 2 |
| Moseley | 14 | 1 | 55 | 2 |
| Alleyne | 14 | 1 | 62 | 5 |
| Stephenson | 4 | 0 | 31 | 1 |

**West Indian XI 2nd innings**

| | | | |
|---|---|---|---|
| EN Trotman | c Pollock | b Watson | 4 |
| AE Greenidge | c Kourie | b Kuiper | 43 |
| EH Mattis | | b Watson | 32 |
| MA Lynch | c Jennings | b Rice | 7 |
| CL King | c sub | b Rice | 42 |

| | | | |
|---|---|---|---|
| †DA Murray | c Pollock | b Rice | 3 |
| *AI Kallicharran | c Pollock | b Watson | 7 |
| FD Stephenson | c Jennings | b Kuiper | 20 |
| EA Moseley | c Hanley | b Watson | 14 |
| ST Clarke | not out | | 23 |
| HL Alleyne | not out | | 0 |
| Extras | | (lb 3, w 2, nb 5) | 10 |
| Total | (9 wkts, 53.2 overs) | | 205 |

FoW: 1-4, 2-72, 3-86, 4-94, 5-97, 6-99, 7-143, 8-172, 9-200

| | O | M | R | W |
|---|---|---|---|---|
| Watson | 16.2 | 3 | 63 | 4 |
| Hanley | 9 | 1 | 27 | 0 |
| Rice | 12 | 0 | 50 | 3 |
| Kuiper | 11 | 0 | 32 | 2 |
| Kourie | 5 | 1 | 23 | 0 |

**4th 'Test' South Africa v West Indian XI**
St George's Park, Port Elizabeth
27,28,30,31 January 1984
Result: West Indian XI won by 6 wickets

South Africa won toss
Umpires: HR Martin and CJ Mitchley

**South Africa 1st innings**

| | | | |
|---|---|---|---|
| SJ Cook | c Murray | b Stephenson | 26 |
| M Yachad | c Murray | b Moseley | 6 |
| PN Kirsten | c Murray | b Clarke | 0 |
| RG Pollock | c Mattis | b Clarke | 0 |
| KS McEwan | c Kallicharran | b Moseley | 120 |
| *CEB Rice | c Murray | b Clarke | 23 |
| AP Kuiper | c Murray | b Stephenson | 5 |
| AJ Kourie | not out | | 63 |
| †DJ Richardson | lbw | b Alleyne | 13 |
| WK Watson | c Murray | b Clarke | 8 |
| RW Hanley | | b Clarke | 0 |
| Extras | | (b 2, lb 8, w 3) | 13 |
| Total | (all out, 82 overs) | | 277 |

FoW: 1-11, 2-16, 3-16, 4-54, 5-100, 6-117, 7-205, 8-264, 9-277

| | O | M | R | W |
|---|---|---|---|---|
| Clarke | 23 | 7 | 36 | 5 |
| Moseley | 20 | 2 | 93 | 2 |
| Stephenson | 18 | 2 | 61 | 2 |
| Alleyne | 16 | 2 | 55 | 1 |
| King | 5 | 1 | 19 | 0 |

**West Indian XI 1st innings**

| | | | |
|---|---|---|---|
| SFAF Bacchus | c Kirsten | b Rice | 66 |
| EN Trotman | c Pollock | b Hanley | 43 |
| EH Mattis | c Kourie | b Kuiper | 15 |
| AI Kallicharran | c Cook | b Watson | 16 |

| | | | |
|---|---|---|---|
| CL King | c Kuiper | b Watson | 0 |
| *LG Rowe | lbw | b Kuiper | 16 |
| †DA Murray | run out | | 8 |
| FD Stephenson | not out | | 19 |
| EA Moseley | c Kourie | b Kuiper | 4 |
| ST Clarke | c Kuiper | b Watson | 0 |
| HL Alleyne | lbw | b Kourie | 4 |
| Extras | | (b 1, lb 5, w 1, nb 1) | 8 |
| Total | (all out, 81 overs) | | 199 |

FoW: 1-83, 2-113, 3-136, 4-136, 5-160, 6-170, 7-176, 8-180, 9-185

| | O | M | R | W |
|---|---|---|---|---|
| Watson | 24 | 10 | 46 | 3 |
| Hanley | 15 | 4 | 30 | 1 |
| Kourie | 11 | 1 | 23 | 1 |
| Kuiper | 18 | 3 | 57 | 3 |
| Rice | 13 | 2 | 35 | 1 |

**South Africa 2nd innings**

| | | | |
|---|---|---|---|
| SJ Cook | c Murray | b Clarke | 2 |
| M Yachad | lbw | b Alleyne | 31 |
| PN Kirsten | | b Clarke | 4 |
| RG Pollock | c Murray | b Clarke | 42 |
| KS McEwan | c Murray | b Alleyne | 0 |
| *CEB Rice | c Clarke | b Stephenson | 12 |
| AP Kuiper | c Alleyne | b Clarke | 14 |
| AJ Kourie | c Murray | b Stephenson | 4 |
| †DJ Richardson | | b Stephenson | 3 |
| WK Watson | not out | | 4 |
| RW Hanley | | b Clarke | 0 |
| Extras | | (b 3, lb 4, w 2, nb 2) | 11 |
| Total | (all out, 46.4 overs) | | 127 |

FoW: 1-4, 2-9, 3-66, 4-87, 5-103, 6-109, 7-117, 8-122, 9-124

| | O | M | R | W |
|---|---|---|---|---|
| Clarke | 13.4 | 3 | 32 | 5 |
| Moseley | 8 | 1 | 22 | 0 |
| Stephenson | 15 | 2 | 47 | 3 |
| Alleyne | 10 | 3 | 15 | 2 |

**West Indian XI 2nd innings**

| | | | |
|---|---|---|---|
| SFAF Bacchus | c sub | b Watson | 76 |
| EN Trotman | c Kuiper | b Kirsten | 77 |
| EH Mattis | lbw | b Hanley | 1 |
| AI Kallicharran | not out | | 32 |
| CL King | c sub | b Kourie | 1 |
| *LG Rowe | not out | | 10 |
| Extras | | (lb 4, w 2, nb 3) | 9 |
| Total | (4 wkts, 49 overs) | | 206 |

DNB: †DA Murray, FD Stephenson, EA Moseley, ST Clarke, HL Alleyne
FoW: 1-130, 2-133, 3-182, 4-186

| | O | M | R | W |
|---|---|---|---|---|
| Watson | 9 | 0 | 46 | 1 |
| Hanley | 8 | 0 | 38 | 1 |
| Kourie | 19 | 5 | 65 | 1 |
| Kuiper | 4 | 0 | 25 | 0 |
| Rice | 3 | 0 | 9 | 0 |
| Kirsten | 6 | 1 | 14 | 1 |

## Australian XI, 1985–86

**1st 'Test' South Africa v Australian XI**
Kingsmead, Durban
26,27,28,29 December 1985
Result: Match drawn

South Africa won toss
Umpires: DH Bezuidenhout and OR Schoof

**South Africa 1st innings**

| | | | |
|---|---|---|---|
| SJ Cook | lbw | b Hogg | 52 |
| HR Fotheringham | c Rixon | b Hogg | 70 |
| PN Kirsten | c Rixon | b Hogg | 2 |
| RG Pollock | c Hughes | b Rackemann | 108 |
| KS McEwan | c Rixon | b Rackemann | 4 |
| *CEB Rice | c Dyson | b Hogg | 11 |
| AJ Kourie | c Haysman | b Hogg | 1 |
| GS Le Roux | c Rixon | b Rackemann | 9 |
| †RV Jennings | c Rixon | b Rackemann | 46 |
| ST Jefferies | not out | | 43 |
| HA Page | c Hogan | b Rackemann | 10 |
| Extras | | (b 11, lb 17, w 5, nb 4) | 37 |
| Total | (all out, 119.1 overs) | | 393 |

FoW: 1-124, 2-130, 3-133, 4-148, 5-184, 6-186, 7-237, 8-327, 9-359.

| | O | M | R | W |
|---|---|---|---|---|
| Hogg | 32 | 13 | 88 | 5 |
| Rackemann | 42.1 | 6 | 115 | 5 |
| Hogan | 16 | 4 | 62 | 0 |
| Maguire | 24 | 2 | 79 | 0 |
| Hohns | 5 | 2 | 21 | 0 |

**Australian XI 1st innings**

| | | | |
|---|---|---|---|
| J Dyson | c Jennings | b Jefferies | 29 |
| G Shipperd | | b Kourie | 59 |
| MD Haysman | lbw | b Jefferies | 0 |
| *KJ Hughes | c Pollock | b Page | 38 |
| MD Taylor | c Jennings | b Jefferies | 109 |
| TV Hohns | c Kourie | b Rice | 10 |
| †SJ Rixon | c Rice | b Jefferies | 20 |
| TG Hogan | c Rice | b Kirsten | 53 |
| JN Maguire | c Kirsten | b Page | 10 |

| | | | |
|---|---|---|---|
| CG Rackemann | c Jennings | b Le Roux | 8 |
| RM Hogg | not out | | 12 |
| Extras | | (lb 5, w 3, nb 3) | 11 |
| Total | (all out, 119.3 overs) | | 359 |

FoW: 1-51, 2-51, 3-115, 4-160, 5-185, 6-236, 7-315, 8-331, 9-343

| | O | M | R | W |
|---|---|---|---|---|
| Le Roux | 24 | 1 | 77 | 1 |
| Jefferies | 34 | 10 | 100 | 4 |
| Page | 25.3 | 6 | 84 | 2 |
| Rice | 8 | 1 | 21 | 1 |
| Kourie | 27 | 6 | 72 | 1 |
| Kirsten | 1 | 1 | 0 | 1 |

**South Africa 2nd innings**

| | | | |
|---|---|---|---|
| SJ Cook | c Haysman | b Hogg | 2 |
| PN Kirsten | c Rixon | b Hogg | 5 |
| KS McEwan | c Haysman | b Rackemann | 5 |
| RG Pollock | b Rackemann | | 6 |
| *CEB Rice | c Hogan | b Rackemann | 9 |
| HR Fotheringham | not out | | 100 |
| AJ Kourie | run out | | 44 |
| GS Le Roux | c Haysman | b Hogan | 28 |
| Extras | | (b 3, nb 1) | 4 |
| Total | (7 wkts dec., 63.4 overs) | | 203 |

DNB: †RV Jennings, ST Jefferies, HA Page
FoW: 1-2, 2-7, 3-16, 4-23, 5-30, 6-130

| | O | M | R | W |
|---|---|---|---|---|
| Hogg | 13 | 6 | 26 | 2 |
| Rackemann | 15 | 4 | 28 | 3 |
| Hogan | 14.4 | 1 | 77 | 1 |
| Maguire | 9 | 1 | 22 | 0 |
| Hohns | 8 | 1 | 38 | 0 |
| Haysman | 4 | 1 | 9 | 0 |

**Australian XI 2nd innings**

| | | | |
|---|---|---|---|
| G Shipperd | lbw | b Le Roux | 6 |
| J Dyson | c Cook | b Page | 4 |
| MD Haysman | not out | | 3 |
| *KJ Hughes | not out | | 17 |
| Extras | | (lb 1, nb 1) | 2 |
| Total | (2 wkts, 11 overs) | | 32 |

DNB: MD Taylor, TV Hohns, †SJ Rixon, TG Hogan, JN Maguire, CG Rackemann, RM Hogg
FoW: 1-4, 2-12

| | O | M | R | W |
|---|---|---|---|---|
| Le Roux | 6 | 2 | 24 | 1 |
| Page | 5 | 2 | 7 | 1 |

**2nd 'Test' South Africa v Australian XI**
Newlands, Cape Town
1,2,3,4 January 1986
Result: Match drawn

South Africa won toss
Umpires: DA Sansom and DD Schoof

**South Africa 1st innings**

| | | | |
|---|---|---|---|
| SJ Cook | lbw | b McCurdy | 91 |
| HR Fotheringham | c Rixon | b Rackemann | 10 |
| PN Kirsten | | b Rackemann | 72 |
| RG Pollock | b Hogg | | 79 |
| *CEB Rice | c Haysman | b McCurdy | 21 |
| KA McKenzie | lbw | b Hogg | 20 |
| AJ Kourie | c Rixon | b Rackemann | 8 |
| GS Le Roux | c Dyson | b McCurdy | 45 |
| †RV Jennings | c Dyson | b McCurdy | 9 |
| ST Jefferies | c Hughes | b Rackemann | 22 |
| HA Page | not out | | 33 |
| Extras | | (b 5, lb 8, nb 7) | 20 |
| Total | (all out, 126.2 overs) | | 430 |

FoW: 1-37, 2-169, 3-204, 4-287, 5-287, 6-308, 7-352, 8-367, 9-384

| | O | M | R | W |
|---|---|---|---|---|
| RM Hogg | 29 | 6 | 85 | 2 |
| CG Rackemann | 37.2 | 3 | 118 | 4 |
| RJ McCurdy | 30 | 1 | 133 | 4 |
| TG Hogan | 30 | 6 | 81 | 0 |

**Australian XI 1st innings**

| | | | |
|---|---|---|---|
| J Dyson | c Jennings | b Kirsten | 95 |
| G Shipperd | | b Jefferies | 17 |
| MD Haysman | | b Jefferies | 4 |
| *KJ Hughes | | b Kirsten | 53 |
| RM Hogg | c Jennings | b Page | 0 |
| MD Taylor | | c & b Kirsten | 22 |
| GN Yallop | | b Le Roux | 51 |
| †SJ Rixon | | b Le Roux | 11 |
| TG Hogan | lbw | b Le Roux | 28 |
| RJ McCurdy | not out | | 4 |
| CG Rackemann | | b Le Roux | 2 |
| Extras | | (lb 10, nb 7) | 17 |
| Total | (all out, 98.3 overs) | | 304 |

FoW: 1-25, 2-30, 3-135, 4-142, 5-171, 6-230, 7-255, 8-260, 9-302

| | O | M | R | W |
|---|---|---|---|---|
| Le Roux | 20.3 | 3 | 56 | 4 |
| Jefferies | 19 | 3 | 59 | 2 |
| Page | 16 | 3 | 39 | 1 |
| Kourie | 16 | 3 | 58 | 0 |
| Rice | 10 | 3 | 21 | 0 |
| Kirsten | 17 | 3 | 61 | 3 |

**South Africa 2nd innings**

| | | | |
|---|---|---|---|
| SJ Cook | c Rixon | b Rackemann | 70 |
| HR Fotheringham | | b Rackemann | 31 |
| PN Kirsten | c Haysman | b Rackemann | 20 |
| RG Pollock | c Dyson | b McCurdy | 3 |
| *CEB Rice | not out | | 27 |
| GS Le Roux | c Haysman | b Rackemann | 15 |
| KA McKenzie | not out | | 18 |
| Extras | | (lb 15, nb 3) | 18 |
| Total | (5 wkts dec., 52 overs) | | 202 |

DNB: AJ Kourie, †RV Jennings, ST Jefferies, HA Page
FoW: 1-86, 2-121, 3-128, 4-156, 5-176

| | O | M | R | W |
|---|---|---|---|---|
| Hogg | 14 | 2 | 43 | 0 |
| Rackemann | 26 | 1 | 106 | 4 |
| McCurdy | 12 | 2 | 38 | 1 |

**Australian XI 2nd innings**

| | | | |
|---|---|---|---|
| G Shipperd | lbw | b Le Roux | 8 |
| J Dyson | c Jennings | b Page | 33 |
| MD Haysman | lbw | b Rice | 33 |
| *KJ Hughes | not out | | 97 |
| MD Taylor | c McKenzie | b Kourie | 17 |
| GN Yallop | not out | | 24 |
| Extras | | (lb 10, w 1, nb 1) | 12 |
| Total | (4 wkts, 90 overs) | | 224 |

DNB: RM Hogg, †SJ Rixon, TG Hogan, RJ McCurdy, CG Rackemann
FoW: 1-31, 2-54, 3-106, 4-185

| | O | M | R | W |
|---|---|---|---|---|
| Le Roux | 13 | 3 | 23 | 1 |
| Jefferies | 13 | 4 | 32 | 0 |
| Page | 11 | 2 | 41 | 1 |
| Kourie | 23 | 7 | 54 | 1 |
| Rice | 13 | 3 | 30 | 1 |
| Kirsten | 17 | 4 | 34 | 0 |

**3rd 'Test' South Africa v Australian XI**
New Wanderers, Johannesburg
16,17,18,20,21 January 1986
Result: South Africa won by 188 runs

Australian XI won toss
Umpires: DD Schoof and OR Schoof

**South Africa 1st innings**

| | | | |
|---|---|---|---|
| SJ Cook | | b Hogg | 5 |
| HR Fotheringham | lbw | b Alderman | 19 |
| PN Kirsten | c Rixon | b Rackemann | 12 |
| RG Pollock | c Rixon | b Rackemann | 19 |
| *CEB Rice | c Faulkner | b Rackemann | 9 |
| KA McKenzie | c Rixon | b Rackemann | 72 |

| | | | |
|---|---|---|---|
| AJ Kourie | c Rixon | b Rackemann | 14 |
| GS Le Roux | c Alderman | b Rackemann | 23 |
| †RV Jennings | c Rixon | b Rackemann | 0 |
| HA Page | not out | | 14 |
| CJPG van Zyl | c Rixon | b Rackemann | 13 |
| Extras | | (b 2, lb 8, nb 1) | 11 |
| Total | (all out, 71.4 overs) | | 211 |

FoW: 1-12, 2-31, 3-51, 4-69, 5-86, 6-155, 7-166, 8-166, 9-191

| | O | M | R | W |
|---|---|---|---|---|
| Hogg | 4 | 3 | 3 | 1 |
| Alderman | 28 | 6 | 68 | 1 |
| Rackemann | 26.4 | 3 | 84 | 8 |
| Faulkner | 13 | 4 | 46 | 0 |

**Australian XI 1st innings**

| | | | |
|---|---|---|---|
| SB Smith | c Pollock | b van Zyl | 116 |
| J Dyson | c Rice | b Page | 9 |
| G Shipperd | | b Le Roux | 44 |
| *KJ Hughes | lbw | b van Zyl | 0 |
| MD Taylor | c Jennings | b Page | 21 |
| GN Yallop | c Jennings | b van Zyl | 20 |
| PI Faulkner | c McKenzie | b Rice | 25 |
| †SJ Rixon | lbw | b van Zyl | 3 |
| CG Rackemann | lbw | b Rice | 8 |
| TM Alderman | not out | | 3 |
| RM Hogg | | b Rice | 0 |
| Extras | | (lb 13, w 1, nb 4) | 18 |
| Total | (all out, 106.3 overs) | | 267 |

FoW: 1-45, 2-159, 3-159, 4-192, 5-214, 6-230, 7-237, 8-263, 9-267

| | O | M | R | W |
|---|---|---|---|---|
| Le Roux | 25 | 6 | 68 | 1 |
| van Zyl | 27 | 4 | 83 | 4 |
| Page | 26.3 | 8 | 37 | 2 |
| Rice | 24 | 8 | 43 | 3 |
| Kourie | 4 | 0 | 23 | 0 |

**South Africa 2nd innings**

| | | | |
|---|---|---|---|
| SJ Cook | lbw | b Alderman | 21 |
| HR Fotheringham | c Rixon | b Rackemann | 5 |
| PN Kirsten | | b Faulkner | 10 |
| RG Pollock | not out | | 65 |
| *CEB Rice | c Rixon | b Rackemann | 50 |
| KA McKenzie | c Alderman | b Rackemann | 110 |
| AJ Kourie | lbw | b Alderman | 0 |
| GS Le Roux | c Rixon | b Rackemann | 18 |
| †RV Jennings | run out | | 0 |
| HA Page | lbw | b Alderman | 2 |
| CJPG van Zyl | c Rixon | b Alderman | 2 |
| Extras | | (lb 17, w 2, nb 3) | 22 |
| Total | (all out, 86.1 overs) | | 305 |

FoW: 1-25, 2-31, 3-80, 4-204, 5-207, 6-242, 7-242, 8-258, 9-274

| | O | M | R | W |
|---|---|---|---|---|
| Rackemann | 30.1 | 6 | 107 | 4 |
| Alderman | 37 | 6 | 116 | 4 |
| Faulkner | 19 | 0 | 65 | 1 |

**Australian XI 2nd innings**

| | | | |
|---|---|---|---|
| SB Smith | c Jennings | b van Zyl | 14 |
| J Dyson | not out | | 18 |
| G Shipperd | | b Le Roux | 3 |
| *KJ Hughes | c Jennings | b Le Roux | 0 |
| MD Taylor | lbw | b Le Roux | 0 |
| GN Yallop | | b Rice | 6 |
| PI Faulkner | c Fotheringham | b Rice | 7 |
| †SJ Rixon | | b Page | 2 |
| CG Rackemann | | b Rice | 2 |
| TM Alderman | c Jennings | b Page | 1 |
| RM Hogg | c Jennings | b Page | 0 |
| Extras | | (b 2, lb 5, nb 1) | 8 |
| Total | (all out, 28.4 overs) | | 61 |

FoW: 1-24, 2-29, 3-29, 4-29, 5-36, 6-48, 7-53, 8-60, 9-61

| | O | M | R | W |
|---|---|---|---|---|
| Le Roux | 7 | 2 | 11 | 3 |
| van Zyl | 8 | 3 | 16 | 1 |
| Page | 7.4 | 0 | 19 | 3 |
| Rice | 6 | 2 | 8 | 3 |

## Australian XI, 1986–87

**1st 'Test' South Africa v Australian XI**

New Wanderers, Johannesburg
24,26,27,28 December 1986
Result: South Africa won by 49 runs

South Africa won toss
Umpires: DD Schoof and FE Wood

**South Africa 1st innings**

| | | | |
|---|---|---|---|
| BJ Whitfield | | b Rackemann | 17 |
| SJ Cook | | b McCurdy | 28 |
| PN Kirsten | c Wessels | b McCurdy | 14 |
| BM McMillan | c Rixon | b McCurdy | 1 |
| *CEB Rice | c Rixon | b Rackemann | 61 |
| KA McKenzie | c Wessels | b Rackemann | 12 |
| AJ Kourie | lbw | b McCurdy | 3 |
| †DJ Richardson | c Rixon | b McCurdy | 29 |
| GS Le Roux | lbw | b McCurdy | 42 |
| HA Page | c Rixon | b Faulkner | 5 |
| ST Jefferies | not out | | 27 |
| Extras | | (lb 5, w 4, nb 6) | 15 |
| Total | (all out, 88.5 overs) | | 254 |

FoW: 1-36, 2-56, 3-63, 4-66, 5-103, 6-125, 7-154, 8-188, 9-210

| | O | M | R | W |
|---|---|---|---|---|
| McCurdy | 24.5 | 7 | 67 | 6 |
| Rackemann | 25 | 3 | 70 | 3 |
| Maguire | 18 | 4 | 54 | 0 |
| Faulkner | 21 | 2 | 58 | 1 |

**Australian XI 1st innings**

| | | | |
|---|---|---|---|
| SB Smith | c Richardson | b Rice | 29 |
| J Dyson | | b Jefferies | 5 |
| KC Wessels | c McMillan | b Le Roux | 0 |
| *KJ Hughes | lbw | b Le Roux | 34 |
| MD Taylor | c Richardson | b Rice | 9 |
| MD Haysman | | b Page | 25 |
| PI Faulkner | | b Page | 9 |
| †SJ Rixon | lbw | b Page | 0 |
| JN Maguire | c Richardson | b Rice | 3 |
| RJ McCurdy | not out | | 2 |
| CG Rackemann | | b Rice | 2 |
| Extras | | (b 7, lb 9, w 1, nb 7) | 24 |
| Total | (all out, 63 overs) | | 142 |

FoW: 1-20, 2-24, 3-51, 4-93, 5-99, 6-125, 7-125, 8-137, 9-137

| | O | M | R | W |
|---|---|---|---|---|
| Le Roux | 11 | 4 | 25 | 2 |
| Jefferies | 8 | 0 | 29 | 1 |
| Page | 17 | 3 | 39 | 3 |
| Rice | 16 | 6 | 19 | 4 |
| McMillan | 9 | 3 | 14 | 0 |
| Kourie | 2 | 2 | 0 | 0 |

**South Africa 2nd innings**

| | | | |
|---|---|---|---|
| BJ Whitfield | lbw | b Maguire | 23 |
| SJ Cook | c Rixon | b McCurdy | 1 |
| PN Kirsten | c Rixon | b Maguire | 19 |
| BM McMillan | lbw | b Maguire | 30 |
| *CEB Rice | c Rixon | b Maguire | 18 |
| KA McKenzie | lbw | b Maguire | 40 |
| AJ Kourie | c Haysman | b Maguire | 1 |
| †DJ Richardson | c Rixon | b Rackemann | 33 |
| GS Le Roux | c Rixon | b Rackemann | 0 |
| HA Page | not out | | 7 |
| ST Jefferies | c Rixon | b Rackemann | 0 |
| Extras | | (b 1, lb 6, w 2, nb 1) | 10 |
| Total | (all out, 69.4 overs) | | 182 |

FoW: 1-2, 2-34, 3-49, 4-92, 5-103, 6-115, 7-153, 8-173, 9-182

| | O | M | R | W |
|---|---|---|---|---|
| McCurdy | 19 | 4 | 58 | 1 |
| Rackemann | 19.4 | 3 | 54 | 3 |
| Maguire | 29 | 12 | 61 | 6 |
| Faulkner | 2 | 0 | 2 | 0 |

**Australian XI 2nd innings**

| | | | |
|---|---|---|---|
| SB Smith | c McKenzie | b McMillan | 36 |
| J Dyson | | b Kourie | 16 |
| KC Wessels | c Richardson | b McMillan | 49 |
| *KJ Hughes | not out | | 54 |
| MD Taylor | c Richardson | b Rice | 8 |
| MD Haysman | c Kourie | b Page | 17 |
| PI Faulkner | c McKenzie | b McMillan | 8 |
| †SJ Rixon | | b Page | 16 |
| JN Maguire | c Richardson | b Rice | 3 |
| RJ McCurdy | | b Jefferies | 0 |
| CG Rackemann | c McKenzie | b Rice | 12 |
| Extras | | (lb 15, w 2, nb 9) | 26 |
| Total | (all out, 95.1 overs) | | 245 |

FoW: 1-49, 2-57, 3-107, 4-143, 5-156, 6-169, 7-199, 8-219, 9-224

| | O | M | R | W |
|---|---|---|---|---|
| Le Roux | 14 | 3 | 39 | 0 |
| Jefferies | 17 | 5 | 42 | 1 |
| Page | 20 | 3 | 53 | 2 |
| Rice | 18.1 | 4 | 37 | 3 |
| McMillan | 15 | 2 | 44 | 3 |
| Kourie | 11 | 6 | 15 | 1 |

**2nd 'Test' South Africa v Australian XI**
Newlands, Cape Town
1,2,3,5,6 January 1987 (5-day match)
Result: Match drawn

Australian XI won toss
Umpires: DH Bezuidenhout and OR Schoof

**South Africa 1st innings**

| | | | |
|---|---|---|---|
| SJ Cook | c Rixon | b McCurdy | 6 |
| BJ Whitfield | st Rixon | b Hohns | 77 |
| PN Kirsten | c Hughes | b Hohns | 173 |
| RG Pollock | c sub | b Maguire | 66 |
| *CEB Rice | lbw | b Maguire | 72 |
| KA McKenzie | c Rixon | b Maguire | 24 |
| BM McMillan | run out | | 30 |
| GS Le Roux | c Rixon | b McCurdy | 13 |
| †DJ Richardson | lbw | b Maguire | 1 |
| HA Page | c Smith | b McCurdy | 7 |
| AJ Kourie | not out | | 2 |
| Extras | | (b 5, lb 10, w 1, nb 6) | 22 |
| Total | (all out, 157.4 overs) | | 493 |

FoW: 1-16, 2-177, 3-288, 4-341, 5-407, 6-449, 7-480, 8-483, 9-491

| | O | M | R | W |
|---|---|---|---|---|
| McCurdy | 43 | 8 | 133 | 3 |
| Rackemann | 28 | 7 | 113 | 0 |
| Maguire | 46.4 | 8 | 116 | 4 |
| Hohns | 40 | 6 | 116 | 2 |

**Australian XI 1st innings**

| | | | |
|---|---|---|---|
| SB Smith | c McKenzie | b Le Roux | 2 |
| J Dyson | | run out | 198 |
| KC Wessels | lbw | b Le Roux | 36 |
| *KJ Hughes | c Richardson | b Le Roux | 48 |
| MD Taylor | | c & b Le Roux | 0 |
| MD Haysman | c Kirsten | b Le Roux | 153 |
| TV Hohns | c Kirsten | b McMillan | 0 |
| †SJ Rixon | c Richardson | b McMillan | 1 |
| JN Maguire | c Kirsten | b McMillan | 20 |
| CG Rackemann | c Whitfield | b Rice | 8 |
| RJ McCurdy | not out | | 11 |
| Extras | | (lb 19) | 19 |
| Total | (all out, 202 overs) | | 496 |

FoW: 1-4, 2-78, 3-166, 4-170, 5-395, 6-399, 7-401, 8-453, 9-478

| | O | M | R | W |
|---|---|---|---|---|
| Le Roux | 42 | 13 | 85 | 5 |
| Page | 43 | 8 | 118 | 0 |
| Kourie | 39 | 10 | 87 | 0 |
| McMillan | 36 | 10 | 83 | 3 |
| Rice | 31 | 8 | 60 | 1 |
| Kirsten | 11 | 0 | 44 | 0 |

**South Africa 2nd innings**

| | | | |
|---|---|---|---|
| SJ Cook | | c & b Hohns | 40 |
| BJ Whitfield | c Hughes | b Maguire | 23 |
| PN Kirsten | not out | | 105 |
| KA McKenzie | lbw | b Wessels | 52 |
| BM McMillan | not out | | 17 |
| Extras | | (b 4, lb 14, nb 2) | 20 |
| Total | | (3 wkts, 86 overs) | 257 |

DNB: RG Pollock, *CEB Rice, GS Le Roux, †DJ Richardson, HA Page, AJ Kourie
FoW: 1-48, 2-99, 3-194

| | O | M | R | W |
|---|---|---|---|---|
| McCurdy | 10 | 1 | 42 | 0 |
| Rackemann | 19 | 3 | 54 | 0 |
| Maguire | 16 | 3 | 53 | 1 |
| Hohns | 26 | 6 | 63 | 1 |
| Wessels | 12 | 6 | 18 | 1 |
| Smith | 2 | 0 | 9 | 0 |
| Dyson | 1 | 1 | 0 | 0 |

**3rd 'Test' South Africa v Australian XI**
Kingsmead, Durban
17,19,20,21,22 January 1987 (5-day match)
Result: Match drawn

South Africa won toss
Umpires: KE Liebenberg and LJ Rautenbach

**Australian XI 1st innings**

| | | | |
|---|---|---|---|
| SB Smith | c Page | b Henry | 137 |
| J Dyson | c Richardson | b Le Roux | 1 |
| KC Wessels | c Richardson | b Le Roux | 0 |
| *KJ Hughes | | c & b Le Roux | 25 |
| GN Yallop | c Page | b Henry | 36 |
| MD Haysman | c McKenzie | b Kirsten | 5 |
| TV Hohns | c McKenzie | b Kirsten | 26 |
| †SJ Rixon | c Richardson | b Page | 13 |
| JN Maguire | c Richardson | b Le Roux | 2 |
| RM Hogg | c Richardson | b Page | 6 |
| RJ McCurdy | not out | | 0 |
| Extras | | (lb 3, w 1, nb 9) | 13 |
| Total | (all out, 88.3 overs) | | 264 |

FoW: 1-4, 2-7, 3-80, 4-148, 5-198, 6-220, 7-256, 8-256, 9-264

| | O | M | R | W |
|---|---|---|---|---|
| Le Roux | 13.3 | 1 | 33 | 4 |
| Page | 17 | 1 | 57 | 2 |
| Rice | 10 | 2 | 32 | 0 |
| McMillan | 10 | 0 | 57 | 0 |
| Henry | 23 | 4 | 58 | 2 |
| Kirsten | 15 | 4 | 24 | 2 |

**South Africa 1st innings**

| | | | |
|---|---|---|---|
| SJ Cook | | b Hohns | 44 |
| BJ Whitfield | c Rixon | b Hohns | 59 |
| PN Kirsten | c Yallop | b Hohns | 13 |
| KS McEwan | b McCurdy | | 101 |
| *CEB Rice | c Dyson | b Hohns | 22 |
| KA McKenzie | lbw | b Hohns | 14 |
| BM McMillan | c Haysman | b McCurdy | 15 |
| †DJ Richardson | not out | | 44 |
| GS Le Roux | c Rixon | b McCurdy | 6 |
| O Henry | c Yallop | b Hogg | 7 |
| HA Page | | c & b Hohns | 2 |
| Extras | | (b 8, lb 7, w 1, nb 7) | 23 |
| Total | (all out, 125.4 overs) | | 350 |

FoW: 1-100, 2-127, 3-130, 4-177, 5-197, 6-237, 7-309, 8-319, 9-341

| | O | M | R | W |
|---|---|---|---|---|
| Hogg | 28 | 5 | 87 | 1 |
| McCurdy | 22 | 2 | 76 | 3 |
| Maguire | 28 | 7 | 74 | 0 |
| Hohns | 47.4 | 13 | 98 | 6 |

**Australian XI 2nd innings**

| | | | |
|---|---|---|---|
| SB Smith | | b Page | 5 |
| J Dyson | c McMillan | b Rice | 101 |
| KC Wessels | c Richardson | b Page | 2 |
| *KJ Hughes | lbw | b Page | 9 |
| MD Haysman | | b Rice | 115 |
| TV Hohns | lbw | b Le Roux | 10 |
| GN Yallop | c Henry | b Le Roux | 26 |
| †SJ Rixon | not out | | 42 |
| JN Maguire | run out | | 2 |
| RM Hogg | c McEwan | b Kirsten | 9 |
| RJ McCurdy | c Whitfield | b Kirsten | 0 |
| Extras | | (b 2, lb 14, nb 2) | 18 |
| Total | (all out, 140.4 overs) | | 339 |

FoW: 1-7, 2-11, 3-25, 4-50, 5-253, 6-260, 7-301, 8-304, 9-337

| | O | M | R | W |
|---|---|---|---|---|
| Le Roux | 29 | 5 | 63 | 2 |
| Page | 35 | 6 | 87 | 3 |
| Rice | 19 | 4 | 38 | 2 |
| McMillan | 17 | 3 | 55 | 0 |
| Henry | 26 | 11 | 44 | 0 |
| Kirsten | 14.4 | 3 | 36 | 2 |

**South Africa 2nd innings**

| | | | |
|---|---|---|---|
| SJ Cook | c Rixon | b Hogg | 23 |
| BJ Whitfield | b Hogg | | 26 |
| PN Kirsten | lbw | b Maguire | 33 |
| KS McEwan | | b Hohns | 27 |
| *CEB Rice | lbw | b Hogg | 0 |
| KA McKenzie | | b Hohns | 3 |
| BM McMillan | not out | | 18 |
| †DJ Richardson | | c & b Hohns | 0 |
| Extras | | (b 1, lb 7, nb 5) | 13 |
| Total | (7 wkts, 57.5 overs) | | 143 |

DNB: GS Le Roux, O Henry, HA Page
FoW: 1-29, 2-89, 3-93, 4-102, 5-115, 6-130, 7-143

| | O | M | R | W |
|---|---|---|---|---|
| Hogg | 16 | 4 | 33 | 3 |
| McCurdy | 17 | 3 | 59 | 0 |
| Maguire | 7 | 3 | 16 | 1 |
| Hohns | 17.5 | 6 | 27 | 3 |

**4th 'Test' South Africa v Australian XI**
St George's Park, Port Elizabeth
30,31 January, 2,3,4 February 1987
Result: Match drawn

Australian XI won toss
Umpires: KE Liebenberg and DD Schoof

**Australian XI 1st innings**

| | | | |
|---|---|---|---|
| SB Smith | lbw | b Le Roux | 77 |
| G Shipperd | c Whitfield | b Donald | 53 |
| J Dyson | lbw | b Le Roux | 1 |
| *KJ Hughes | | b Donald | 42 |
| KC Wessels | | b Henry | 135 |
| MD Haysman | c Rice | b Donald | 19 |
| TV Hohns | hit wicket | b Rice | 37 |
| †SJ Rixon | c Page | b Henry | 61 |
| RM Hogg | lbw | b Henry | 0 |
| RJ McCurdy | not out | | 6 |
| Extras | | (b 2, lb 11, nb 11) | 24 |
| Total | (9 wkts dec., 163.5 overs) | | 455 |

DNB: TM Alderman
FoW: 1-123, 2-131, 3-191, 4-192, 5-255, 6-308, 7-442, 8-442, 9-455

| | O | M | R | W |
|---|---|---|---|---|
| Le Roux | 27 | 6 | 67 | 2 |
| Donald | 32 | 7 | 94 | 3 |
| Page | 27 | 4 | 95 | 0 |
| Rice | 19 | 5 | 43 | 1 |
| Henry | 36.5 | 10 | 96 | 3 |
| Kirsten | 22 | 6 | 47 | 0 |

**South Africa 1st innings**

| | | | |
|---|---|---|---|
| SJ Cook | c Dyson | b McCurdy | 84 |
| BJ Whitfield | c Rixon | b Hogg | 4 |
| PN Kirsten | lbw | b Hogg | 34 |
| RG Pollock | | b Hogg | 144 |
| KS McEwan | not out | | 138 |
| HA Page | | b Hohns | 9 |
| *CEB Rice | lbw | b Hogg | 26 |
| †DJ Richardson | lbw | b Hogg | 7 |
| GS Le Roux | lbw | b McCurdy | 20 |
| O Henry | c Hohns | b Alderman | 13 |
| AA Donald | c Haysman | b Hohns | 21 |
| Extras | | (b 2, lb 24, w 1, nb 6) | 33 |
| Total | (all out, 167.2 overs) | | 533 |

FoW: 1-9, 2-64, 3-211, 4-312, 5-329, 6-382, 7-394, 8-446, 9-477

| | O | M | R | W |
|---|---|---|---|---|
| Hogg | 39 | 7 | 97 | 5 |
| Alderman | 37 | 3 | 142 | 1 |
| McCurdy | 40 | 5 | 159 | 2 |
| Hohns | 51.2 | 12 | 109 | 2 |

**Australian XI 2nd innings**

| | | | |
|---|---|---|---|
| SB Smith | | b Rice | 113 |
| G Shipperd | | b Le Roux | 0 |
| J Dyson | c Kirsten | b Le Roux | 8 |
| *KJ Hughes | | b Donald | 44 |

| | | | |
|---|---|---|---|
| KC Wessels | not out | | 105 |
| MD Haysman | not out | | 53 |
| Extras | | (b 4, lb 2, w 1, nb 3) | 10 |
| Total | (4 wkts, 116 overs) | | 333 |

DNB: TV Hohns, †SJ Rixon, RM Hogg, RJ McCurdy, TM Alderman
FoW: 1-26, 2-26, 3-142, 4-198

| | O | M | R | W |
|---|---|---|---|---|
| Le Roux | 16 | 0 | 61 | 2 |
| Donald | 19 | 4 | 71 | 1 |
| Page | 19 | 1 | 64 | 0 |
| Rice | 10 | 1 | 25 | 1 |
| Henry | 35 | 14 | 63 | 0 |
| Kirsten | 15 | 4 | 42 | 0 |
| Cook | 2 | 1 | 1 | 0 |

## English XI, 1989–90

**1st 'Test' South Africa v English XI**
New Wanderers, Johannesburg
8,9,10 February 1990
Result: South Africa won by 7 wickets

South Africa won toss
Umpires: KE Liebenberg and JW Peacock

**English XI 1st innings**

| | | | |
|---|---|---|---|
| BC Broad | c Jennings | b McMillan | 48 |
| CWJ Athey | | b Donald | 3 |
| RT Robinson | c Snell | b McMillan | 31 |
| *MW Gatting | c McMillan | b Snell | 22 |
| AP Wells | | b Snell | 4 |
| KJ Barnett | c Fotheringham | b Donald | 0 |
| †BN French | c Jennings | b Donald | 1 |
| JE Emburey | c Jennings | b Snell | 1 |
| RM Ellison | | b Donald | 6 |
| NA Foster | c Rundle | b Snell | 11 |
| PW Jarvis | not out | | 1 |
| Extras | | (b 4, lb 17, nb 7) | 28 |
| Total | (all out, 65.5 overs) | | 156 |

FoW: 1-15, 2-96, 3-106, 4-118, 5-119, 6-123, 7-132, 8-138, 9-152

| | O | M | R | W |
|---|---|---|---|---|
| Donald | 21 | 10 | 30 | 4 |
| Snell | 22.5 | 11 | 38 | 4 |
| McMillan | 15 | 2 | 41 | 2 |
| Kuiper | 6 | 1 | 21 | 0 |
| Rundle | 1 | 0 | 5 | 0 |

**South Africa 1st innings**

| | | | |
|---|---|---|---|
| *SJ Cook | c Robinson | b Ellison | 20 |
| HR Fotheringham | lbw | b Jarvis | 8 |
| KC Wessels | st French | b Emburey | 1 |
| PN Kirsten | c French | b Jarvis | 4 |
| RF Pienaar | | b Ellison | 13 |
| AP Kuiper | | b Foster | 84 |
| BM McMillan | | b Ellison | 0 |
| †RV Jennings | c Emburey | b Ellison | 23 |
| DB Rundle | c French | b Foster | 23 |
| RP Snell | c French | b Jarvis | 7 |
| AA Donald | not out | | 7 |
| Extras | | (lb 7, w 5, nb 1) | 13 |
| Total | (all out, 72.5 overs) | | 203 |

FoW: 1-23, 2-28, 3-40, 4-40, 5-77, 6-77, 7-148, 8-180, 9-189

| | O | M | R | W |
|---|---|---|---|---|
| Jarvis | 22.5 | 7 | 71 | 3 |
| Foster | 21 | 6 | 54 | 2 |
| Ellison | 15 | 6 | 41 | 4 |
| Emburey | 14 | 5 | 30 | 1 |

**English XI 2nd innings**

| | | | |
|---|---|---|---|
| BC Broad | c Jennings | b Donald | 0 |
| CWJ Athey | lbw | b McMillan | 16 |
| RT Robinson | c Jennings | b McMillan | 17 |
| *MW Gatting | | b Kuiper | 0 |
| AP Wells | c Wessels | b Donald | 11 |
| KJ Barnett | c Donald | b Snell | 24 |
| †BN French | c Jennings | b Donald | 0 |
| JE Emburey | c Jennings | b Snell | 2 |
| RM Ellison | c Cook | b Rundle | 12 |
| NA Foster | c Jennings | b Donald | 21 |
| PW Jarvis | not out | | 0 |
| Extras | | (b 4, lb 11, w 2, nb 2) | 19 |
| Total | (all out, 63 overs) | | 122 |

FoW: 1-2, 2-33, 3-34, 4-42, 5-69, 6-73, 7-78, 8-85, 9-122

| | O | M | R | W |
|---|---|---|---|---|
| Donald | 18 | 5 | 29 | 4 |
| Snell | 15 | 5 | 28 | 2 |
| McMillan | 11 | 6 | 18 | 2 |
| Kuiper | 14 | 4 | 23 | 1 |
| Rundle | 5 | 2 | 9 | 1 |

**South Africa 2nd innings**

| | | | |
|---|---|---|---|
| *SJ Cook | | c & b Gatting | 15 |
| HR Fotheringham | lbw | b Ellison | 38 |
| KC Wessels | lbw | b Gatting | 2 |
| PN Kirsten | not out | | 17 |
| RF Pienaar | not out | | 1 |
| Extras | | (w 3) | 3 |
| Total | | (3 wkts, 24.1 overs) | 76 |

DNB: AP Kuiper, BM McMillan, †RV Jennings, DB Rundle, RP Snell, AA Donald
FoW: 1-56, 2-56, 3-71

| | O | M | R | W |
|---|---|---|---|---|
| Jarvis | 6 | 2 | 25 | 0 |
| Foster | 4 | 0 | 20 | 0 |
| Ellison | 7 | 1 | 13 | 1 |
| Gatting | 6 | 1 | 17 | 2 |
| Athey | 1.1 | 1 | 1 | 0 |

Four informal warm-up matches were played: 9 November: v Northern Transvaal County Districts Invitation XI at Nelspruit, 10 November: v Northern Transvaal County Districts at Nelspruit, 16 November: v Orange Free State County Districts at Virginia, 18 November: v Transvaal County Districts at Orkney

# Bibliography

Jack Bailey, *Conflicts in Cricket*, Methuen, 1989
Hilary Beckles (ed.), *A Spirit of Dominance: Cricket and Nationalism in the West Indies*, University Press of the West Indies, 1998
Douglas Booth, *The Race Game: Sport and Politics in South Africa*, Frank Cass, 1998
Allan Border, *Allan Border: An Autobiography*, Meuthen, 1986
Mihir Bose, *Sporting Colours: Sport and Politics in South Africa*, Robson Books, 1994
Mihir Bose, *A History of Indian Cricket*, Andre Deutch, 2002
Geoffrey Boycott, *In the Fast Lane*, Sphere, 1981
Geoffrey Boycott, *Boycott: The Autobiography*, Macmillan, 1987
Geoff Chapple, *1981: The Tour*, AH & AW Reed, 1984
Jimmy Cook with Frederick Cleary, *The Jimmy Cook Story*, Pelham Books, 1993
Michael Down, *Is it Cricket? Power, money and politics in cricket since 1945*, Queen Anne Press, 1985
Richard Evans, *The Ultimate Test*, Partridge Press, 1990
Roger Fieldhouse, *Anti-Apartheid: A History of the Movement in Britain, 1959–1994*, Merlin, 2004
Bruce Francis, *'Guilty': Bob Hawke or Kim Hughes?*, 1989
Joel Garner, *Big Bird Flying High*, Arthur Barker Ltd, 1988
Graham Gooch, *Out of the Wilderness*, Grafton Books, 1986
Graham Gooch and Frank Keating, *Gooch: My Autobiography*, Collins Willow, 1995
David Gower, *Gower: The Autobiography*, Collins Willow, 1992
Benny Green (ed.), *Wisden Anthology 1963–1982*, Queen Anne Press, 1983
Gideon Haigh, *The Cricket War*, Melbourne University Press, 2007
Peter Hain, *Don't Play with Apartheid*, Allen & Unwin, 1971
Stewart Harris, *Political Football: The Springbok Tour of Australia*, Gold Star, 1971
Chris Harte, *Two Tours and Pollock*, Sports Marketing, 1988
Chris Harte and Warwick Hadfield, *Cricket Rebels*, QB Books, 1985
Chris Harte with Bernard Whimpress, *A History of Australian Cricket*, Penguin, 2003
Rodney Hartman, *Ali: The Life of Ali Bacher*, Penguin, 2004

Omar Henry, *Man in the Middle*, Queen Anne Press, 1994
Michael Holding and Tony Cozier, *Whispering Death: The Life and Times of Michael Holding*, Andre Deutsch, 1993
CLR James, *Beyond the Boundary*, Stanley Paul & Co., 1963
Marc Keech, *International Sport and the End of Apartheid*, PhD Thesis: University of Staffordshire, 1999
Imran Khan, *All-round View*, Chatto & Windus, 1988
Ray Knowles, *South Africa v England: A Test Cricket History*, New Holland, 1995
Alan Knott, *It's Knott Cricket*, Macmillan, 1985
Richard Lapchick, *Apartheid Sport and South Africa's Foreign Policy*, United Nations Centre Against Apartheid, 1976
Tony Lewis, *Taking Fresh Guard*, Headline, 2003
Dennis Lillee, *Over and Out!*, Meuthen, 1984
Simon Lister, *Supercat: The Authorised Biography of Clive Lloyd*, Fairfield, 2007
Michael Manley, *A History of West Indies Cricket*, Andre Deutsch, 2002
Malcolm Marshall, *Marshall Arts: The Autobiography of Malcolm Marshall*, Queen Anne Press, 1988
Trevor McDonald, *The Authorised Biography of Viv Richards*, Pelham, 1984
Trevor McDonald, *Clive Lloyd: The Authorised Biography*, HarperCollins, 1986
Jackie McGlew and Trevor Chesterfield, *South Africa's Cricket Captains: From Melville to Wessels*, Southern Book Publishers, 1995
Leo McKinistry, *Geoff Boycott: A Cricketing Hero*, HarperCollins Willow, 2005
Don Mosey, *Botham*, Sphere, 1987
Stephen Moss (ed.), *Wisden Anthology 1978–2006*, John Wisden & Co., 2006
Rob Nixon, *'Apartheid on the Run'*, *Transition*, vol. 58, pp. 68–88 (1992)
Peter Oborne, *Cricket and Conspiracy*, Time Warner, 2004
Andre Odendaal (ed.), *Cricket in Isolation*, 1977
Andre Odendaal, *The African Game*, David Philip, 2003
Mike Procter, *Mike Procter on Cricket*, Pelham, 1981
Mike Procter, *South Africa in Isolation*, Queen Anne Press, 1994
Simon Rae, *It's Not Cricket*, Faber and Faber, 2001
Barry Richards, *The Barry Richards Story*, Faber, 1978

Vivian Richards and Bob Harris, *Sir Vivian: The Definitive Autobiography*, Penguin, 2001
Christian Ryan, *Golden Boy: Kim Hughes and the bad old days of Australian cricket*, Allen & Unwin, 2009
John Scott, *Caught in Court*, Andre Deutsch, 1989
Ric Sissons, *The Players: A Social History of the Professional Cricketer*, Kingswood Press, 1988
EW Swanton, *As I Said At The Time*, Collins, 1983
Ivo Tennant, *Graham Gooch*, HF&G Witherby, 1993
Richard Thompson, *Retreat from Apartheid : New Zealand's sporting contacts with South Africa*, Oxford University Press, 1975
David Tossell, *Grovel! The Story & Legacy of the Summer of 1976*, Know the Score, 2007
Vince van der Bijl, *Cricket in the Shadows*, Shuter and Shooter, 1984
Marcus Williams (ed.), *Double Century: Cricket in The Times Volume Two, 1935–1990*, Pavillion 1990.
Bob Willis, *Lasting the Pace*, Collins, 1985
Bob Woolmer, *Pirate & Rebel? An Autobiography*, Arthur Baker Ltd, 1984
Bob Woolmer, *Woolmer on Cricket*, Virgin, 2000

## Annuals

*Wisden* (various, 1968–1993)

## Newspapers

Australia: *Adelaide Advertiser, The Age, The Australian, The Herald-Sun, Hobart Mercury, Sydney Morning Herald*
Barbados: *The Daily Nation*
Guyana: *Guyana Chronicle*
Jamaica: *Jamaica News*
South Africa: *Cape Argus, Cape Times, The Citizen, Daily News (Durban), Rand Daily Mail, The Sowetan, The Star (Johannesburg), Sunday Times*
Sri Lanka: *Daily News* (Colombo)
UK: *Daily Express, Daily Mail, Daily Mirror, Daily Telegraph, Guardian, News of the World, The Observer, People, The Sun, Sunday Express, Sunday Mirror, Sunday Telegraph, Sunday Times, The Times*

## Television & Radio

BBC Radio, *Rebel Hell*, first broadcast 8 February 2003

BBC Television, *Empire of Cricket: West Indies*, first broadcast 7 June 2009
British Sky Broadcasting, *Out of the Wilderness: Part II*, first broadcast 19 July 2008

## Websites

www.cricinfo.com and specifically the following articles:

'The Unforgiven' by Siddhartha Vaidyanathan, first published 2 August 2007 at http://content.cricinfo.com/westindies/content/story/286356/html.
'Eighty-three once more' by Ayaz Memon, first published 24 June 2008 at http://content.cricinfo.com/magazine/content/story/355915.html.
www.news.com.au and specifically the following article:
'Rebels still live in shame, despair' by Robert Craddock, first published 14 April 2007 at http:// www.news.com.au/heraldsun/story/0,21985,21552339-11088,00.html.
www.indianexpress.com and specifically the following article:
'The rebel with a grouse', first published 21 August 1997 at http: www.indianexpress.com/ie/daily/19970822/23450553.html.

# Index